African American Coping
in the Political Sphere

SUNY series in African American Studies

John R. Howard and Robert C. Smith, editors

African American Coping
in the Political Sphere

Jas M. Sullivan and Moriah Harman

Foreword by
Sherman James

Cover photo taken in downtown Atlanta during the George Floyd protest on May 31, 2020.

Published by State University of New York Press, Albany

For information, contact State University of New York Press, Albany, NY
www.sunypress.edu

Library of Congress Cataloging-in-Publication Data

Names: Sullivan, Jas M., 1975– author. | Harman, Moriah, 1994– author.
Title: African American coping in the political sphere / Jas M. Sullivan, Moriah Harman.
Description: Albany, NY : State University of New York Press, [2023] | Series: SUNY series in African American Studies | "John Henryism Active Coping Scale, or JHAC." | Includes bibliographical references and index.
Identifiers: LCCN 2022060957 | ISBN 9781438494920 (hardcover : alk. paper) | ISBN 9781438494937 (ebook)
Subjects: LCSH: African Americans—Attitudes. | Agent (Philosophy)—Political aspects. | African Americans—Politics and government. | African Americans—Psychology. | Race discrimination—United States—Psychological aspects. | Black nationalism—United States. | Resilience (Personality trait) | Henry, John (Legendary character)—Influence. | American Dream. | Work ethic.
Classification: LCC E185.615 .S855 2023 | DDC 320.089/96073—dc23/eng/20230222
LC record available at https://lccn.loc.gov/2022060957

10 9 8 7 6 5 4 3 2 1

Dedicated to Malik—
and to all those who persist and overcome
—Jas M. Sullivan

Dedicated to my family—
and to all those who inspire us
—Moriah Harman

Contents

Contents

Illustrations

Tables

Figures

Acknowledgments

A couple of years prior to the height of the racial justice protests, the COVID-19 pandemic, and the 2020 presidential election, I had written a paper using the John Henryism Active Coping measure to understand the ways coping might influence support for race-specific policies. Once I completed the paper, I sent an email to Dr. Sherman A. James—who had dedicated his academic career to exploring the influence of psychosocial stressors and coping on psychological and health outcomes among African Americans. Since I had not personally met Dr. James, I was expecting a cursory reply message. To my surprise, he sent a detailed note about the research and his interest in the findings. From there, our mutual research interest led to many phone conversations and subsequent meetings when our time overlapped in Atlanta. From our discussions, I gained a deeper understanding about coping research (specifically, John Henryism Active Coping) and its potential effects on political life. Consequently, I want to thank Dr. James for his kindness, and his willingness to share his knowledge.

I also would like to thank my colleagues at Louisiana State University. Fall 2022 academic term will be my sixteenth year at LSU, and I am continuously challenged to think more deeply, broadly, and interdisciplinary about my research by my colleagues in political science, psychology, and African and African American studies. As a community of scholars, I am inspired by their research and overall dedication to their profession.

This research would also not be possible without the National Survey of American Life (NSAL) data. Having been involved in conducting a national survey, I am keenly aware of the time and energy devoted to them. Therefore, I would like to thank all the investigators who were part of the NSAL data collection team. In many ways, the data are still providing important information on the experiences of African Americans. I would also like to thank SUNY Press for their support throughout the process.

Finally, I want to thank my family. During the writing of this book, we were living in a two-bedroom apartment in Decatur, Georgia. At that time, there wasn't much known about COVID-19, so stay-at-home policies were implemented for almost a year, and my workspace was the kitchen table. During the weekdays, about every fifty minutes there would be an interruption to my writing—with my son's snack breaks since school was online for the entire year. Oh, the things I learned about him, his teachers, and all his classmates that year! At the same time, we were exposed to the horrible murders of Ahmaud Arbery, George Floyd, and Breonna Taylor. I was devastated, as was the rest of the country. The Arbery case affected me the most since I, too, am an avid runner. I just couldn't fathom how a young man, minding his own business, could be chased for nearly four minutes, harassed, followed by car, and ultimately get shot and killed. Many questions percolated through my mind: What kind of society do we live in? How do I protect my son from such cruelty? In addition, the country was in the middle of a nasty, divided presidential election. Collectively, this was a difficult time for all of us—emotionally and psychologically. It wouldn't be a stretch to say that, as I wrote this book, I personally experienced a great number of varying emotions at that kitchen table due to these circumstances—joy, deep sorrow, and anger. It was the lighthearted moments and the laughter we shared as a family that helped me cope and encouraged me to continue writing this book. Malik, my son, you bring me the greatest joy, and everything that I do is for you. Keep persisting, challenging, and succeeding in this often-chaotic world. Last, but most importantly, I thank God for the immense grace and favor he has shown me throughout my life.

—Jas Sullivan

Throughout the past two years or so, while deeply exploring the literature on coping and its effects on various social, psychological, and health outcomes, at the same time that the COVID-19 pandemic raged on, I found myself frequently thinking about and relying on coping strategies. Raised to work hard, give my all to everything I do, and believe in myself, I relate to the core themes captured in measures of active coping, and particularly in the measure used in this book, John Henryism Active Coping (JHAC). Both in my research on this topic, and in my life experiences, I have become acutely aware that there are both benefits and trade-offs to the way we choose to deal with, or handle, stressors and challenges in our lives. There is no "one-size-fits-all" approach to coping, and there are both advantages and disadvantages to most coping strategies. Learning more about the factors that shape individuals' coping styles and how coping affects a range of behaviors and attitudes, I had many exciting conversations with Jas that centered on a surprise and curiosity as to why/how coping, and particularly active coping, has been understudied in political science.

The rise in cases of police brutality, racial discrimination, and police killings of African Americans, which inspired large-scale protests demanding change and calls for justice throughout the United States and around the world in 2020 and 2021, combined with the COVID-19 pandemic—and the social, political, health, and economic disparities exacerbated by it—made the connections between coping and politics even clearer to us. We argue and show that beyond affecting social, psychological, and health outcomes, coping also plays a role in shaping political attitudes and behaviors. It is our hope that this book will inspire future research on coping in the political sphere.

I am indebted to Sherman A. James, whose work continues to inspire a wealth of research on active coping, including my work with Jas Sullivan. His research on coping, including the development of the John Henryism Hypothesis and the JHAC measure, made this book possible. I also thank him for writing a thoughtful and constructive foreword to this book, for which I am truly grateful. Similarly, I am grateful to all those whose time, effort, energy, and curiosity contributed to the collection of the NSAL data, and I thank them for generously sharing it. I, too, would like to sincerely thank SUNY Press for their support throughout this process—and a special thank you to the editors and anonymous reviewers who validated the importance and relevance of this work and offered suggestions that improved it.

Moreover, I thank Jas for making my first experience coauthoring a book a truly rewarding experience—you have always treated me as a strong and equal cocontributor, and though completing this book came with many challenges and hurdles, I am grateful for the many conversations that inspired and motivated this research. I have grown both personally and professionally throughout this process, and it has been a joy working with you, Jas, from initial ideas to final edits. I also thank our generous colleagues in the Department of Political Science at LSU who kindly provided feedback on portions of this book.

Finally, I would like to thank my family for always inspiring me to pursue my passions and for motivating me to work hard, believe in myself, and overcome any challenges I face. I am grateful for their patience, love, and support, without which I would not be where I am today. I would also like to thank my four-legged family member, Max, whose spunky personality and love of sunshine, walks, and playing fetch has made all the difference for my mental health the past few years.

—Moriah Harman

Foreword

> One ever feels his two-ness—an American, a Negro; two souls, two
> thoughts, two unreconciled strivings; two warring ideals in one dark
> body, whose dogged strength alone keeps it from being torn asunder.
>
> —W. E. B. Du Bois, *The Souls of Black Folk*[2]

With a nod to the great W. E. B. Du Bois, in *African American Coping in
the Political Sphere*, Sullivan and Harman present a fascinating portrait of
the "two-ness" in the souls of African Americans more than 100 years after
Du Bois's characteristically astute observation. The authors' comprehensive
analysis of data from the National Survey of American Life, a nationally
representative sample of African Americans conducted between 2001 and
2003, revealed, among other things, how much African Americans believe
in the American Dream (does hard work lead to success?); the diversity of
their political ideologies (are you conservative, moderate, or liberal?); and
the degree of their support for various social policies designed to mitigate
or undo historical racial injustices (do you support reparations for slavery?).
Sullivan and Harman break entirely new ground, however, by positing that
the degree to which individual African Americans say they confront adversity
with high-effort coping, by which is meant with energy, optimism, and a
determination to succeed, influences their political ideology, their social
policy preferences, and whether they are actively engaged in the political
arena. As a cutting-edge work in Black political psychology, *African American*

Coping in the Political Sphere illuminates, in quantitative terms, what DuBois' "two-ness" in the souls of Black folk looked like in the first few years of the twenty-first century.

I was asked to write the Foreword to *African American Coping in the Political Sphere* because, in the early 1980s, I coined the term *John Henryism* to connote the "high-effort coping" personality predisposition that forms the through line of this book. I was formally trained in personality and social psychology, but I spent my entire academic career teaching and conducting research in schools of public health and public policy on what, in recent years, has come to be called the "social determinants of health." Systemic anti-Black racism is one of the most important examples of a "social determinant" of health, because the laws, social policies, and social norms through which it manifests put *shape-shifting* economic, social, and political barriers between African Americans and the life-enhancing resources so essential for healthy human development and well-being. John Henryism, I have argued, is a historically rooted, *learned* cultural response by African Americans, especially working-class African Americans, to anti-Black, systemic racism. It is, as it were, a refusal on their part to submit to *permanent*, systemic racial subjugation.[3]

I discovered "John Henryism" by accident in the summer of 1978, while interviewing a then seventy-one-year-old retired, North Carolina Black farmer named John Henry Martin. Five years out of graduate school, I was a young, assistant professor of epidemiology at the University of North Carolina–Chapel Hill. In the pre-HIV/AIDS and pre-COVID-19 years of the 1970s, untreated and uncontrolled high blood pressure and its potent contribution to premature death from strokes and heart attacks was one of the most pressing problems in US medical and public health circles. By the late 1970s, however, new and safe medication to treat high blood pressure had become available; but then, as always, the challenge was how to reach segments of the population most in need. In the case of untreated high blood pressure and its potentially devastating effects on the heart, brain, and kidney, the population "most in need" were poor and working-class Americans, especially Black Americans, and in particular, working-class Black men. A research team was therefore assembled to write a grant application to the National Institutes of Health to conduct a high blood pressure control program in a mostly rural, eastern North Carolina county located in a region of the state with well-documented high mortality from strokes, especially in the Black population. We prioritized reaching Black men, many of whom in the absence of any other discomforting health problem, would likely be unaware that they had high blood pressure. To incorporate the views and concerns of Black men already under treatment for high blood pressure into how we developed the interventions, a physician colleague, at my request, identified six of his Black male patients for me to interview. A "Mr. John Martin" (I was not initially aware of his middle name) was my first interviewee.

For two hours, as we sat in his backyard, Mr. Martin, a masterful raconteur, told me his life story.[4] Born into a dirt-poor sharecropper family in 1907, and unable to attend school beyond the second grade, Mr. Martin vowed at an early age that, unlike his father, he would not be a perpetually in debt sharecropper all of his life. Around age thirty-five, after years of sharecropping himself, Mr. Martin obtained a bank mortgage to purchase seventy-five acres of farmland. Although he had forty years to pay off the mortgage, by working sixteen-hour days, often six days per week, he paid it off completely in just five years. Referring to stomach ulcers that he developed in his fifties, and to the debilitating osteoarthritis he had developed by his mid-sixties, Mr. Martin reasoned that his health "went bad" because he had "pushed himself too hard in the fields." Around this time, his wife came to the door and called out, "John Henry—it's time for lunch, and bring your guest with you." Astonished, I looked at him and asked, "Your name is 'John Henry'?" Yep, "John Henry Martin," he replied. Almost immediately, Mr. Martin's life story struck me as an echo of the legend of "John Henry—the steel-driving man" who, in the early 1870s, allegedly defeated a mechanical steam drill in an epic steel-driving contest but then dropped dead from complete exhaustion.[5] John Henry Martin also competed against "the machine"—the exploitative sharecropper labor system of the Jim Crow South; and, like the legendary steel-driver, John Henry Martin "won," but at a cost—the early deterioration of his physical health.

Growing up, in the rural South of the 1950s, I was surrounded by Black adults just like John Henry Martin—hard-working, determined, conscientious people—literal embodiments of Du Bois's "dogged strength." Many also had high blood pressure, and many died or became disabled from stroke or congestive heart failure. Was John Henry Martin's story not also their story, and that of African Americans writ large? Thus, the construct of John Henryism was born, which I defined as a strong behavioral predisposition to engage in high-effort coping with adversity, and to do so with both optimism and a determination to succeed. The John Henryism hypothesis (which builds on pioneering 1970s laboratory and field research by others) posits that such determined, high-effort coping with adversity, when repeated over many years, accelerates the deterioration of one's physical (but not necessarily mental) health. A growing literature documents that John Henryism, as measured by the twelve-item John Henryism Active Coping (JHAC) scale, is widespread among African Americans and frequently, though not always, identifies which community members are most likely to have, or develop, high blood pressure and related physical health problems relatively early in adult life.

Given that John Henryism is a fairly widespread phenomenon among African Americans, investigating its significance in arenas of life besides public health seems logical. With verve, Sullivan and Harman extend research on John Henryism in African Americans to a most important arena, the political sphere.

What follows is a commentary on some of the authors' major research findings. First, I discuss a cluster of research findings that paint a fairly coherent picture of African Americans, viewed from a national standpoint, who seem strongly inclined to confront adversity with high-effort coping, that is, "John Henryism." Second, I comment on observed statistical associations between "high" (i.e., above the median) scores on the John Henryism Active Coping scale, and African Americans' endorsement of certain "core" American Values, for example, being "proud to be American," and believing that "America is the land of opportunity for those willing to work hard." Third, I discuss reported associations between JHAC scores and support among African Americans for social policies such as "reparations for slavery" or other government-level initiatives that target historical racial inequities. Fourth, I comment on relationships between JHAC scores and African Americans' political participation, such as voting and working for political candidates, in the 2000 presidential and local elections. I will then conclude with a brief methodological note, which has implications for future social science as well as public health research.

Overall, JHAC scores in the NSAL were skewed toward higher values, a finding consistent with my own research as well as that by others. For example, a striking 94 percent of NSAL participants responded "completely true" or "somewhat true" to this very first JHAC statement: "I've always felt that I could make of my life pretty much what I wanted to make of it." Hence, the overwhelming majority of NSAL respondents possess a strong sense of agency, and if we take their response at face value, presumably they are prepared to act on it. Again, consistent with prior research, NSAL participants with less education or income scored *higher* on the JHAC scale than those more educated and with higher incomes. Scores on the JHAC scale were similar for men and women. This is another common finding in the literature and suggests that the strong predisposition among African Americans to engage in high-effort coping with adversity is cultural, not gender-specific, even if some important health and social outcomes related to JHAC scores prove to be sex or gender-specific.

African Americans in the South, that is, those residing in the eleven states of the former Confederacy, had higher JHAC scores than those in the non-South. This regional difference in JHAC scores is a new finding, one that only a national study like the NSAL could uncover. Beyond this interesting regional difference, African Americans with high JHAC scores were more likely to consume Black media (newspapers, magazines, radio and TV, etc.), and more likely to seek entertainment (e.g., movies) that feature Black performers. High scorers on JHAC were also more likely to advocate for "buying Black" (i.e., shopping at Black-owned stores), and "voting Black" (i.e., voting for Black candidates for political office), views Sullivan and Harman equate with "Black nationalism." Nevertheless, about one-third of NSAL participants described themselves as "conservative," one-third as "moderate," and one-third as "liberal." Although "liberals" were about equally divided between high and low JHAC scorers, high JHAC scorers were somewhat underrepresented among "moderates" and overrepresented among "conservatives."[6] Hence, the national portrait that emerges of African Americans with high JHAC scores is as follows: they are just as likely to be female as male, more likely to be Southern, more likely to be working class, and somewhat more likely to be "conservative." High scorers on the JHAC scale are also more likely to be strong supporters of economic and cultural institutions that their forebears created to, as much as possible, buffer Black communities from the widespread injuries of anti-Black racism.

"One ever feels his two-ness—an American, a Negro . . ." Du Bois wrote in *Souls*. Few of Sullivan and Harman's findings better illustrate this key insight by Du Bois than how African Americans, especially high JHAC scorers, answered NSAL questions about "American Values." In analyses that controlled for education, income, gender, region, and so on, high JHAC scorers were more likely to say they were "very proud" to be American and that in America—the land of opportunity—"hard work pays off." That high JHAC scorers more strongly endorse the "work ethic" is not surprising since, from the beginning, I viewed a strong work ethic as a defining feature of John Henryism. The authors' more specific finding, however, that JHAC main effects for "work ethic" were most pronounced for "conservatives," compared to "moderates" and "liberals," illuminates what being "conservative" actually signifies for the third of all African Americans who embrace this ideology. It would appear that "conservative" African Americans are more likely than others to place a high value on *industry*, *frugality*, and *personal responsibility*.[7] With this in mind, then, juxtaposing this cluster of *positive* associations between high JHAC scores and "strong work-ethic," "pride in America," and seeing "America as the land of opportunity" against similarly *positive* associations between high JHAC scores and "Black nationalist" sentiments (i.e., preferring to "buy Black" and "vote Black") makes it clear that Du Bois's century-old insight about a "two-ness" in the souls of Black folk endures.

African Americans with high JHAC scores were not only more likely to endorse economic and cultural "Black nationalist" sentiments, they also expressed more support for government policies that "help Blacks," along with policies that increase the number of Blacks in Congress by, for example, creating more "majority-minority congressional districts." Although a high JHAC score was not, in itself, associated with stronger support for "reparations for slavery," among high JHAC scorers such support for reparations increased monotonically with age and also with increasing lifetime encounters with racial discrimination. Hence, for these two groups of African Americans with high JHAC scores, their stronger support for reparations probably signals a classic "fight, not flight," response to *racialized* adversity that they, themselves, or members of their age cohort experienced while growing up in "Jim Crow" America.

JHAC scores did not predict political participation in the presidential, state, and local elections closest to the time (presumably 2000 and 2002) when the NSAL was conducted. Since 1980, polls indicate,[8] voter turnout has been higher among women and individuals with more education and income. Sullivan and Harman observed similar gender and social class differences in political engagement among African Americans in the NSAL data. While it is possible that a strong predisposition to engage in high-effort coping with adversity—John Henryism—has no bearing, at any time, on political engagement by African Americans, it is also possible that JHAC main effects on political engagement (voting, working for political candidates, etc.) are conditional on the nature and perceived strength of *external threats* facing African Americans *as a whole*. In other words, the degree to which the US political culture is *racially fraught* during a given election cycle could determine whether JHAC main effects on voting behavior or other forms of political engagement will show up in the data. After all, the US political culture in the early 2000s, when NSAL data were collected, was not especially fraught, racially. It was highly fraught, however, with tension and anxiety about how the nation should respond to the recent September 11, 2001 terrorist attacks. In retrospect, the country was uncharacteristically unified along racial lines in the early 2000s, and these broad feelings of "national unity" may have generated more "favorable" attitudes among African Americans toward White Americans, especially among the more "conservative," high-JHAC scoring African Americans.

If comparable NSAL data existed for the three election cycles of 2008–2010, 2016–2018, and 2020–2022, when the trajectory of the US political culture was becoming increasingly racially fraught, it is likely that the high turnout by Black voters in 2008 to help elect Barack Obama would have swamped JHAC main effects, especially with regard to voting. However, the "White backlash" against what Obama's presidency foreshadowed—so crudely represented by the election of Donald Trump to the US presidency in 2016, and by the sweeping, racially targeted, voter suppression laws following Trump's defeat for reelection in 2020, is precisely the kind of *external threat* that "high-JHAC" African Americans have been taught by history to confront with a sense of urgency. African American women, it seems, are moving to the front lines of this confrontation.

African American Coping in the Political Sphere is an important contribution to scholarship on the political psychology of African Americans. The authors have a keen appreciation of the "classical" stress and coping literature in psychology and the growing literature on John Henryism—defined as repeated high-effort coping with systemic adversity—in both public health and psychology. That such a predisposition to engage in high-effort coping with adversity might also illuminate the behavior of African Americans in the political sphere was a notable leap of imagination by Sullivan and Harman. That there has been no diminution in the systemic stressors African Americans have had to face—because of their race—since NSAL data were collected in the early 2000s is made clear by the authors' sobering account in the book's opening pages of events that make the Black Lives Matter Movement a necessity.

Finally, an important, but unavoidable, methodological limitation of the authors' research is the NSAL's relatively small sample size. Dividing JHAC scores at the median to determine who is predisposed to engage in "high-effort coping," and who is not, obscures an important "middle" group; namely, the individuals presumably more inclined to carefully "pick their battles." In the political, as in the public health sphere, understanding who the African Americans in this "middle" group are, and how they move through the world, could be important.

Introduction

"We don't exist and when we do exist, we exist as a threat. This is exhausting."[9] These are the words of Michelle Obama, the former First Lady of the United States. In her podcast, Obama elaborates, "What the white community doesn't understand about being a person of color in this nation is that there are daily slights in our workplaces where people talk over you, or people don't even see you."[10] As an example, Obama told a story about waiting in line with her two daughters and a friend at an ice cream parlor and another customer cutting in line. When she addressed the situation with the customer who jumped in line, Obama observed the following: "The woman didn't apologize, she never looked me in my eye, she didn't know it was me. All she saw was a Black person, or a group of Black people, or maybe she didn't even see that. Because we were that invisible."[11]

Psychosocial stressors are a part of the human condition. For African Americans, however, there are added stressors that impact daily functioning, due to no fault of their own. These stressors include, but are not limited to, discrimination, microaggressions, and police brutality, as well as income, health, and education inequalities. There isn't a debate about the mere existence and the devastating impact of these stressors on African Americans, as illustrated by Michelle Obama. Research has shown that these stressors often have negative effects on physical and mental health outcomes, among others. In fact, Sherman James coined the "John Henryism Hypothesis" (JHH)—which is rooted in the assumption that individuals of lower socioeconomic status, and especially African Americans, frequently face psychosocial stressors that necessitate they expend substantial energy on a daily basis in order to manage the stress that stems from these circumstances—in order to help explain and/or predict the prevalence of high blood pressure within these groups.[12] Importantly, the JHH is also rooted in the assumption that not all individuals facing routine psychosocial stressors consistently respond with the same amount or level of effort; those who do constantly put forth considerable effort in the midst of stressful, challenging circumstances are engaging in high effort coping (or high John Henryism), while those less inclined to exert consistent energy to manage psychosocial stressors are reflective of low effort coping (or low John Henryism).[13] Inspired by the JHH, and more broadly, the research on John Henryism, this book explores the influence coping has on African Americans' political attitudes and behaviors.

Active Coping Measure

Coping in this book is measured using the John Henryism Active Coping scale, which is extensively detailed in chapters one and two.[14] John Henryism is defined as "a strong behavioral predisposition to cope actively [(vs. passively)] with psychosocial environmental stressors."[15] This measure, developed by Sherman James, taps the type of effort (low or high) one exerts to overcome stressors. High-effort copers are actively (rather than passively) trying to overcome obstacles, and these individuals show sustained, persistent cognitive and emotional engagement in achieving their goal.[16] Similar to the folk legend, John Henry, who inspired the concept, individuals who score high on JHAC (high-effort or active copers) are known to put forth hard work, strenuous effort, relentless determination, and impressive vigor in the midst of challenging circumstances, and they reflect a high level of personal efficacy.[17]

Before we present the outline for this book, the goal in the first part of this introduction is to highlight some of the stressors (in their various manifestations) that African Americans confront, often on a daily basis, and subsequent reactions to these stressors. Due to data limitations, we are not able to attribute the responses to these recent events to active or passive coping; rather, the cases we highlight serve as illustrative examples of stressors, such as discrimination and police brutality, that African Americans face. However, we believe these cases shine light on the need for future studies to consider and incorporate measures of coping, such as JHAC. Using data from the National Study of American Life (conducted in 2001 and 2003), our findings suggest that coping has much to offer in the study of the political sphere. Following the illustrative examples of recent cases of psychosocial stressors, we discuss the purpose of the book and explain our contribution to the literature on coping and specifically, its influence on political attitudes and behavior. Then, we provide a brief outline of the chapters.

Ahmaud Arbery: "A Modern-Day Lynching"[18]

On February 23, 2020, Ahmaud Arbery went jogging. With the temperature in the sixties, in Brunswick, Georgia, it was perfect running weather. Arbery's intent was to stay in shape. So, for this twenty-five-year-old, running was familiar; something he liked to do.[19] Little did he know that a simple jog around a familiar city would cost him his life. Around 1:00 p.m., according to the Glynn County Police Department's report,[20] Arbery was chased, yelled at, physically assaulted, and gunned down by three white men. Much about the encounter is clear, since it was captured on a cell phone video, provided to the police department and subsequently made public. In the video,[21] as Arbery was running, a white truck was parked in front of him. Standing on the back of the truck bed was Gregory McMichael, a former police officer, while Travis McMichael, the son of Gregory McMichael, was standing in front of the open driver's door with a shotgun in a pointed position. Behind him, in another car, was William Bryan Jr., who was filming the incident. According to the police, Bryan wasn't relegated to simply recording the event; he used his vehicle to "confine and detain Arbery without legal authority."[22] As Arbery approached the truck, after being chased for nearly four minutes,[23] he moved to the right side of the road to go around the truck—most likely to avoid the gun-toting Travis McMichael. As Arbery went around the right side of the truck, McMichael ran to confront Arbery. At this point a scuffle ensued between the two, and there was a fight for the gun McMichael was holding. The fight ended with McMichael shooting Arbery three times with the shotgun. Arbery was shot in the "center of his chest, upper left chest around the armpit and his right wrist."[24] Autopsy reports showed that there were no alcohol or drugs in Arbery's system.

Reactions to Arbery's killing varied from peaceful protests, anger, and sadness toward those who committed this despicable act, but also toward a justice system that had initially justified their actions. For African Americans, it was especially difficult both psychologically and emotionally. James Ravenell, an avid runner, explains, "I'm legitimately just tired of it. It's a lot of trauma to constantly know that people see you and they just feel threatened by you, by nothing that you have done."[25] He further says, "Running is a thing that allows us to escape, even just for a little bit, from all the craziness. Here's a thing that so many of us are trying to do . . . just so we can stay physically fit and mentally fit. To have this type of assault on us is just really exhausting."[26] John Piggott, a marathon runner, states, "I saw the video and I can't get it out of my mind. This guy wasn't doing anything but being himself and that could have been me, that could have been anybody. He did nothing wrong to anyone."[27] Anthony Reed, a cofounder of the National Marathoners Association, "hopes it brings visibility to the fact that . . . Blacks have a different experience when we go for a run. We would like to run to relieve the stress, but in the back of our minds that same run can be stressful."[28]

Similar sentiments were expressed in an article published in *Mic*, wherein Vanessa Taylor asked runners to share their thoughts. Here are some of their feelings.

> I cannot help but feel enraged that my safety is contingent upon my invisibility. . . . It's a grim reminder that your very existence as a Black person in this country puts you in constant danger, and all you can do is continue trying to live the life you want in spite of it. . . . It brings about a sense of frustration, hopelessness, anger, and I find it so sad that I and so many others have to legitimately consider the risks of being outside merely because of the color of our skin and others' perception of it.[29]

These reactions speak to the stress that discriminatory experiences and racial injustices inflict on those involved or observing, whether directly or indirectly, and the physical and psychological wear and tear that such circumstances have on both the individual as well as on groups. These emotions and lived experiences are described as haunting, exhausting, demoralizing, frustrating, and saddening, and they suggest an awareness that requires considerable energy to manage the stress associated with these conditions.

George Floyd: "I Can't Breathe"[30]

On May 25, 2020, in Minneapolis, Minnesota, forty-six-year-old George Floyd, an African American man, went into Cup Foods, a grocery store he frequented often, to buy a pack of cigarettes.[31] This mundane activity set the wheels in motion to what would be Floyd's last evening alive. Suspecting the twenty dollars Floyd used to buy his cigarettes was a counterfeit bill, a teenage Cup Foods employee called police to report it, and a transcript of the call to 911 reveals that the employee reported Floyd refused to give the cigarettes back, and the employee accused him of being inebriated and out of control.[32] Minutes later, two police officers arrived and found Floyd and two other people sitting in a car.[33] One of the officers, Thomas Lane, approached the car, pulled his gun out, and gave Floyd an order to show his hands, which he allegedly repeated around ten times before Floyd was ordered to exit the vehicle.[34]

Following the police officers' arrival, an initially cooperative and apologetic Floyd became distressed as he resisted handcuffs and being put into a squad car, informing the officers—who grew in number over the course of the arrest—that he was claustrophobic.[35] After he was pulled away from the passenger side by another officer, Derek Chauvin, Floyd fell to the ground and lay there in handcuffs face down.[36] The officers restrained Floyd while onlookers started filming the incident.[37] It was at this time that Chauvin "placed his left knee between [Floyd's] head and neck,"[38] an act that lasted eight minutes and forty-six seconds.[39]

During those eight minutes and forty-six seconds, Floyd's last moments alive, he repeated over twenty times to the officers that he could not breathe, begged "Please, please, please,"[40] and called out for his mother.[41] In one gasp, Floyd pleaded, "You're going to kill me, man,"[42] to which Chauvin responded, "Then stop talking, stop yelling. It takes a heck of a lot of oxygen to talk."[43] Floyd went on to say, "Can't believe this, man. Mom, love you. Love you. Tell my kids I love them. I'm dead."[44] It was six minutes into the restraint that Floyd became silent and nonresponsive, while onlookers pleaded for the officers to check his pulse.[45] Officer Kueng, when checking Floyd's right wrist, informed the other officers that he "couldn't find [a pulse],"[46] but no one moved. After Chauvin finally removed his knee from Floyd's neck, a motionless Floyd was put into an ambulance and taken to Hennepin County Medical Center, where "he was pronounced dead about an hour later."[47] The four officers involved in Floyd's arrest were ultimately fired, and the video of his arrest went viral on social media.[48]

Reactions to the killing of Floyd were swift. Demonstrators poured into the streets of Minneapolis.[49] Some marched in peaceful protest of Floyd's unjust murder, while others vandalized police cars and the police station.[50] In the days and weeks that followed, demonstrations spread across the country, with protestors in Atlanta, Memphis, Los Angeles, Portland, and other cities across all fifty states and DC, taking to the streets to protest, with some lying face down, similar to Floyd, with their hands behind them, chanting the words of desperation he uttered repeatedly, "I can't breathe."[51] The police station in Minneapolis, where the officers involved in Floyd's arrest worked, was taken over by protestors and set on fire.[52] For many protestors, who varied in age, race, ethnicity, and gender, it was their first time taking to the streets, and they felt emotionally compelled to do so after witnessing the viral video of the incident.[53] For other protestors, it was the countless cases of racial discrimination that inspired them to march, including the recent case of Ahmaud Arbery, and that of Breonna Taylor, a twenty-six-year-old African American health worker who was killed in her own home in Kentucky by police officers.[54]

Even with curfews imposed by many US cities, the protests did not come to an end. The outrage continued, and by the eighth night of protests, the number of demonstrators was now in the tens of thousands across the US.[55] While most demonstrations remained peaceful, there were demonstrations that turned violent, with one man driving his car into protestors in Brooklyn.[56] Protests were also seen around the world. Tens of thousands of protestors marched throughout Australia, France, Germany, Spain and the UK.[57] Protestors chanted and held up signs that read, "I can't breathe," "Racism is suffocating us," and "Black Lives Matter."[58] Government officials from around the globe largely expressed their support for what they deemed legitimate demonstrations, and condemned the "abuse of power" and racial violence in the US, as well as President Trump's military threats.[59] The protests, both violent and nonviolent, featured prominently across social media platforms.

The police killing of Floyd took a particularly overwhelming emotional toll on African Americans. Eugene Robinson of the *Washington Post* wrote that he wanted to "throw something" and "scream";[60] Oprah Winfrey expressed that "I haven't been able to get the image of the knee on his neck out of my head";[61] Rihanna wrote, "The magnitude of devastation, anger, and sadness I've felt has been overwhelming to say the least";[62] Kevin Hart expressed that "we deserve the right to feel safe";[63] and Kelly Rowland wrote, "I can't sit still. I'm angry. I'm hurt. At times feeling hopeless."[64]

Breonna Taylor: "Say Her Name"[65]

On March 13, 2020, at around midnight, twenty-six-year-old Breonna Taylor, an emergency medical technician, was sleeping in her Louisville, Kentucky home with her boyfriend when police officers executed a "no-knock" warrant, broke down her door, and stormed into her home.[66] "Believing they were intruders, [Taylor's] boyfriend fired one shot at the officers using a handgun he legally owned. The officers responded by firing 22 bullets, killing Taylor."[67] It was later revealed that Taylor had been shot eight times, and that police officers had lied to obtain the warrant they used to raid her house, violating federal civil rights laws and leading to her death.[68] While Taylor's family claimed the police had the wrong address, authorities claimed her apartment was raided due to an alleged connection with a suspect believed to be hiding drugs in (or receiving them in packages at) the apartment; however, no drugs were found in her apartment during or after the raid.[69] The incident report revealed numerous errors made by the police, including the lack of body camera footage from the raid and the incorrect assertion that officers had not forcibly entered the home.[70]

The events of that fateful night have been widely disputed by the police officers involved, but following the raid, at least four former and current police officers (at the time of this writing) have been federally charged with offenses ranging from civil rights violations to use of excessive force, conspiracy, and obstruction.[71] Moreover, the city of Louisville agreed to a twelve-million-dollar settlement to be paid to the Taylor family in response to the wrongful death lawsuit they filed.[72] Three months after Taylor was killed, no-knock search warrants were banned in Louisville after city council members passed "Breonna's Law."[73]

Though the killing of Floyd arguably received wider attention given the virality of his murder, people throughout the country and in several places around the world flocked to the streets in 2020 to protest police brutality and racial injustice in the United States, while holding up signs and chanting phrases that also drew attention to Taylor's killing, such as "Say her name."[74] Protestors, and Taylor's family, have demanded police reform and accountability. The reactions to the killings of Taylor, Floyd, and Arbery shine light on the mental, emotional, and physical toll such cases have on African Americans; events that should be rare are unfortunately commonplace, and this reality is something African Americans are forced to grapple with.

Purpose of the Book

The cases mentioned above exemplify one form of psychosocial stressor (discriminatory experiences) that African Americans confront on a daily basis and the emotional reactions elicited by such stressors. However, there are many other types of stressors experienced by African Americans—including, but not limited to, income inequality, health disparities, poor education, and lack of upward mobility in jobs. There is a tremendous amount of research on African Americans and coping, but this research has been primarily relegated to psychology and public health. The question this book seeks to answer is: If coping mechanisms affect general social, psychological, and health outcomes, why wouldn't they affect political attitudes and behavior? However, we know much less about the ways coping influences actions and attitudes in the political sphere.

Throughout this book, we shed light on the ways in which coping can inform and enrich studies within the field of political science. More specifically, we explore how coping influences reactions to discrimination, the consumption of Black information, support for race-specific policies, attitudes toward American values, intragroup and ideological beliefs, and political participation. We offer theoretical and empirical evidence supporting our argument that coping plays an important role in the study of political behavior and political psychology. Moreover, coping has applicability to studies on public opinion and decision making, among others. We show throughout this book that coping is intertwined with the ways in which individuals react to distressing situations, the types of information they seek and consume, the ideological views and attitudes they embrace, and the types of (race-specific) policies they support. We firmly believe that studying coping within the field of political science is crucial at present and will become even more important in the future.

Book Outline

In chapter 1, we explore coping in its various forms. We trace its theoretical roots and show how scholars have defined and approached it in different ways. Along the way, we make clear through references to previous research that coping plays a significant role in a number of outcomes, including (but not limited to) social, psychological, and health outcomes. We draw from the coping literature the particular form of coping known as John Henryism Active Coping, which we argue is missing from the political science literature. An overview of the literature on JHAC shows its wide application, and sets the stage for us to explore its influence on political attitudes and behaviors.

In chapter 2, we offer a more detailed overview of the JHAC measure and the empirics associated with it. We discuss our data and methods at large, which appear throughout the book in various analyses, and present a series of tables that help to put our findings into perspective.

In chapter 3, we explore the role coping plays in reactions to discrimination. We begin with an example of a recent event that occurred in May 2020 to illustrate the significance and relevance of discriminatory experiences before moving into a brief overview of the literature on reactions to discrimination. We expect to find that individuals who are high-effort copers will be more likely to react to discrimination in a handful of ways (for example, doing something about it, praying about it), and we run a series of models to test our expectations. We find that, controlling for the effects of other variables, high-effort copers are more likely than low-effort copers to pray, to work harder to prove other wrongs, and to try to do something about experiences of discrimination. We discuss the implications of these findings as well as potential explanations for them and offer ideas for future research.

In chapter 4, we explore the relationship between coping and ideological views. More specifically, we explore the relationship between coping and Black nationalism, as well as coping and American values. We begin this chapter, much like the preceding and subsequent empirical chapters, with an example illustrating the modern-day significance of this topic. We expect high-effort copers to be more likely than low-effort copers to embrace ideological views that fall under the umbrellas of Black nationalism and American values and find support for this in our empirical results. We discuss potential explanations for our findings along with implications.

In chapter 5, we explore the role coping plays in policy preferences. More specifically, we explore the effect of coping on African Americans' race-specific policy positions and preferences. We expect high-effort copers to be more likely than low-effort copers to support race-specific policies and find empirical support for this. We discuss implications of our findings and limitations in our study, and we suggest ideas for future research.

In chapter 6, we explore the relationship between coping and Black information consumption. We draw from studies concerning identity, racial orientation, and socialization, as well as from those concerning media consumption and information sources. In doing so, we further expand our argument that coping plays a role in a multitude of contexts: in this case, in the information individuals consume. We expect to find that high-effort copers will be more likely to consume Black information than low-effort copers (and consume them more often), and our empirical results show support for this hypothesis. We offer potential explanations, implications, and limitations of this study.

In chapter 7, we explore the role coping plays in political participation. Based on the political science literature on efficacy, and the literature on JHAC, we expect to find that high-effort copers will be more likely to participate in politics than low-effort copers. However, our empirical results do not align with this expectation. We offer potential explanations for this unexpected finding; most notably, we argue that when it comes to political participation, context matters. While coping and political participation are not strongly related in this study under the years for which we have data available, we argue that more recent years are likely to show a strong relationship between coping and political participation. Importantly, these results, which do not align with theoretical expectations in the ways that those in the preceding empirical chapters do, are a clear illustration of why/how it is essential to expand the study of JHAC. This measure does not, to our knowledge, appear in recent surveys, but we argue that it would be extremely insightful if incorporated into future studies, given the relevance and rise in significance of coping in a variety of contexts.

In our final chapter, we wrap up the book by briefly highlighting our argument and the theoretical and empirical contribution it makes to the study of coping and the political science literature. We reiterate why studying coping matters, and how the JHAC measure in particular can expand our knowledge and understanding of the role coping plays in the political sphere. We again highlight limitations of our work, implications of our findings, and potential avenues for future research.

Ultimately, it is our goal in this book to start a conversation and advance the incorporation of coping into political science. We strive to make it clear that coping plays an essential role in the political world, including in the study of political attitudes and behavior, and this book offers a first look at how political science and related fields can benefit from including coping in relevant studies. It is our hope that future surveys and studies in political science will take JHAC into consideration and use it, allowing for more data and richer analyses using this measure in the future. We argue that in addition to affecting social, psychological, and health outcomes, coping also affects political outcomes, and future research would be enriched by its inclusion. In presenting numerous cases that highlight the modern relevance of psychosocial stressors and the frequency at which certain groups face (and have to manage) them, along with empirical tests of the role JHAC plays in the political world, we show throughout this book that coping has long been important to the study of politics, and its significance is bound to increase in the polarized era we live in.

CHAPTER 1

Coping

Coping is measured using the John Henryism Active Coping scale in this book, and we are therefore most interested in JHAC and its applicability to political studies. We demonstrate its usefulness and significance in the study of political science in the subsequent empirical chapters. However, this chapter first serves as a broad overview of the literature on coping, which spans multiple disciplines. We trace its historical roots, how it has been studied over time, and briefly discuss different measures of it, before more extensively detailing JHAC. In doing so, we build the argument that coping matters—it has been shown to affect a multitude of outcomes—and political science would do well to start incorporating measures, such as JHAC, that capture its complexity and the role it plays in the political sphere.

Many studies have explored coping through either the animal model of stress and control, or the psychoanalytic ego psychology model.[1] The former approach reflects Darwinian thought in that it explores coping through a survival standpoint of animal behavior.[2] This model largely focuses on drive or arousal, and behavioral responses such as avoidance and escape.[3] Through this lens, "coping is frequently defined as acts that control aversive environmental conditions, thereby lowering psychophysiological disturbance."[4] While this model has its place and purpose, its limitations with regard to explaining human coping and defense mechanisms—and more specifically the complexity of cognitive coping—have led many scholars to favor or embrace other models (such as the psychoanalytic ego psychology model).[5]

In the psychoanalytic ego psychology model, behavior is still examined, but more focus is given to cognition.[6] In this model, "coping is defined as realistic and flexible thoughts and acts that solve problems and thereby reduce stress."[7] Studies involving such models place particular emphasis on ego defenses and some include a hierarchy wherein coping is often viewed as the highest ego process.[8] In one such study, Karl Menninger[9] identifies coping devices such as talking about or thinking through things—strategies at the top of the hierarchy that may lessen tensions resulting from common occurrences while keeping a sense of balance and order.[10]

Psychoanalytic ego psychology models have heavily influenced the literature on coping theory and measurement.[11] While this type of model allows for a better understanding of cognitive coping and human defense mechanisms than the animal model, it also has limitations for studying coping.[12] One of the issues with studying coping through this approach is that it, too, can be a bit simplistic.[13] When such models are applied to coping theory and measurement, they can be limited to classifications of people and predictions about coping behavior, and as a result, coping may be viewed and measured as a steady trait or style rather than as a process susceptible to change.[14]

Coping as a Trait or Style

Coping styles and traits are similar in that they paint a picture of how an individual will relate or react to others and certain situations. Coping styles tend to be broader than traits and often refer to the pervading ways in which individuals relate to certain types of people (e.g., those with power and those without), while traits are narrower and refer to personal qualities that predispose individuals to respond in specific ways depending on the type of situation.[15] Among the most prominent traits in the coping litera-ture[16] are repression-sensitization[17] and coping-avoiding.[18] Through the trait approach, researchers often view coping "as habitual problem-solving thoughts and actions."[19] This perspective often presents coping as a static concept.

Scholars commonly use interviews and questionnaires to tap into defini-tions of traits and styles in order to make inferences or assumptions about how people will cope in certain situations.[20] Drawing from psychoanalytic theory, Michael Goldstein explains, "Defenses such as intellectualization, reaction formation, and projection might be classified as coping styles which would result in greater vigilance for threat, while repression and denial represent attempts to avoid awareness of threat."[21] Within this framework, scholars make predictions about how an individual, who reflects a certain trait or embraces a certain style, may respond to a particular situation. A variety of trait measures are used to study coping and include (but are not limited to) the sentence completion method,[22] the repression-sensitization scale (Byrne R-S scale),[23] and the defense mechanisms inventory,[24] among others.[25]

Scholars who study coping through the trait approach focus mainly on personalities and how they shape responses, but trait measurements are often limited in that they do not always provide information on or accurately predict an individual's actual coping processes.[26] Frances Cohen and Richard Lazarus's 1973 study[27] examining the coping dispositions and active coping processes of sixty-one surgical patients (with comparable medical issues) reflects this limitation of traits as predictors.[28] Prior to surgery, the patients were interviewed and their emotional state, knowledge concerning the operation, and additional desired information was assessed.[29] In directly assessing coping—by examining actual thoughts and actions at the time of the threat—this study went beyond what most trait measures are capable of.[30] Each patient was given a coping disposition measure, ranging in dimension from extreme avoidant coping (they did not know much about the operation, nor did they want to know), to extreme vigilant coping (they knew a lot about the operation and desired to know even more).[31] Patients were placed into one of three groups—avoidance, vigilance, or both.[32]

Similar coping disposition measures for preoperative anxiety and prior life stress were included, and a standard trait measure—the Byrne R-S scale—was administered.[33] In order to test the relationship between coping dispositions (and processes) and recovery from surgery, Cohen and Lazarus used five variables for recovery: number of days in the hospital, number of pain medications, minor medical complications, negative psychological reactions, and the sum of these.[34] Their results indicate that the trait measure and recovery were not clearly or consistently related, but that the process measure was related to two of the recovery outcomes (number of days in the hospital and minor medical complications).[35]

In general, trait measures of coping, which frequently assess coping along only one dimension, often fail to account for the full complexity of coping and variations in coping efforts.[36] While people may be prone to certain behaviors or thoughts in response to stressful situations, these thoughts and behaviors may vary depending on a variety of factors, including the situation at hand, the individual, and the environment. Rudolf Moos and Vivien Davis Tsu[37] highlight the complexity of coping with the example of physical illness.[38] When dealing with physical illness, a patient faces multiple stressors, such as the environment (e.g., a hospital), pain associated with the illness, stress and anxiety surrounding any potential or necessary procedures, the demands of the individuals involved (e.g., medical professionals), maintaining relationships (e.g., with family and friends) and self-image, and navigating emotions.[39] Thus, when facing multiple stressors, such as in the case of physical illness, an individual is likely to rely on more than one coping strategy, which is difficult to capture in a single measure.[40]

Another issue within the psychoanalytic ego psychology model of coping (as well as the animal model) is that coping is often considered as having a positive connotation and associated with mastery or success.[41] When coping and defense are situated in a hierarchical fashion with coping at the top, as in some psychoanalytic ego psychology models, the impression is given that some processes are better than others and associated with certain outcomes.[42] With that said, an emphasis on mastery is not necessarily problematic enough on its own to render a certain definition or measurement of coping obsolete. Take, for example, "John Henryism (JH)" and "its strong emphasis on environmental mastery," which Sherman A. James, Sue A. Hartnett, and William D. Kalsbeek explain as being similar to the concepts of personal efficacy and locus of control.[43] The contexts in which definitions and measures of coping are developed and deployed matter, as they also play a role in strengthening or weakening the construct. This is particularly evident when comparing the strengths of the JH measure to the weaknesses of some trait measures of coping. One way of overcoming some of the weaknesses associated with certain measures of coping is to consider the multifaceted nature of it and to study it using more than one dimension, which is what Lazarus and Folkman do.[44] In addition, they advocate for studying coping processes separately from coping outcomes and recognizing that these can differ from person to person or even within the same individual across different contexts.[45]

Coping as a Process

In reviewing the weaknesses of some definitions and measurements of coping, Lazarus and Folkman[46] put forth their own cognitive theory of coping wherein they argue that it is a complex process. Paying careful attention to the prior literature and addressing many of the limitations they identified in existing definitions, Lazarus and Folkman[47] define coping as "constantly changing cognitive and behavioral efforts to manage specific external and/ or internal demands that are appraised as taxing or exceeding the resources of the person."[48] While coping definitions do vary across and within disciplines, in psychology, Lazarus and Folkman's definition is widely accepted.[49]

An important part of this research is recognizing the conscious effort involved in coping responses and distinguishing them from automatized responses.[50] In addition, this definition of coping "involves efforts to alter the stressful situation (i.e., problem-focused coping) as well as efforts to regulate the emotional distress associated with the situation (i.e., emotion-focused coping)."[51] An example of problem-focused coping is seeking information, while an example of emotion-focused coping is turning to others for emotional support.[52] Problem-focused and emotion-focused coping efforts have been widely studied in coping research following the contributions of Lazarus and Folkman.[53] While the two forms of coping are different, it has been argued that people rely on both when they encounter stressful situations, and that both can alleviate psychological distress.[54] Moreover, unlike the trait approach, this approach is concerned with direct assessments of actual thoughts and actions within a particular context, as well as how the process changes or may change over time.[55] The process approach suggests that how people cope depends on multiple factors, including situational (e.g., controllability) and individual (e.g., self-confidence) factors.[56]

To paint a fuller picture of the coping as a process approach, it is important to discuss appraisal theory. This theory is featured in the work of Lazarus and Folkman and plays an important role in stress and coping theory.[57] Appraisal theory "suggests that emotions are elicited as a result of people's assessments of a given event or situation."[58] The assessments themselves, an evaluation of whether a situation relates to their well-being or not, come about through a process known as cognitive appraisal.[59]

Cognitive appraisal includes primary appraisals and secondary appraisals, and while the terminology may erroneously imply there is an order to them, Lazarus and Folkman[60] warn against viewing them in such a manner. A primary appraisal is an evaluation of whether a certain situation is relevant (challenging, threatening, or stressful) to individuals (for instance, whether or not it has ramifications for their well-being, goals, or sense of self), while a secondary appraisal is an assessment of the options (such as coping potential and resources) available for dealing with the situation.[61] Importantly, appraisals can occur simultaneously; for example, an individual may assess a situation as both challenging and threatening.[62] In addition, appraisals are susceptible to change, as are emotions.[63] It is for these reasons, among others, that Lazarus and Folkman advocate for the coping as a process approach. To better understand how and why an individual copes a certain way, understanding first how they appraise a situation can be insightful.

Additional Definitions and Measurements

There are many variations in how coping is defined and measured. While a complete list and full breakdown is beyond the scope of this chapter, it is worth briefly mentioning some of these additional definitions and measurements of coping. For example, the relationship between culture and coping has been explored, and a cultural coping research program has emerged.[64] Scholars have looked at how people differ in their coping processes, how these differences may reflect "patterns across national, racial, and ethnic groups," and how "cultural dimensions, such as collectivism-individualism" may influence coping.[65] One concept within this literature is "collective coping," which is described as "a form of coping extending beyond social support that encompasses the action of multiple group members to resolve a single problem."[66]

In studies exploring cultural dimensions such as individualism and collectivism, scholars have found notable differences in coping.[67] For example, while collectivists are more prone to relying on their in-group(s) for support and resources, and often embrace emotion-focused coping and/or avoidance coping,[68] individualists are more likely to use methods that center the individual, such as active coping and problem-focused coping.[69] A number of measures have been created to address cultural-based variability in coping.[70] These include, but are not limited to, the Collectivistic Coping scale, created by Christine Yeh et al.,[71] the Collectivist Coping Styles inventory,[72] the Cross-Cultural Coping Scale,[73] the Collectivistic Coping Style measure,[74] and others.[75]

Another measure of coping is the Mainz Coping Inventory (MCI).[76] Building on the coping research that follows the personality or trait approach and emphasizes two main constructs (vigilance and avoidance), and similar in that sense to the Byrne R-S scale,[77] the MCI was designed to overcome the one-dimensional nature of previous measures through the use of a two-dimensional measure of coping.[78] The MCI "is devised as a stimulus-response inventory. It originated from the model of coping modes (MCM),[79] which describes and explains individual differences in behavioral regulation under stressful conditions."[80]

Moreover, drawing on the distinction between approach and avoidance, the Miller Behavioral Style Scale (MBSS)[81] is another measure that enables scholars to study coping styles and responses to stressors. More specifically, the MBSS distinguishes between "monitors (information seekers) [and] blunters (distractors)";[82] it presents scenarios that potentially evoke stress, and respondents are asked to select which statements (four of a monitoring variety, and four of a blunting variety) are applicable to them based on the scenario. In addition, there is the Coping Orientation to Problems Experienced (COPE) inventory,[83] and the subsequent Brief COPE.[84] Both the original COPE inventory and the Brief COPE are multidimensional measures designed to evaluate various coping strategies,[85] and have been largely used in public health studies with some success in linking certain coping responses to certain health predictors. The Brief COPE contains fourteen scales with two items in each scale, and each scale has a different conceptual focus (for example, active coping and denial are two of the scales).[86]

The list of coping scales and questionnaires continues to grow. Additional measures include (but are not limited to) the Coping Strategies Inventory,[87] the Ways of Coping checklist,[88] the Coping Strategy Indicator,[89] the Coping Self-Efficacy Scale,[90] the Brief Resilient Coping Scale,[91] and the Proactive Coping Inventory.[92] While some coping measures are broad and applicable to a variety of purposes and participants, others are narrower and designed for particular purposes and participants, or focus on specific coping behaviors.[93] For example, scales designed to measure specific coping behaviors include (but are not limited to) the Emotional Eating Scale,[94] and more recently, the Spending as Social and Affective Coping scale.[95] Thus, scholars can (and do) study coping through a variety of approaches and measures. Next, we turn our focus to the literature on John Henryism Active Coping, which has wide applicability, and is the form of coping we focus on in this book.

John Henryism Active Coping

Featuring prominently in public health research, where the concept and associated hypothesis originated, the term *John Henryism* refers to "a strong behavioral predisposition to cope actively with psychosocial environmental stressors."[96] It is synonymous with active coping, and the terms are used interchangeably throughout this book.[97] A series of papers published in the 1970s, which established that " 'high effort' coping (that is, sustained cognitive and emotional engagement) with difficult psychosocial stressors produces substantial increases in heart rate and systolic blood pressure, increases which persist as long as individuals actively work at trying to eliminate the stressor,"[98] inspired an area of research that has been thriving ever since.

Drawing from this research, Leonard Syme[99] noted that the lower an individual's socioeconomic status (SES)—particularly in the case of African Americans in economically disadvantaged positions—the more likely they are to face challenging psychosocial environmental stressors frequently in comparison to individuals with higher SES.[100] Thus, Syme[101] hypothesized, "prolonged, high effort coping with difficult psychosocial stressors could be the most parsimonious explanation of both the inverse association between SES and hypertension typically observed in U.S. communities and the increased risk for this disorder in Black Americans."[102] Sherman James studied the research on high-effort coping, and, combined with meeting a retired African American farmer named John Henry Martin—whose name and story brought to James's mind the folktale of the steel driver John Henry, the man who beat the machine at the expense of his life—it inspired him to coin the John Henryism Hypothesis (JHH).[103] The stories of both men reflect high-effort or active coping with challenging psychosocial stressors for a prolonged period of time.[104] Given that some groups face challenging psychosocial stressors, such as financial strain and job insecurity, more often than others, this form of coping takes a toll on those individuals in particular, as it requires constant effort and energy.[105]

Importantly, the JHH is not limited in application to individuals who reflect high-effort coping. While some individuals (e.g., high-effort copers) facing routine psychosocial stressors will engage in high-effort coping consistently over time, especially those fueled by their success, others (e.g., low-effort copers) may either not put forth the same amount of energy and effort, or may do so for a certain amount of time, but ultimately give up; it is the high-effort, active copers who are predicted to increase the prevalence of high blood pressure in lower SES groups.[106] Through this lens, it is predicted that individuals who are of low SES, and who embrace a high level of John Henryism (high-effort copers), are more likely to have high blood pressure levels than individuals who score low on the John Henryism scale (low-effort copers).[107] Originally consisting of only eight items,[108] the updated twelve-item scale known as " 'The John Henryism Scale for Active Coping,' or "The John Henryism Active Coping scale," is used to measure John Henryism.[109] Inspired by scholarly works on the legend,[110] the twelve items in the scale were designed to capture and reflect three particular themes of John Henryism.[111]

The three themes captured in the JHAC scale are: "(1) efficacious mental and physical vigor; (2) a strong commitment to hard work; and (3) a single-minded determination to succeed."[112] Individuals read the twelve items that reflect these themes, and are asked to provide a response ranging from 1 (completely false) to 5 (completely true).[113] Therefore, overall scores on the scale range from 12 at the lowest (for individuals who respond with "completely false" for every item) to 60 at the highest (for individuals who respond with "completely true" for every item).[114] Individuals who score above the sample median are classified as "high" in JH, while individuals who score at or below the sample median are classified as "low" in JH.[115] A sample item from the scale, as provided by James, is "I've always felt that I could make of my life pretty much what I wanted to make of it."[116] Individuals with "a high John Henryism orientation," unlike those with a low John Henryism orientation, "believe that just about any obstacle can be overcome through hard work and a strong determination to succeed."[117] The exact twelve items that make up the JHAC scale are listed in the subsequent chapter.

The JHAC measure appears frequently in the coping literature, and has held up strongly over time. We argue that this measure captures the complexity of coping, including the component that mainly focuses on beliefs, as well as the degree of effort an individual puts forth that shapes their behavior. Thus, it is likely to capture aspects of both emotion- and problem-focused coping. In the next portion of this chapter, we focus on the effects of coping acknowledged in this literature.

Effects of Coping

Regardless the coping definition or measure used, it has been established that how people cope with stress affects a variety of outcomes, including their psychological, physical, and social well-being.[118] "Coping· researchers argue that how people deal with stress can reduce or amplify the effects of adverse life events and conditions, not just on emotional distress and short-term functioning, but also long-term, on the development of physical and mental health or disorder."[119] As a result, a bulk of the literature on coping focuses on its relationship with health.

Both problem-focused and emotion-focused coping strategies have demonstrated significant correlations with overall health outcomes—the former often associated positively with overall health outcomes, and strategies such as distancing, avoidance, and confrontive coping, each often negatively correlated with overall health outcomes.[120] Individuals often use both types of coping strategies.[121] In addition, just as Lazarus and Folkman have argued, there are a variety of factors that influence the outcomes associated with certain coping strategies, and not all individuals will experience the same outcome even if they employ the same strategy. Situational characteristics, such as the type of stressor, whether it is controllable or uncontrollable, and the stressor duration can all play a role.[122] JHAC is a good example of this. While it has been linked to a number of health outcomes, including hypertension,[123] increased risk for cardiovascular disease,[124] and tobacco use behavior,[125] research shows that its effect varies.

Physical Health Outcomes

Given what is known about how stress affects an individual, a number of studies examine the relationship between coping and health outcomes. Among these are studies assessing the relationship between John Henryism (JH) and health.[126] Some of the earliest studies examining this relationship focused on JH's interaction with blood pressure, and more specifically hypertension, and the related risk for cardiovascular disease among individuals of a low SES.[127] However, the results have been mixed.[128]

While some studies have found some support for the interaction between John Henryism and low SES affecting blood pressure and cardiovascular functioning,[129] other studies have not found the same John Henryism effect.[130] However, it is important to note that the differences in findings across empirical studies testing the effect of John Henryism on health outcomes may boil down to differences in approach (testing an interactive effect of John Henryism, as the JHH advances, versus testing an independent effect of John Henryism), or differences in population samples.[131] This echoes the literature that argues coping is complex and involves multiple factors. Just as James originally hypothesized, other factors, such as socioeconomic status, should be considered.

Moreover, Bennett et al. point out that the empirical studies that have found support for the JHH "have largely been conducted among subjects drawn from the Southeastern United States, which may provide some support for the view[132] that sociocultural aspects of this region may be significantly implicated in the expression of JH."[133] While the effect of John Henryism on health outcomes has held up in studies focusing on low-SES African American men in rural areas, other studies have also found support for it in different populations and areas.[134] For example, Duijkers et al. find that high John Henryism is associated with higher blood pressure in men in a sample of Dutch men and women.[135] Gupta, Belanger, and Phillips also find support for the hypothesis in a sample of low-income individuals from Saint-Hyacinthe, Quebec,[136] suggesting that the effects of John Henryism are not limited to a certain population or region.

Though some studies suggest John Henryism is linked to a higher risk for a number of negative health outcomes, other studies find that its effects are mixed or even result in positive health outcomes.[137] For example, Bonham, Sellers, and Neighbors, in examining the relationship between John Henryism and self-reported health status among a group of high-SES African American men, find that it is actually a beneficial resource and has positive effects on health.[138] Importantly, however, and similar to other studies, the authors note that high-SES plays a role in their results; individuals from such a category are more likely to have better health care and more resources (on account of their economic and/or educational success) than those from a low-SES group.[139]

In addition, van Loon et al., in their study examining the relationships between personality, coping, and lifestyle risk factors for cancer among 2,514 men and women aged twenty to sixty-five in the Netherlands,[140] found an association between John Henryism and smoking cessation among women. In a study examining the association of John Henryism and education on smoking behavior and nicotine dependence in a Black population,[141] Fernander et al. find that low levels of education and low levels of JHAC are associated with higher nicotine dependence scores. Interestingly, the levels of nicotine dependence were lowest at the initial stage of the study for individuals with low levels of education but high active coping scores, suggesting that high John Henryism has its benefits in certain contexts.[142]

Other scholars have found additional positive health outcomes associated with high levels of John Henryism. Jelena Čvorović and Sherman James found that higher levels of John Henryism are associated with better self-reported health among a sample of low-income Serbian Roma, particularly among Roma females.[143] Moreover, Bronder et al., in an examination of the relationships between psychological distress, well-being, and John Henryism among a diverse sample of Black women, found that John Henryism is positively related to and beneficial for mental health outcomes.[144]

Going beyond JHAC and its effects on physical health, scholars have also found that other forms of coping affect health outcomes. Coping strategies such as distancing, denial, and avoidance pose potentially serious physical health risks, for example, when they result in delayed medical treatment.[145] Moreover, individuals who embrace these coping styles may also embrace risky behaviors, such as alcohol and/or drug (ab)use.[146] On the other hand, self-control is a coping strategy that can have positive effects on physical health, particularly when it inspires individuals to use problem-focused coping and/or reach out for social support.[147]

Psychological Outcomes

Life stressors are associated with psychological and physical distress,[148] which means that beyond physical health outcomes, coping can also affect psychological outcomes in a variety of ways. Bronder et al. found in a diverse sample of Black women that higher levels of John Henryism were associated with lower levels of depressive symptoms.[149] However, they also acknowledge that John Henryism may serve as a buffer or mask for depressive symptoms among Black women, who face pressure to be strong. In another study examining how coping may affect depressive symptoms, Holahan et al. found a link between avoidance coping and future problems (chronic and acute life stressors), as well as future depressive symptoms.[150] Not only were individuals who relied on avoidance coping likely to have more life stressors four years later, they were also more likely to present depressive symptoms ten years later.[151] These results reflect the dynamic nature of coping and how it can affect individuals not only in the short term, but also in the long run.

In an examination of coping profiles and perceived stress and health-related behaviors among 578 French students, Doron et al. found that high copers and avoidant copers demonstrated higher levels of perceived stress than adaptive copers and low copers.[152] In addition, they found that high copers and avoidant copers (in comparison to low copers and adaptive copers) participated more in unhealthy behaviors. This study is yet another that speaks to the variability in coping strategies and outcomes, in that individuals who were actively coping and individuals who were embracing avoidance coping were both found to display greater perceived stress and unhealthy behaviors than their fellow participants embracing other forms of coping.[153] However, this study also reinforces the argument that people often combine coping strategies, and they do this differently depending on the situation and the person.

In addition to avoidance, coping forms such as denial and distancing are also associated with distress and depression.[154] Choosing to avoid a situation or not think about a certain stressor, for example, may be comforting in the moment, but may result in negative consequences later on. These coping strategies may also lead an individual to turn to alcohol or drugs for comfort, or other risky behaviors that may increase their risk of disease.[155] Moreover, scholars who study the relationship between coping and psychological outcomes note the lack of access to quality mental health care, especially among individuals who are more likely to experience frequent challenging stressors (including African Americans and more broadly, the poor).[156] This is worth noting because a lack of resources, particularly in terms of health care, has the potential to affect an individual's psychological outcomes just as much as, if not more than, the coping strategy they choose to embrace. In addition, a lack of resources can limit an individual's coping options.

Monitoring, another form of coping, can also affect psychological outcomes. Scholars have found that in comparison to blunters, monitors are more prone to anxiety[157] and depression.[158] This may be due, in part, to their tendency to seek more information, some of which may not be pleasant or positive. Monitors are also more likely than blunters to be distressed during invasive screening exams,[159] and are more prone to anticipating physical pain and discomfort throughout medical procedures.[160]

An emotion-focused coping strategy, such as seeking social support, may benefit the health of individuals in certain contexts, such as in the workplace.[161] By seeking and receiving social support in the form of informational help with a work-related problem, for example, an individual is less likely to feel distress and uncertainty.[162] Seeking social support may also reduce an individual's feelings of isolation and loneliness when dealing with job-related stressors.[163]

Social Outcomes

Social factors can both affect and be affected by how people cope. Leonard Pearlin explains,

> Many stressful experiences . . . don't spring out of a vacuum but typically can be traced back to surrounding social structures and people's locations within them. The most encompassing of these structures are the various systems of stratification that cut across societies, such as those based on social and economic class, race and ethnicity, gender, and age. To the extent that these systems embody the unequal distribution of resources, opportunities, and self-regard, a low status within them may itself be a source of stressful life conditions.[164]

Scholars acknowledge that certain groups, particularly African Americans, experience racism and social and economic adversity far more often than others.[165] The stress and hardships that come with living in an oppressive society may be reason enough to explain the mental and physical health disparities between African Americans and whites, but may also explain why individuals from oppressed groups may embrace high-effort, or active coping styles such as John Henryism in an attempt to take back some sense of control.[166] Research has shown that African Americans tend to demonstrate John Henryism more often, on average, than whites,[167] and the research that inspired the JHH shows why that may be the case.

Individuals who frequently confront psychosocial stressors, such as African Americans, are constantly trying to overcome social and economic disadvantages. Social and environmental stressors may thus influence coping styles and make certain individuals or groups more likely to embrace high-effort coping, and the combination of the stressors and the forms of coping employed has effects on social outcomes. For example, individuals who constantly face psychosocial stressors, but who believe anything can be accomplished with hard work and motivation (high-effort copers), may be more likely to advance in their careers due to their commitment to overcome challenges and their belief in their ability to succeed. Similarly, low-effort copers, who are less likely to believe that factors are within their control, may not perform at the same level as high-effort copers in the workplace because they may not see opportunity for mobility as something they can control. Recent studies that have found an association between John Henryism and high SES with greater self-reported health and overall well-being lend some support to this idea.[168]

Some individuals seek social support when dealing with stressors, which has been positively associated with overall well-being and quality of health.[169] Culture also plays a role in social outcomes. While some individuals may turn to family and/or close friends for support, which contributes to and helps to maintain close bonds, others may withdraw and isolate themselves so as to not be a burden. In individualistic societies, for example, people may be more likely to turn to strangers (such as therapists) than to friends in order to navigate stressors in life, while in collectivistic societies, this is not often the case.[170]

Moreover, scholars have found that relationships and relationship dynamics can affect social processing and coping behavior, which in turn can affect both relationships and relationship dynamics.[171] When dealing with health-related stressors in a relationship, such as couples dealing with early-stage breast cancer, Manne et al. found that for both individuals in the couple, perceptions of their partner's unsupportive behavior had an effect on their social and health outcomes.[172] They found that individuals who perceived their partner as being unsupportive were more likely to hold back from sharing concerns and more likely to disengage, thus negatively affecting one another's cognitive and social processing of the disease. These findings demonstrate that coping behavior in a relationship can affect communication, both partners, and the relationship itself.

The Gap

In this chapter, we have provided an overview of the literature on coping, paying particular attention to the models, theories, definitions, measurements, and effects of coping studied within the fields of psychology, behavioral medicine, and public health, and to a lesser extent, within the fields of biology and sociology. The research makes clear that coping is defined and measured in a variety of ways, and its effects on health, psychological, and social outcomes are well documented. However, an important gap appears to remain in that coping, particularly John Henryism Active Coping, has not been given the same attention in the field of political science. In the following chapters, we continue to build on our argument that coping, and JHAC in particular, influences an additional area of life: political behaviors and attitudes.

CHAPTER 2

Measuring and Analyzing the Influence of John Henryism Active Coping

As discussed in chapter 1, prior research shows that the way one copes with psychosocial stressors affects a host of social, psychological, and health outcomes. For this reason, we believe coping research has the potential to shed light on why people act in a certain way or hold certain beliefs in the political sphere.

In this chapter, our discussion focuses on active coping, as measured with John Henryism Active Coping and the empirics associated with it. The measure that we use was developed by Sherman James.[1] As highlighted in the previous chapter, JHAC refers to "a strong behavioral predisposition to cope actively with psychosocial environmental stressors,"[2] which is synonymous with active coping.[3] Examples of such stressors include unemployment/underemployment, chronic financial strain, unrelenting family obligations, and discrimination. The John Henryism Hypothesis is rooted in the assumption that individuals of lower socioeconomic status, and especially African Americans, frequently face psychosocial stressors that require them to expend substantial energy on a daily basis in order to manage the stress that stems from these circumstances.[4]

However, the JHH is also rooted in the assumption that not all individuals facing routine psychosocial stressors consistently respond with the same amount or level of effort; those who do constantly put forth considerable effort to manage their stressors are reflective of high-effort, active coping (or high John Henryism), and are often fueled by their success, while individuals who either do not put forth high effort or only do so for a certain amount of time, before giving up, are reflective of low-effort, passive coping (or low John Henryism).[5] Throughout this book, we often refer to individuals who score high on John Henryism, also known as high copers or active copers, as "high-effort copers," and to individuals who score low on John Henryism, also known as low copers or passive copers, as "low-effort copers." Unlike low-effort copers, high-effort copers believe that "just about any obstacle can be overcome through hard work and a strong determination."[6]

Since the introduction of the JHAC construct in the mid-1980s, research on it has flourished, and much of the proliferation has been relegated to health-related and psychological topics—such as blood pressure,[7] hypertension,[8] cardiovascular reactivity,[9] physical activity,[10] cholesterol,[11] depressive symptoms,[12] and tobacco use behavior.[13] Consequently, studies show empirical support for the JHAC. The extensive use of JHAC in health and psychological research makes it possible to apply it to different contexts, such as the political sphere. Thus, throughout this book, we do just that.

For our analysis, we use the JHAC scale developed by James[14] as a measure of active coping. JHAC is measured by means of twelve items; see table 2.1 for the exact wording of these items. Again, these items measure "atypical mental and physical vigor; a focused determination to realize one's goals; and an unrelenting commitment with hard work."[15] Responses were coded on a four-point Likert scale—from "completely false = 1" to "completely true = 4," resulting in total scores that could range from 12 to 48. Respondents were classified as "low" on JHAC if they scored at or below the sample median and "high" if they scored above the median.[16] Among adult samples, reliability coefficients for JHAC range from 61 to 80.[17] A comprehensive study assessing the reliability and validity of JHAC shows that the measure is reliable, and Fernander et al. concluded their study with the following statement: "The study provides evidence that the JHAC is a psychometrically sound measure of active coping."[18]

In our study, the JHAC scale was again found to be highly reliable (α = .80). In using JHAC, our goal is to show that studies of African American political behavior and attitudes should also account for active coping, in addition to the usual sociodemographic, political, and psychological measures. Doing so allows us to fully capture the experiences and thought processes, as well as variation in coping styles, that shape decisions and beliefs in the political sphere. That said, as has been demonstrated in previous studies using this measure,[19] its applicability is not limited to the study of African Americans; indeed, future work can and should consider incorporating it as long as there is justification for it (for example, it would also be applicable to the study of political behavior and attitudes among individuals with a lower SES, other minority groups, and so on).

Data

In the following chapters, we use data from the National Study of American Life, a public health survey from the National Institute of Mental Health's Collaborative Psychiatric Epidemiology Survey, and the Program for Research on Black Americans at the University of Michigan.[20] Conducted in 2001 and 2003, the NSAL used a nationally representative sample of African Americans. Specifically, "data were collected using a stratified and clustered sample design, and weights were created to account for unequal probabilities of selection, non-response, and post-stratification."[21] All of the respondents were age eighteen and over. In the first phase, data were collected using face-to-face interviews and a computer-assisted program. After the initial face-to-face interviews were concluded, all respondents who participated in the first phase were invited to participate in the second phase—completing a self-administered questionnaire, which was referred to as the NSAL Adult Re-Interview (RIW). The total sample included 3,570 African Americans, 1,621 African Caribbeans (Blacks of Caribbean descent), and 891 whites. Of the 3,570 African Americans, 2,137 completed the RIW. For this research, we focus on the African American respondents who took both the initial NSAL and the RIW.

The major feature that makes the NSAL and the NSAL RIW unique is that "the study includes a large, nationally representative sample of African Americans, permitting an examination of the heterogeneity of experience across groups within this segment of the African American population."[22] Additionally, "all respondents were selected from the targeted catchment areas in proportion to the African American population, distinguishing a first national sample of different ethnic groups within Black America who live in the same contexts and geographical area in which African Americans are actually distributed—both high and low density, urban and rural, inner-city and suburban, for example."[23] Consequently, these data allow us to draw more robust generalizations from our analysis and make more confident claims regarding the role of JHAC in shaping attitudes and behaviors.

The sample of 2,137 respondents came from twenty-eight states plus Washington, DC. Georgia had the highest number of respondents in the sample with 230, followed by North Carolina (174), Louisiana (158), Michigan (131), and South Carolina (123). Of the twenty-two states without any respondents, only two, Arkansas and Delaware, had an Africa American population in the 2000 Census greater than 10 percent, and Arkansas was the only southern state without any respondents. Arizona, Oregon, and

Minnesota were the only states with an African American population of less than 5 percent with respondents in the sample. Overall, the number of respondents and the percentage of a state's population that is African American correlated at .62.

The NSAL queried respondents regarding "intra- and inter-group racial and ethnic differences in mental disorders, psychological distress and informal and formal service use, as they are manifested in the context of a variety of stressors, risk and resilient factors, and coping resources."[24] The survey also included social, cultural, psychological, and political questions ranging from voting habits to policy positions to questions about discrimination. While these questions make up a small part of the project, the survey provides an excellent and unique opportunity for analysis, given the nationally representative sample of African Americans and the inclusion of JHAC.[25]

Descriptives

The central focus of this book is to explore the effect JHAC has on African American political behavior and beliefs. However, in this chapter, we highlight the JHAC measure and provide an empirical overview. As stated previously, JHAC is a twelve-item scale that measures active coping. Responses are coded from "completely false" (1) to "completely true" (4). Thus, the total score can range from 12 to 48.

Table 2.1 presents responses to each of the twelve items. As the table shows, a majority of the respondents indicated "somewhat true" or "completely true" for each of the questions. For example, for question 1 ("I've always felt that I could make of my life pretty much what I wanted to make of it"), 93.8 percent of the respondents either indicated that it was somewhat or completely true. There is a bit more variability in responses to questions 4, 5, 11, and 12—with 22.7 percent, 20.2 percent, 20.1 percent, and 12.9 percent, respectively, indicating "completely false" or "somewhat false."

Only those who answered all of the JHAC items were included in our analysis. The sample median score was 40. Respondents then were further categorized as low or high—"low" on the JHAC scale if they scored at or below the sample median and "high" if they scored above the median.[26] 1,108 respondents (54 percent) were in the low JHAC group, while 923 respondents (46 percent) were in the high JHAC group.

Table 2.1. John Henryism Active Coping Scale

	n (wt. %)			
	Completely false	Somewhat false	Somewhat true	Completely true
I've always felt that I could make of my life pretty much what I wanted to make of it.	27 (1.30)	101 (4.95)	1,061 (49.83)	919 (43.92)
Once I make up my mind to do something, I stay with it until the job is completely done.	19 (0.76)	100 (4.75)	890 (41.91)	1,102 (52.57)
I don't let my personal feelings get in the way of getting a job done.	30 (1.27)	178 (8.60)	873 (42.30)	1,023 (47.83)
It's important for me to be able to do things in the way I want to do them rather than in the way other people want me to do them.	86 (3.57)	400 (19.15)	892 (42.88)	728 (34.40)
Sometimes I feel that if anything is going to be done right, I have to do it myself.	103 (4.54)	325 (15.68)	849 (40.85)	837 (39.93)
I like doing things that other people thought could not be done.	63 (3.24)	215 (9.80)	948 (44.46)	875 (42.50)
I feel that I am the kind of individual who stands up for what he [or she] believes in, regardless of the consequences.	32 (1.46)	139 (6.20)	883 (42.25)	1,057 (50.09)
Hard work has really helped me to get ahead in life.	61 (2.21)	191 (9.07)	812 (38.31)	1,045 (50.42)
When things don't go the way I want them to, that just makes me work even harder.	47 (2.23)	223 (10.60)	988 (46.81)	845 (40.36)

continued on next page

Table 2.1. Continued.

	n (wt. %)				
	Completely false	Somewhat false	Somewhat true	Completely true
It's not always easy, but I manage to find a way to do the things I really need to get done.	9 (0.30)	61 (2.96)	868 (41.58)	1,177 (55.16)
Very seldom have I been disappointed by the results of my hard work.	77 (3.82)	347 (16.28)	1,082 (51.18)	604 (28.71)
In the past, even when things got really tough, I never lost sight of my goals.	45 (1.99)	246 (10.89)	905 (43.25)	915 (43.86)

Source: Author created.

JHAC and Other Characteristics

In subsequent chapters, we test the explanatory power of JHAC on various dependent variables—such as social, psychological, and political behaviors and beliefs. We present chi-square tests between JHAC (low vs. high) and common attitudinal and behavioral variables to highlight the relationship between them. In table 2.2, we provide demographic characteristics for each of the independent variables used in the various models throughout the book. We provide total sample, weighted percent, mean, and standard deviation (when appropriate).

The sample consists of 2,135 respondents. Of those, 43.9 percent identified as male and 56.1 percent as female. JHAC across gender shows

Table 2.2. Sociodemographic and Other Characteristics of Participants, 2001–2003 National Survey of American Life

	Sample
Gender, n (wt. %)	
Male	693 (43.9)
Female	1,442 (56.1)
Age, wt. mean (SD)	42.4 (15.8)
Education, n (wt. %)	
≤ 11 years	563 (24.8)
12 years	795 (36.3)
13–15 years	480 (24.5)
≥ 16 years	297 (14.4)
Income, n (wt. %)	
≤ $9,999	419 (15.8)
$10,000–$14,999	258 (10.0)
$15,000–$24,999	456 (19.3)
$25, 000–$49,999	626 (31.5)
≥ $50, 000	376 (23.4)
Political party, n (wt. %)	
Republican	116 (7.3)
Democrat	1,472 (92.7)

continued on next page

Table 2.2. Continued.

	Sample
Political ideology, _n_ (wt. %)	
Conservative	553 (30.7)
Moderate	705 (38.7)
Liberal	585 (30.6)
Region, _n_ (wt. %)	
Non-South	912 (49.0)
South	1,223 (51.0)
Linked fate, _n_ (wt. %)	
No	791 (37.2)
Yes	1,300 (62.9)
Race relations, _n_ (wt. %)	
Very dissatisfied	205 (10.2)
Somewhat dissatisfied	575 (26.5)
Somewhat satisfied	992 (47.9)
Very satisfied	330 (15.5)
Frequency of religious attendance, _n_ (wt. %)	
Once a year or less	195 (11.5)
Few times a year	404 (21.2)
Few times a month	524 (26.6)
At least once a week	743 (35.8)
Nearly every day	119 (5.0)
Racial centrality, _n_ (wt. %)	
Low	745 (35.4)
High	1,319 (64.6)
Public regard, _n_ (wt. %)	
Low	1,455 (69.7)
High	615 (30.3)
Social dominance orientation, wt. mean (SD)	8 (2.9)
Feelings toward Whites, wt. mean (SD)	59.7 (22.3)
Everyday discrimination, wt. mean (SD)	20.3 (8.1)
Lifetime discrimination, wt. mean (SD)	1.5 (1.7)

Source: Author created.

that among those with low JHAC, 54.3 percent were female, while 45.7 percent were male. Among those with high JHAC, 57.1 percent were female, while 42.9 percent were male. The results show that there is not a significant relationship between JHAC and gender ($p = 0.316$).

Age is a continuous variable, with a mean score of forty-two years. The results show that there is not a significant relationship between JHAC and age. Descriptive statistics show that there is a variation in educational attainment: 24.8 percent of respondents had up to eleven years of education, 36.3 percent had twelve years, 24.5 percent had between thirteen and fifteen years, and 14.4 percent had sixteen or more years. JHAC across education shows that among those with low JHAC, 20.7 percent were in the 0–11 years of education category, 34.9 percent in the 12 years category, 27.8 percent in the 13–15 years category, and 16.6 percent in the 16(+) years category. Among those with high JHAC, 29.6 percent were in the 0–11 years of education category, 37 percent in the 12 years category, 21 percent in the 13–15 years category, and 12.5 percent in the 16(+) years category. The results show that there is a significant relationship between JHAC and education ($p = 0.000$).

There is also quite a bit of variation in income earned. Most respondents in the sample fall into two income categories: those earning $25,000 to $49,999 (31.5 percent) and those earning greater than or equal to $50,000 (23.4 percent). JHAC across income shows that among those with low JHAC, 12.8 percent were in the less than or equal to $9,999 income category, 9.8 percent in the $10,000–$14,999 category, 19.4 percent in the $15,000–$24,999 category, 34 percent in the $25,000–$49,999 category, and 24.1 percent in the $50,000 or more category. Among those with high JHAC, 18.7 percent were in the less than or equal to $9,999 income category, 9.8 percent in the $10,000–$14,999 category, 19.2 percent in the $15,000–$24,999 category, 29.4 percent in the $25,000–$49,999 category, and 23 percent in the $50,000 or more category. The results show that there is a significant relationship between JHAC and income ($p = 0.033$).

In terms of political party affiliation, an overwhelming majority of the respondents indicated that they were Democrats (92.7 percent). JHAC across political party shows that among those with low JHAC, 8.1 percent were Republicans, while 92 percent were Democrats. Among those with high JHAC, 6.4 percent were Republicans, while 93.6 percent were Democrats. The results show that there is not a significant relationship between JHAC and political party ($p = 0.312$). There is more variability with respect to political ideology: 30.7 percent were conservative, 38.7 percent were moderate, and 30.6 percent were liberal. JHAC across political ideology shows that among those with low JHAC, 26.8 percent were conservative, 41.3 percent were moderate, and 31.9 percent were liberal. Among those with high JHAC, 34.5 percent were conservative, 35.9 percent were moderate, and 29.6 percent were liberal. The results show that there is a significant relationship between JHAC and political ideology (p = 0.016).

Region was categorized as non-South or South. Southern states include ten of the eleven original confederate states: Alabama, Florida, Georgia, Louisiana, Mississippi, North Carolina, South Carolina, Tennessee, Texas, and Virginia. Data were not collected for Arkansas. The rest of the states included in the sample were considered non-South. Overall, 49 percent of the respondents were from the non-South, while 51 percent of the respondents were from the South. JHAC across region shows that among those with low JHAC, 51.9 percent were from the non-South, while 48.1 percent were from the South. Among those with high JHAC, 46 percent were from the non-South, while 54.1 percent were from the South. The results show that there is a significant relationship between JHAC and region (p = 0.029).

Linked fate was measured by asking respondents whether they think what happens generally to Black people in this country will have something to do with what happens in their life.[27] Responses were either "no" or "yes"; 37.2 percent indicated "no," while 62.9 percent indicated "yes." JHAC across linked fate shows that among those with low JHAC, 34.4 percent indicated "no," while 65.6 percent indicated "yes." Among those with high JHAC, 40.4 percent indicated "no," while 59.7 percent indicated "yes." The results show that there is a significant relationship between JHAC and linked fate (p = 0.023).

For the race relations measure, respondents were asked how satisfied they were with race relations in their city or town. Responses ranged from "very dissatisfied" to "very satisfied." Overall, 10.2 percent reported they were very dissatisfied with race relations, 26.5 percent reported they were somewhat dissatisfied, 47.9 percent reported they were somewhat satisfied, and 15.5 percent reported they were very satisfied with race relations. JHAC across race relations shows that among those with low JHAC, 10.3 percent were very dissatisfied, 30.3 percent were somewhat dissatisfied, 50.2 percent were somewhat satisfied, and 9.3 percent were very satisfied. Among those with high JHAC, 10.5 percent were very dissatisfied, 22.1 percent were somewhat dissatisfied, 45.2 percent were somewhat satisfied, and 22.3 percent were very satisfied. The results show that there is a significant relationship between JHAC and race relations (p = 0.000).

Frequency of religious attendance was measured by asking respondents how often they attended church. Responses comprised: once a year or less, a few times a year, a few times a month, at least once a week, and nearly every day. The largest group of respondents (35.8 percent) indicated that they attended church at least once a week. The second and third largest categories were those who attended church a few times a month (26.6 percent) and those who attended a few times a year (21.2 percent). JHAC across religious attendance shows that among those with low JHAC, 11.5 percent attended church once a year or less, 25 percent attended a few times a year, 25 percent attended a few times a month, 33.4 percent attended at least once a week, and 5.1 percent attended nearly every day. Among those with high JHAC, 11.4 percent attended church once a year or less, 17.3 percent attended a few times a year, 28.2 percent attended a few times a month, 38.2 percent attended at least once a week, and 4.9 percent attended nearly every day. The results show that there is a significant relationship between JHAC and religious attendance ($p = 0.015$).

Racial identity (that is, racial centrality) and public regard are measured using the modified version of the Multidimensional Inventory of Black Identity (MIBI) scale developed by Sellers et al.[28] MIBI captures "the significance and qualitative meaning that individuals attribute to their membership in the African American racial group within their self-concepts."[29] The first measure of identity is centrality, and it measures the extent to which an individual normatively defines themselves with regards to race. The following four questions were included: "Being Black is a large part of my life," "My life depends on other Black lives," "No strong ties to other Blacks," and "Being Black is not an important part of identity." The second measure of identity is public regard, and it measures the extent to which an individual perceives the way that others view their group. Public regard was measured using three questions: "Whites do not respect Blacks," "Whites do not think Blacks add to US," and "Minorities do not think Blacks are smart." All of the questions were coded on a four-point Likert scale—from 1 ("strongly disagree") to 4 ("strongly agree"). Mean scores for each of the racial identity measures were created, and these scores were then placed into four categories, ranging from 1 (low) to 4 (high), and then further distilled into two categories (low and high). Higher values indicate greater agreement.

For racial centrality, 35.4 percent indicated low centrality, while 64.6 percent indicated high centrality. In terms of public regard, 69.7 percent indicated low public regard, while 30.3 percent indicated high public regard. The results show that there is not a significant relationship between JHAC and racial centrality ($p = 0.249$), nor is there a significant relationship between JHAC and public regard (p = 0.363). Respondents were also asked about their feelings toward whites, measured on a thermometer scale from 0 to 100, wherein a higher score reflects a more positive feeling. The mean score was 59.7. The results show that there is not a significant relationship between JHAC and feelings toward whites (p = 0.133).

In this research, we include both everyday and lifetime forms of discrimination. Everyday discrimination measures respondents' experiences with "routine and relatively minor day-to-day interpersonal experiences of unfair treatment."[30] Instances of everyday discrimination are often referred to as "microaggressions,"[31] and they involve "character assaults."[32] Nine measures were used to capture the frequency of experiencing unfair treatment: being treated with less courtesy than others; being treated with less respect than others; receiving poorer restaurant service than others; being treated as if you are not as smart as others; others being afraid of you; being perceived as dishonest by others; people acting like they are better than you; being called names and insulted by others; and feeling threatened or harassed. Response categories ranged from "never" (score = 1) to "almost every day" (score = 6). Responses were summed and ranged from a low of 9 to a high of 54. Higher scores indicate higher frequencies of day-to-day (everyday) discrimination. The mean score was 20.3. The results show that there is a significant relationship between JHAC and everyday discrimination (p = 0.024).

Lifetime discrimination measures "lifetime discrimination experiences that may have occurred many years ago and that, for the most part, involve major interference with advancing socioeconomic positions."[33] Another set of nine questions captured whether respondents had received unfair treatment, namely: being fired from a job; not being hired for a job; being denied a promotion; being hassled by police; being discouraged from continuing education by a teacher or adviser; being prevented from moving into a neighborhood; having life made difficult by neighbors; being denied a loan; and receiving unusually bad service from a repairman. The response categories were "no (0)" or "yes (1)," with total scores thus ranging from 0 to 9. Higher scores indicated more experiences of lifetime discrimination. The mean score was 1.5. The results show that there is a significant relationship between JHAC and lifetime discrimination (p = 0.000).

The concept of social dominance orientation (SDO) is defined as "the degree to which individuals desire and support group-based hierarchy and the domination of 'inferior' groups by 'superior' groups."[34] SDO was measured using the following four items: "winning is more important than playing the game"; "get ahead by any means necessary"; "war sometimes is necessary"; and "inferior groups should stay in their place." All responses were coded using a four-point Likert scale, from (1) "strongly disagree" to (4) "strongly agree." Sum scores across the four items were calculated. Thus, sum scores range from 4 to 16; the higher values indicate higher social dominance orientation. The mean score was 8. The results show that there is a significant relationship between JHAC and social dominance orientation ($p = 0.000$).

Analytical Strategy

General Expectations

To provide a baseline for our analytical expectations, we discuss the general relationships we expect to emerge for JHAC (see table 2.3 for our general expectations). Within each upcoming chapter, we provide specific hypotheses based on the dependent variables that are tested, as well as greater context for understanding these relationships. In every analysis, we code the various dependent variables so that stronger agreement equates to stronger attitudes or behaviors. Therefore, when we discuss a positive relationship, we are referring to one in which as the strength of JHAC increases, so does the strength of agreement with the attitude or behavior tested. Conversely, a negative relationship denotes that as the strength of JHAC increases, the disagreement with the dependent variable under question becomes stronger. Throughout the analysis, we generally expect a positive relationship for JHAC and the outcome variables. A detailed discussion of each expectation is provided in each of the empirical chapters.

Methods

Again, each empirical chapter presents a detailed discussion of the dependent variable and analytical strategies used. Nonetheless, in this section, we give a brief overview of the methods and analysis used in the book. The concepts we analyze mostly come in a Likert-scale format where respondents picked their level of agreement with a given statement. In our case, most of the survey items had four responses to choose from: "strongly disagree," "somewhat disagree," "somewhat agree," and "strongly agree." In other cases, the response categories ranged from "never" to "very often"—again, four categories. In some chapters, we rely on dichotomous coding. For

Table 2.3. General Expectations

	high JHAC (vs. low JHAC)
Chapter 3: Coping in Reactions to Discrimination	
Prayed about it	+
Tried to do something about it	+
Worked harder to prove others wrong	+
Chapter 4: Coping and Ideological Views	
Black nationalism	+
National pride	+
Authoritarianism	+
Work ethic	+
Chapter 5: Coping and Policy Preferences	
Need political districts to elect minorities	+
Government should help Blacks	+
Government should pay reparations	+
Chapter 6: Coping and Black Information Consumption	
Overall measure of Black information consumption	+
Black radio	+
Black TV	+
Black newspapers	+
Black magazines	+
Black literature	+
Black movies	+
Chapter 7: Coping and Political Participation	
Vote in presidential election	+
Vote in state and local elections	+
Ever worked for a political party	+
Ever contacted government about problems	+
Involved in neighborhood Black organizations	+
Member of a national Black organization	+

Source: Author created.

example, in chapter 3 (reactions to discrimination) and chapter 7 (political participation), the response options were coded 1 for someone indicating "yes" and 0 for someone indicating "no." Nonetheless, we stay consistent in the analysis and presentation of results. We do this to allow the reader the opportunity to see the results in a comparable and common format and, hopefully, to lessen the statistical confusion for anyone not well acquainted with social science statistical methodology. In the rest of this section, we briefly discuss the methodological details of the upcoming analysis so we can focus on the substantive relationships between JHAC and attitudes and behaviors in the remaining chapters.

When the outcome for a dependent variable was binary (as in chapters 3 and 7), we ran logistic regression models. To understand the meaning of the coefficients, we turn to postestimation predicted probabilities to provide a substantive understanding of the model findings.[35] When the outcome for a dependent variable was ordered with more than two categories (as in chapters 4, 5, and 6), we ran ordered logistic regression models. We then use the results from these models in a second set of estimates that calculate the marginal effect of independent variables under specific conditions, such as at a single level of the dependent variable. In addition, when there were significant interaction effects, we used predicted probabilities to provide a substantive understanding of the model findings. Chapter 6 uses both linear regression (continuous dependent variable) and ordered logistic regression models. In the case of a continuous dependent variable, we used linear regression models and present predicted probabilities.

In all the predicted probability figures (which we present after running logistic and linear regression models), we present the influence of JHAC for the average respondent in the sample. This allows us to show the most generalizable influence as we hold all the other variables at the mean for interval variables or modal categories for categorical variables. Finally, we include 95 percent confidence intervals in the bar charts.

All of the results are reported as odds ratios (OR) rather than as beta coefficients. For the interpretation of odds ratios, if the odds ratio is less than 1, the odds are decreased for an outcome; if the ratio is greater than 1, the odds are increased for an outcome; and if the odds ratio is exactly 1, then there is no effect. In all the empirical chapters, we report the odds ratios as percentages. To convert the odds ratios to percentages, if the ratio is greater than 1, subtract 1 from the ratio. If the odds ratio is less than 1, subtract the ratio from 1. For example, if the odds ratio were 1.51 (greater than 1), the calculation would be 1.51 - 1 = 51 percent. If the odds ratio were 0.76 (less than 1), the calculation would be 1 - 0.76 = 24 percent.

Control Variables

An important component of any analysis is controlling for competing factors that may also influence an attitude or behavior. Within each chapter, we discuss specific variables that relate to the concept and discuss their role in explaining the concept. In table 2.2, we list the control variables used in the various analyses along with summary statistics. The most common control variables are the standard demographic characteristics for the respondents. Looking at table 2.2, we see the average respondent is a forty-two-year-old female with a high school education who lives in the South and has an annual household income of between $25,000 and $50,000.

Conclusion

This chapter has provided the details of our data, measures, and analytical strategy. It has also provided details about the major independent variable of focus in the book—JHAC. We have highlighted the demographic, political, and psychological measures used in the analysis. This chapter is the reference for understanding the analytical details provided in chapters 3–7. Subsequent chapters show the influence of JHAC across a range of attitudes and behaviors while controlling for multiple alternative factors of influence.

CHAPTER 3

Coping in Reactions to Discrimination

On Monday, May 25, 2020, fifty-seven-year-old Christian Cooper, a Harvard graduate, avid birdwatcher, and board member of New York City's Audubon Society, was bird-watching in Central Park near an area known as the Ramble, when he encountered Amy Cooper and her unleashed dog.[1] Given the dog leash law in the city and in the Ramble, Christian Cooper politely requested that Amy Cooper leash her dog.[2] She refused, and Christian Cooper offered the dog a treat (in a bid to get it out of a plant bed and to get Amy Cooper to leash it), and he began filming the interaction.[3] Amy Cooper asked Christian Cooper to stop filming her, and when he refused, she grabbed her dog by the collar and moved away to call the police.[4] Amy Cooper then told the 911 operator that an African American man was threatening her and her dog, an assertion she repeated more than once while emphasizing Christian Cooper's race.[5] Once Amy Cooper leashed her dog, Christian Cooper politely said, "Thank you," and stopped filming the incident.[6] He was gone by the time the officers arrived and later expressed that while he refused to participate in her dehumanization of him at the time, he had no desire to file a complaint against her afterward.[7]

The viral video of the incident in Central Park led the district attorney to charge Amy Cooper with filing a false police report.[8] It also sparked intense discussions on social media platforms over the tendency of white people to racially discriminate and file false reports against African Americans, a problem that New York lawmakers are attempting to address in new legislation that grants people the right to act if and when someone calls the police on them in a discriminatory manner.[9] Christian Cooper's reaction was, "If this painful process helps to correct, or takes us a step further toward addressing the underlying racial, horrible assumptions that we African Americans have to deal with, and have dealt with for centuries, that this woman tapped into, then it's worth it."[10] The reaction from the mayor of New York City, Bill de Blasio, was: "She called the police BECAUSE he was a Black man. Even though she was the one breaking the rules. She decided he was the criminal and we know why. This kind of hatred has no place in our city."[11] Sapna V. Raj, deputy commissioner of the Law Enforcement Bureau, said that "efforts to intimidate Black people by threatening to call law enforcement draw on a long, violent and painful history. . . . At a time when the devastating impacts of racism in Black communities have been made so painfully clear . . . it is appalling to see these types of ugly threats directed at one New Yorker by another."[12]

On social media networks, users expressed their outrage over the racism displayed by Amy Cooper, and demanded she be fired from her job at Franklin Templeton Investments—a demand that was ultimately met.[13] The viral video led to comparisons of racial injustice wherein Black men have been falsely accused of crimes in the past. Cooper himself acknowledged that after Amy Cooper emphasized his race, he was not going to be racially intimidated by her and compared it to the assumptions made in the death of Ahmaud Arbery.[14] Christian Cooper's sister, Melody Cooper, posted the video taken by her brother to create awareness of the racism African Americans have to deal with. She stated, "When I saw my brother's video, it was personal, I just imagined what happened to Mike Brown or George Floyd happening to him, and I wanted to make sure no Black person would have to go through that kind of weaponization of racism from her. If the cops showed up, they wouldn't have seen his resume or known his job. This kind of racism can kill people. It could've killed my brother."[15]

The cases of Ahmaud Arbery, George Floyd, and Breonna Taylor exemplify in extreme forms the discrimination (e.g., hate crimes and police brutality) that African Americans confront on a daily basis. Instances like Christian Cooper experienced are more subtle forms of discrimination but can also lead to severe psychological and emotional trauma. Consequently, the culmination of these discriminatory incidents became a catalyst to wide-ranging reactions among African Americans throughout the country—both in major cities and in small towns.[16] There were nonviolent and violent forms of protests. While most of the protests were in the form of peaceful marches, some involved rioting, looting, and destruction of property, in which several state governors ordered National Guard units to secure the streets. Additionally, these cases raised discussions in homes, on television news, and on social media platforms that revealed the anger, disgust, and disappointment at the discriminatory treatment of African Americans. Another type of reaction was boycotts. For example, Black-Out-Day 2020, which occurred on July 7, advocated that African Americans spend their money at African American–owned businesses such as banks, grocery stores, and hair salons.[17] Reactions, such as threats of boycotts, spilled onto college campuses. For example, Kansas State, Florida State, and Oklahoma State football players threatened to boycott team practices until their universities acted on issues dealing with diversity and racism.[18] In addition, the country witnessed boycotts of businesses such as CrossFit, Facebook, and the NFL.[19]

Broadly speaking, people have faced discrimination directed at a variety of features, including (but not limited to) race, ethnicity, language, sexual orientation, gender, age, and mental and/or physical differences or disabilities.[20] Discrimination is often blatant, but it also manifests in subtle and/or unconscious forms, such as "microaggressions or everyday discrimination."[21] Given its universal and destructive nature, policies designed to prohibit it exist in most countries.[22] Nevertheless, it remains prevalent and its consequences are as wide-ranging as it is itself. In the United States, the presence and effects of racial discrimination are particularly profound. As Carter et al.[23] explain, "Racial discrimination is a unique type of stressor in that it is chronic and multifaceted (biological, social, and psychological) and associated with an array of factors (behavioral, sociodemographic, and psychological) that influence behavior and thought."[24] Therefore, in order to better understand why and how people differ in their reactions to discrimination, it is essential to first understand the various factors associated with it.

Perhaps one of the most concerning consequences of discrimination is its effect on physical and mental health.[25] Scholars have increasingly studied the association between discrimination and health (as well as health care) in the United States over the past couple of decades, particularly in terms of disparities resulting from racism.[26] Research shows African Americans often do not receive the health care they need, and when they are treated, they may not receive quality care on account of implicit bias or outright racial discrimination.[27] Scholars have explored the connection between discrimination and cardiovascular disease, as well as disparities in treatment relating to the disease.[28] One such study, by Chae et al.,[29] found that racial discrimination and negative internal attitudes about one's racial group are two risk factors concerning cardiovascular health that African American men face.

Moreover, research shows an association between (perceived) discrimination and premature biological aging,[30] lower infant birth weight and higher infant mortality rates among African American mothers,[31] a higher overall mortality rate for African Americans,[32] inflammation and elevated blood pressure,[33] depressive symptoms,[34] increased stress and/or psychological distress,[35] and poorer self-rated and/or overall health.[36] In addition, research shows that individuals who experience racial discrimination may embrace certain behaviors, such as (ab)using tobacco, alcohol, and/or illegal substances, as a way to deal with it.[37]

Beyond the areas of health and health care, discrimination, particularly racial discrimination, runs rampant across a variety of domains in the United States, including (but not limited to) employment (from hiring practices to promotions), housing, the criminal justice system (e.g., policing), and education.[38] In a study by Nancy Krieger and Steven Sidney,[39] 50 percent of African American women and 60 percent of African American men experienced racial discrimination in three or more of the following seven situations: in school, at work, getting a job, getting a house, getting medical care, on the street or in a public setting, and from the police or in the courts. An even higher number of African American individuals (77 percent) experienced racial discrimination in at least one of these situations.[40]

Scholars have explored the association between discrimination and jobs, particularly hiring practices; they have found that stereotypes can lead employers to look down on minorities and favor whites, and that white applicants are more likely to be called back for jobs (and receive positive comments from interviews) than minority candidates, even when they have similar backgrounds and skills.[41] In addition, despite legal efforts to reduce racial discrimination associated with housing, racial gaps in mortgage loan denial and mortgage cost (among other discriminatory practices) persist, making it more difficult for marginalized groups such as African Americans to acquire suitable housing.[42] Education is another area wherein individuals experience discrimination.[43] Chavous et al.[44] explain that given social structures within schools, and the lack of multicultural education training (among other things), it is perhaps unsurprising that African American adolescents report racial discrimination in school settings, from receiving lower grades or evaluations from instructors to being more strictly disciplined.

Furthermore, discriminatory practices in policing remain a salient issue in the United States. African American men are far more likely than white men to be incarcerated, subjected to or threatened by deadly force, and killed by police officers.[45] Moreover, in an experimental examination of racial bias and the decision to shoot, Correll et al.[46] found that college-aged participants "were faster to shoot armed African American targets than armed White targets, and they were faster to decide not to shoot unarmed White targets than unarmed African Americans."[47] In another study, Ashby Plant and Michelle Peruche[48] found similar results for police offers in their decisions to shoot.[49] Referencing this study, Sadler et al. explain that despite showing racial bias initially in their decision to shoot, police officers' racial bias did decrease with practice.[50] Drawing inspiration from the previous studies by Correll et al. and Plant and Peruche, Sadler et al. conducted their own study, but incorporated Latino and Asian male targets as well. They found that similar to the previous studies, "racial bias in response times to decide whether or not to shoot African American targets was pervasive."[51] However, they also found that racial bias in deciding to shoot is not limited to anti-Black sentiment, but is connected to racial stereotypes.[52]

While the presence and frequent occurrence of discrimination across a variety of domains is well documented in the literature, along with its effects on health in particular, there is less research that specifically focuses on reactions to discrimination. That said, some studies have explored racial and gender differences in response to unfair treatment and reported discrimination,[53] emotional and/or psychological reactions to racism,[54] regional differences in African Americans' reactions to discrimination,[55] and post-traumatic reactions to racial discrimination.[56] Our aim in this chapter is to contribute to this body of literature.

In their 1996 study, Krieger and Sidney found that "gender-mediated responses to unfair treatment may influence blood pressure," and that those who accept discrimination as a part of life may be more likely to experience elevated blood pressure as a result of their internalized reaction.[57] African American males, who experienced more discrimination in the workplace than their female counterparts, were more likely to have elevated blood pressure, and the differences in their reactions to discrimination may result from feelings concerning expression, with females more likely than males to feel free enough to express themselves in a way that gives them validation.[58] Gerrard et al. also explore how experiences of and reactions to discrimination may negatively affect health.[59] "Perceived racial discrimination is associated with increases in both internalizing and externalizing emotional responses," they explain, "and these reactions, in turn, are associated with deterioration in health status and increases in unhealthy behavior (drinking frequently and problematic drinking)."[60] Their findings show that women who do not do something about it, and try to avoid thinking about their experiences with discrimination, are more likely to drink more frequently and report problematic drinking at a higher rate than women who cope differently.[61]

While this may be effective in the short term, in the long term it has det-rimental effects on health.[62]

Robert Carter and Jessica Forsyth explore emotional and psychological reactions to racism, as well as help-seeking behaviors, across five different minority racial groups.[63] They distinguish between discrimination and harass-ment, and ask specific questions about the types of racism experienced, the environment in which it was experienced, and how people reacted to it. Work and school were the most frequent places where participants expe-rienced racist incidents, and in terms of emotional reactions, 75 percent of participants reported that they felt disrespected, 74 percent felt angry, 60 percent felt insulted, and 51 percent felt disappointed.[64] Participants also reported feeling helpless, demoralized, and inferior, among other emo-tions, although to a lesser extent.[65] While Carter and Forsyth found that psychological reactions did not differ much across various types of racist incidents, they did find that some respondents experienced more intense or traumatic stress reactions when experiencing workplace hostility and harassment. "Experiences categorized by respondents as harassment were associated with more Hypervigilant and Anxious reactions than were those categorized as discrimination," they explain, and "these results suggest that reactions to different types of racism can be complex."[66] Finally, in terms of help-seeking behaviors, Carter and Forsyth's study reveals that participants who experienced racial discrimination and harassment were not likely to turn to professionals for help; they often kept it to themselves or spoke only to their closest friends or family members about it.[67]

Similarly, Henson et al. explore psychological reactions to discrimi-nation.[68] Their study, which focuses on African American undergraduates, found that "individual differences (based on race-based rejection sensitivity and social constraints in talking with others about racism) are associated with reactions to being the target of racial discrimination."[69] More specifically, they found that individuals who score high on race-based rejection sensitivity are more likely to have a negative response to discrimination that is intense, aligning with the research that such individuals tend to be hypervigilant and hypersensitive when it comes to racial discrimination, which results in quick, defensive reactions that tend to be intense emotionally and cognitively.[70] Additionally, individuals with higher social constraints in talking with others about racism are more likely to feel distress, and individuals who score high on either race-based rejection sensitivity or social constraints are likely to experience negative affect and be less inclined to forgive the perpetrator.[71]

In terms of regional differences, Jas Sullivan found that African Amer-icans in the South were more likely than those in the non-South to "pray about it" when experiencing discrimination, while African Americans in the non-South were more likely than those in the South to "try to do some-thing" and "g[e]t mad" when experiencing discrimination.[72] He posits that socialization—and the survival reasons associated with it—may explain why African Americans differ in their reactions to discrimination across regions.[73] In addition, he explains that given the South's history with racism and discrimination, it may be that the frequency with which African Americans experience discrimination in the South makes them more inclined to accept that it is beyond their control and/or a burden not worth their energy.[74]

Expectations

Prior research has shown that discrimination exists in various manifestations. Studies have also offered evidence of the social, psychological, and economic effects discrimination has on African Americans. Less clear, however, other than in anecdotal evidence, are the types of reactions among African Americans in response to acts of discrimination and how these reactions may differ by the way one copes. Thus, we ask the following question: Do high-effort copers react to discrimination differently than low-effort copers? In particular, we examine three different reactions to discrimination: praying about it, trying to do something about it, and working harder to prove the discriminators wrong. Our general hypothesis is that there will be an association between reactions to discrimination and coping. More specifically, we expect those who score high on JHAC to be more likely to pray about it, try to do something about it, and/or work harder to prove others wrong. High-effort copers are persistent and do not give up and will likely believe that to react (in one or more of these three ways) is to do something to overcome the discrimination that may ultimately lead to some form of success. On the other hand, we predict that individuals who score low on JHAC will be less likely to react in any of these ways, since they are not persistent in their efforts to overcome psychosocial stressors.

Methods

Here the dependent variables are reactions to discrimination. The NSAL queried African American respondents on their reactions to experiences of discrimination. The exact wording of the question is as follows: "How did you respond to this/these experience(s) of discrimination? Please tell me if you did each of the following things." The three reactions examined as dependent variables are as follows: (1) prayed about it, (2) tried to do something about it, and (3) worked harder to prove others wrong. Responses were "no" or "yes" for each item.

Figure 3.1 presents the responses for African Americans' reactions to discrimination. Findings indicate that 61.1 percent prayed about it, while 38.9 percent did not. Further, 50 percent did not work harder to prove others wrong, while 49.9 percent said they did. In terms of trying to do something about it, 29.5 percent indicated they did try, while 70.5 percent indicated they did not.

Chi-square tests were analyzed to compare differences between low and high JHAC in response to the reaction to discrimination questions (see table 3.1). The findings show a significant relationship between coping and two of the reactions to discrimination variables. For example, the findings show that there is a significant relationship between JHAC and praying about it (p = 0.000). Additionally, there is a significant relationship between JHAC and working harder to prove others wrong (p = 0.000). There was not a significant relationship between JHAC and trying to do something about discrimination (p = 0.712).

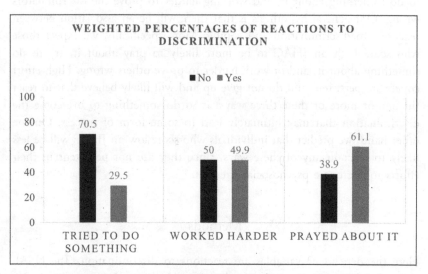

Figure 3.1. Reactions to Discrimination. *Source*: Author created.

Table 3.1. Reactions to Discrimination by JHAC

| | n (weighted %) | | |
	Low JHAC	High JHAC	p-value
Prayed about it			0.000**
No	339 (44.7)	192 (32.2)	
Yes	515 (55.3)	486 (67.8)	
Total	854	678	
Worked harder to prove others wrong			0.000**
No	467 (54.9)	315 (43.7)	
Yes	385 (45.1)	363 (56.3)	
Total	852	678	
Tried to do something about it			0.712
No	617 (70.9)	476 (69.9)	
Yes	238 (29.1)	202 (30.2)	
Total	855	678	

$*p < 0.05$; $**p < 0.0001$

Source: Author created.

Analytical Strategy and Model Selection

Since the outcome variables are binary (two response options, "no" and "yes"), we estimated models for each of the three reactions to discrimination with logistic regression. For each type of reaction to discrimination, three separate models were analyzed—that is, praying about it, working harder to prove others wrong, and trying to do something about it. In addition, we included demographic, political, race identity, and psychosocial controls. We also tested whether coping interacts with these control variables in influencing reactions to discrimination. In figures 3.2, 3.4, and 3.6, we present results that do not include interaction terms. These figures include odds ratio estimates. We also analyzed predicted probabilities for the reaction to discrimination questions. Sample weights were created and used to account for nonresponse variations.

Results

PRAYING ABOUT IT

We find a statistically significant association between coping and "praying" as a reaction to discrimination (see figure 3.2). More specifically, high-effort copers are 60 percent (OR: 1.60; 95% CI: 1.20, 2.14; p = 0.001) more likely to pray about it than low-effort copers. Compared to males, African American females are 112 percent more likely (OR: 2.12; 95% CI: 1.58, 2.85; p = 0.000) to pray as a reaction to discrimination. Older respondents (OR: 1.02; 95% CI: 1.01, 1.03; p = 0.002), those residing in the South (OR: 1.89; 95% CI: 1.42, 2.51; p = 0.000), and those experiencing greater frequency of everyday discrimination (OR: 1.02; 95% CI: 1.00, 1.04; p = 0.034) are more likely to pray about it. In other words, those higher in age are 2 percent more likely to pray about it, those whose reside in the South are 89 percent more likely to pray about it, and those experiencing everyday discrimination more often are 2 percent more likely to pray about it.

Figure 3.3 presents the predicted probabilities for JHAC and praying as a reaction to discrimination. These predicted probabilities were estimated from the model presented, while setting all variables at their modal category or mean value. This allows us to isolate the association of JHAC for the average respondent. Predicted probabilities show that those in the low-JHAC category have about a 57 percent chance of praying as a reaction to discrimination. On the other hand, those in the high-JHAC category have about a 68 percent chance of praying as a reaction to discrimination. There is a significant difference between the low and high categories (p = 0.001). In other words, those more strongly predisposed to respond to social and economic adversity with high-effort coping show the strongest agreement with praying as a reaction to discrimination.

WORKING HARDER TO PROVE OTHERS WRONG

We find a statistically significant association between coping and "working harder to prove others wrong" as a reaction to discrimination (see figure 3.4). More specifically, high-effort copers are 55 percent (OR: 1.55; 95% CI: 1.18, 2.02; p = 0.001) more likely than low-effort copers to work harder to prove others wrong. As age increases (OR: 0.99; 95% CI: 0.98, 1.00; p = 0.004), the less likely a respondent was to report working harder to prove

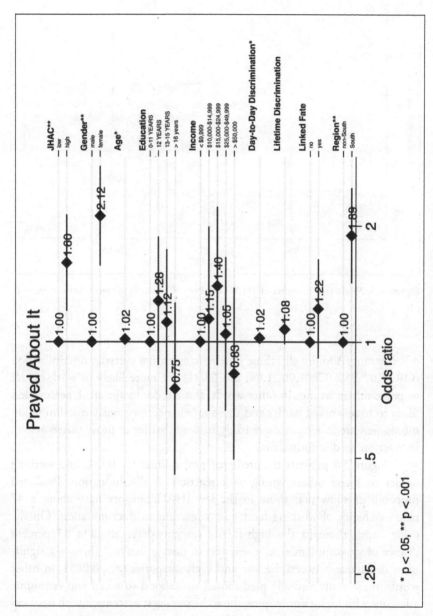

Figure 3.2. JHAC on Prayed about it. *Source:* Author created.

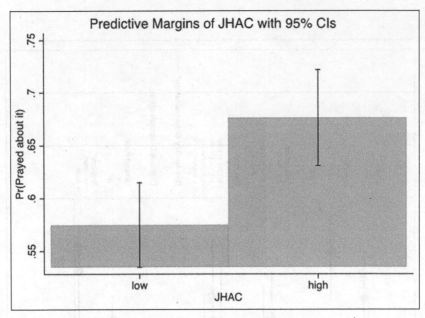

Figure 3.3. Predictive margins of JHAC on Prayed about it. *Source*: Author created.

others wrong. Additionally, those experiencing greater everyday discrimination (OR: 1.02 95% CI: 1.00, 1.04; p = 0.021) are more likely to work harder to prove others wrong. In other words, those older in age are 1 percent less likely to have worked harder and those experiencing everyday discrimination more often are 2 percent more likely to work harder to prove others wrong in reaction to discrimination.

Figure 3.5 presents the predicted probabilities for JHAC and working harder to prove others wrong as a reaction to discrimination. Predicted probabilities show that those in the low-JHAC category have about a 47 percent chance of working harder as a reaction to discrimination. On the other hand, those in the high-JHAC category have about a 57 percent chance of working harder as a reaction to discrimination. There is a significant difference between the low and high categories (p = 0.001). In other words, those more strongly predisposed to respond to social and economic adversity with high-effort coping show the strongest agreement with working harder as a reaction to discrimination.

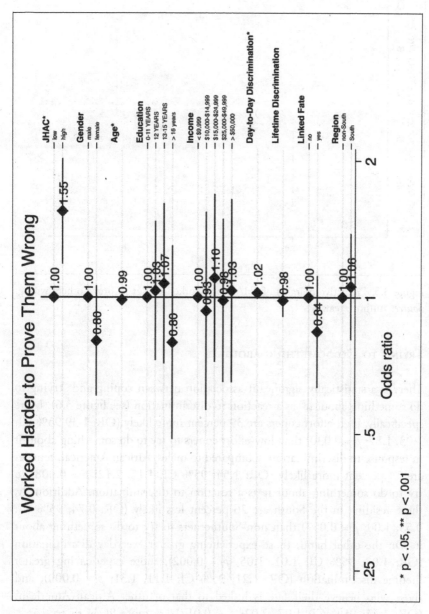

Figure 3.4. JHAC on Worked harder to prove others wrong. *Source.* Author created.

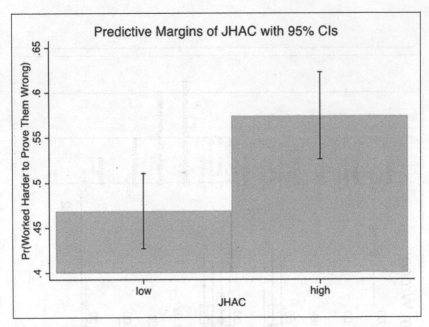

Figure 3.5. Predictive margins of JHAC on Worked harder to prove others wrong. *Source*: Author created.

Trying to Do Something about It

There is a statistically significant association between coping and "trying to do something about it" as a reaction to discrimination (see figure 3.6). More specifically, high-effort copers are 39 percent more likely (OR: 1.39 95% CI: 1.03, 1.87; p = 0.030) than low-effort copers to try to do something about it in response to discrimination. Compared to males, African American females are 54 percent more likely (OR: 1.54; 95% CI: 1.12, 2.12; p = 0.008) to try to do something about it as a reaction to discrimination. Additionally, those residing in the South are 26 percent less likely (OR: 0.74; 95% CI: 0.55, 1.00; p = 0.057) than non-Southerners to try to do something about it. On the other hand, those experiencing greater everyday discrimination (OR: 1.03; 95% CI: 1.01, 1.05; p = 0.002), those experiencing greater lifetime discrimination (OR: 1.21; 95% CI: 1.11, 1.31; p = 0.000), and those who believe their fate is linked to that of other African Americans (OR: 1.47; 95% CI: 1.07, 2.02; p = 0.017) are more likely to try to do something about it, by 3 percent, 21 percent, and 47 percent, respectively.

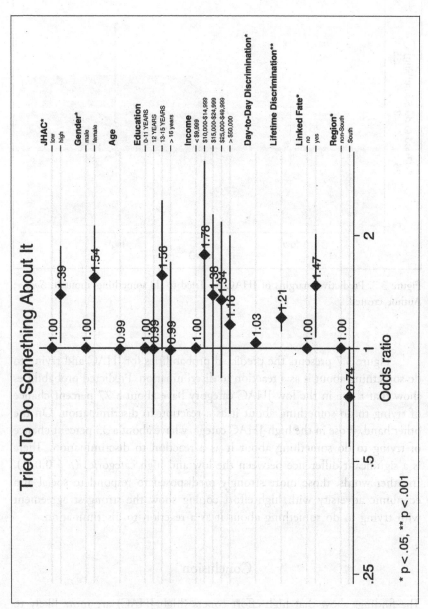

Figure 3.6. JHAC on Tried to do something about it. *Source:* Author created.

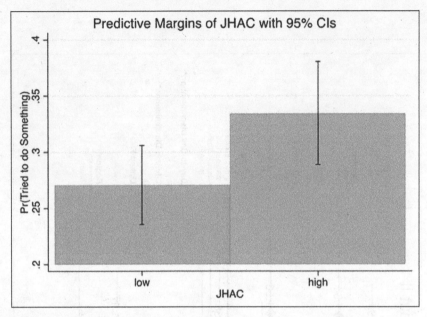

Figure 3.7. Predictive margins of JHAC on Tried to do something about it. *Source*: Author created.

Figure 3.7 presents the predicted probabilities for JHAC and trying to do something about it as a reaction to discrimination. Predicted probabilities show that those in the low-JHAC category have about a 27 percent chance of trying to do something about it as a reaction to discrimination. On the other hand, those in the high-JHAC category have about a 33 percent chance of trying to do something about it as a reaction to discrimination. There is a significant difference between the low and high categories ($p = 0.031$). In other words, those more strongly predisposed to respond to social and economic adversity with high-effort coping show the strongest agreement with trying to do something about it as a reaction to discrimination.

Conclusion

The findings show that high-effort copers (high JHAC) are more likely to pray, to work harder to prove others wrong, and to try to do something about experiences of discrimination. This finding is not surprising, since we are keenly aware that high-effort copers are more likely than low-effort copers to act and find ways to alleviate stressors. These reactions, in their own way, are themselves mechanisms for alleviating stressors. High-effort copers are "fighters"; they don't easily give up on their goals, even in the midst of "trials and tribulations"—in this case, discrimination. In addition, for high-effort copers, these findings may reflect a greater sense of optimism that discrimination is not, or should not be, a part of life, and is possibly something within their control. Yet, it is worth noting that the type of discrimination and the environment in which it occurs may play a role as well.[75] For example, Krieger and Sidney found differences between working- and professional-class individuals in their responses to unfair treatment,[76] wherein the latter may have more resources and feel more capable of doing something about it than the former.

For those low on JHAC, this finding could have several possible explanations. It is possible that low-effort copers, in accepting discrimination as a part of life, may be so resigned to it that they simply do not choose to react to it in the ways that high-effort copers do, because they have either become immune to it (given the frequency at which they experience it), or because they have decided it is beyond their control and their energy and time is better invested in other things.[77] For low-effort copers, this finding may be indicative of a loss of hope, or a reluctance to react in a way that may put them at risk, whether mentally or physically.[78] This could negatively affect the mental health of African American males, which in turn could impact their physical health—whether in the form of increased risk for elevated blood pressure and cardiovascular disease, or in the form of behaviors (such as drinking or smoking) adopted to cope with discrimination and/or health challenges that arise from experiencing it.

Regardless the way one copes, the literature on the connection between discrimination and cardiovascular risk factors, including blood pressure, along with psychological distress, depressive symptoms, and certain detrimental behaviors (such as turning to alcohol, drugs, or fatty foods), among other things, suggests that the potential consequences of our findings may be that discrimination is capable of negatively affecting the health of African Americans, depending on their reactions to it. For example, Krieger and Sidney's findings suggest that being able to talk about unfair treatment may lower individuals' likelihood to experience elevated blood pressure in comparison to an internalized response, wherein one accepts it as a part of life and/or keeps it to oneself.[79] This overlaps to some extent with Chae et al.'s finding that internalized negative beliefs about one's racial group and discrimination increase the risk for cardiovascular disease.[80] Therefore, a more specific potential consequence of our findings is that African Americans may be at greater risk of elevated blood pressure on account of accepting discrimination as a part of life and the potential, negative internalized beliefs that may be associated with that reaction.

Moreover, in their study on the emotional and psychological reactions to racism across multiple racial groups, Carter and Forsyth found that overall, 78 percent of participants who experienced racist incidents found them to be stressful, even months or a year after the events occurred.[81] The emotional reactions to incidents of racism found in Carter and Forsyth's study align with the literature on discrimination's association with stress and emotional distress,[82] and speak to its ability to remain with those who encounter it for a long time, possibly resulting in experiences of traumatic stress.[83] Therefore, African Americans, regardless their reaction to discrimination, are at risk of increased stress and emotional distress.

When we reflect on African Americans' reactions to Christian Cooper's experience with discrimination, it is clear that many individuals voiced their anger (e.g., on social media) and/or were determined to do something about it (e.g., Christian Cooper's sister explained that uploading the video to social media was her way of doing something about it, while other individuals took it upon themselves to demand Amy Cooper be fired from her job). We also see on the policy level that Christian Cooper's case inspired a new law that is designed to prevent the false reporting of crimes based on an individual's race. From expressing anger online, to advocating for boycotts, taking to the streets to protest, and demanding structural change, individuals react to discrimination (experienced by them or others) in various ways, as this case illustrates. Future research could benefit from incorporating coping measures such as JHAC into studies on various behaviors and attitudes. While we do not have the ability to test the relationship directly, due to data limitations, we argue that coping could potentially explain and/or help predict how people react in circumstances such as those experienced by Christian Cooper. As our results in this chapter show, people react differently depending on how they cope (passively vs. actively). As unfortunate as it is, we know from cases like Christian Cooper's experience that discrimination occurs frequently, and future research would be enriched by looking at the role coping plays in reactions to discrimination.

While our findings provide a clearer understanding of the role coping plays in the types of reactions to discrimination, there is much work to be done, generally, in the study of discrimination and reactions to it. First, a possible reaction to discrimination in this study was measured by asking if respondents tried to do something about it. "Tried to do something about it" is vague. Future research could explore the specific ways one copes with discrimination. For example, protesting is a form of coping, as is seeking a psychotherapist. In this respect, for example, are high-effort or low-effort copers more likely to participate in a particular type of protest—either nonviolent (e.g., marching) or violent (e.g., looting, rioting, destruction of property)? Second, we do not control for the ways in which racial identity influences reactions to discrimination. A possible question is: What is the effect of racial centrality or public regard on engaging in marches (or riots)? What we have done in this study is begin a conversation on an important topic—reactions to discrimination—at a crucial period in American history, and we have shown some of the ways in which coping influences such reactions.

CHAPTER 4

Coping and Ideological Views

When considering ideological views, one's first thought may be political ideology: a concept and measure of whether an individual identifies, for example, as a conservative, moderate, or liberal. However, ideological views are complex and can capture or reflect a number of beliefs, ideas, and values. In this chapter, we explore specific ideological views concerning Black nationalism and American values. Before illustrating the current relevance of these ideological views, we offer an overview of what each means and refers to, beginning with Black nationalism.

Black Nationalism

Black nationalism can take more than one form and be defined and understood in various ways depending on the context, but a general description of its most basic idea is that in the United States, Black nationalism "is the philosophy that African Americans should be both self-defining and self-determined vis-à-vis the remainder of American society."[1] In another light, it measures a "commitment to African culture and the degree to which blacks should confine their social relationships to other blacks."[2] In our analyses, the measure of Black nationalism is based on the summary of responses to at least three out of four questions, including the extent to which participants agreed or disagreed with statements such as "Blacks should shop Black-owned stores" and "Blacks should vote for Blacks."

So, why does it matter? Historically, Black nationalism and movements related to it (or ideas it is associated with) can be viewed, at least in one sense, as a response to the nation's long-standing history of racism. "Nationalistic feelings, organizations, and movements among, for, and by African Americans have existed virtually since Africans were captured, imported, and enslaved for the purpose of building a nation that has but reluctantly accepted their descendants."[3] While racial tensions existed centuries ago in the United States, in tandem with slavery, the outlawing of slavery did not bring racism to an end.[4] We can reflect on the civil rights movement, and events that occurred throughout it, including the 1961 Freedom Rides,[5] as examples of movements and events that reflect sentiments of Black nationalism. Such ideological views are a part of our nation's history and continue to shape attitudes and behaviors. We can turn to more recent events to illustrate this point.

During the summer of 2020, numerous cases of racial discrimination, police brutality, and police killings of African Americans went viral and sparked protests throughout the United States and the world, even as the COVID-19 pandemic continued. While modern movements that reflect Black nationalism, such as Black Lives Matter (BLM) and Buy Black, existed prior to summer 2020, such movements gained even more traction and attention during this time. The BLM movement, for example, "took center stage, from global protests to a renamed plaza in Washington, DC, to murals adorning neighborhoods throughout the country."[6] Millions of people in the United States and across the globe attended protests following the deaths of George Floyd, Breonna Taylor, and Ahmaud Arbery. In these protests, we see the power of movements and the calls for change. Some even suggest that BLM may be the biggest movement in our nation's history, given its geographic spread, the duration of the protests, and the number of individuals turning out: for example, at the protests' peak on June 6, 2020, "half a million people turned out in nearly 550 places across the United States."[7]

These protests, and the BLM movement more broadly, are intended to speak to injustices in the country and demand change. In a statement given to *Vox*'s Fabiola Cineas in November 2020, Kentucky state representative Attica Scott expressed what the BLM movement stands for and how its mission will continue, and illustrated the relevance of Black nationalism today.

> Regardless of who is in the White House in January, Black folks are going to be louder than we've ever been; Black folks are going to run for office in numbers that are larger than we have ever done before; Black people are going to be working on advocacy and public policy way more than we've ever done

before. . . . And we're turning all of these systems and structures on their head. We're very clear about structural racism and
the fact that we are not going to keep living with the foot of
injustice on our necks.[8]

While this sentiment reflects Black nationalism, it also reflects a theme in
John Henryism Active Coping and in efficacy more broadly: the idea that
an individual has control over outcomes.

Beyond social and political action, African Americans are also embracing
Black nationalism when it comes to making financial decisions. For example,
the Buy Black movement is designed to encourage African Americans to
shop at stores owned by African Americans, a call that also has historical
significance. "Buying black has been at the center of the fight for civil rights
since Reconstruction. . . . Over the years, every prominent figure in the
movement for racial equality implored their brothers and sisters to spend
money within the community,"[9] and it seems to be on the rise once more.
Take, for example, watch brands. "Black-owned watch brands are having
an unprecedented year . . . [and] most say they have no doubt that, in the
wake of social justice demonstrations across the country, the #BuyBlack
movement has played a part. Searches for Black-owned businesses skyrocketed
this summer."[10] This action is one way to combat racism while embracing
and supporting one's racial identity, and it speaks to the ideological views
that reflect Black nationalism, as well as the ideological beliefs that some
African Americans hold.

American Values

When one thinks of American values, patriotism may be the first thing that
comes to mind. However, American values can take more than one form
and may have a different meaning from person to person. In our analyses,
we use three items from the data set to measure American values, including
the extent to which a participant agreed or disagreed with the following
statements: (1) "I am very proud to be an American" (national pride); (2)
"America is the land of opportunity in which you only need to work hard
to succeed" (work ethic); and (3) "Obedience and respect for authority are
the most important virtues children should learn" (authoritarianism). As
is apparent from these statements, American values in this study capture
notions of patriotism, belief in the American Dream, and the belief that

respect for authority and obedience are critical virtues for children to learn. In a country with such deep-rooted racism, it may come as a surprise that African Americans would embrace these ideological views pertaining to American values.

However, much like with Black nationalism, we can reflect on past events that have shaped and continue to shape these beliefs and ideas to understand their current and future significance and why/how they are associated with African Americans who score high on JHAC. In reflecting on the protests and activism that occurred in the lead up to and throughout the civil rights movement, it is clear that there was a "commitment to, and enthusiasm for, patriotic protest. Indeed, black leaders sought consistently to fuse respectable tactics—such as dressing smartly, behaving peacefully, and maintaining dignity even in the face of white supremacist provocation and violence—with appeals to Americanism."[11] This notion or theme of peaceful and patriotic protest is clear in recent events as well. A report using data from the *US Crisis Monitor*, a joint project between the Armed Conflict Location and Event Data Project (ACLED) and the Bridging Divides Initiative at Princeton University, reveals that more than 93 percent of BLM protests (based on those that took place between May 26 and August 22, 2020, of which there were more than 7,750 in all fifty states and Washington, DC) have been peaceful, involving "non-violent demonstrators."[12] These protests associated with the BLM movement, which occurred throughout the summer of 2020 in the face of blatant racial discrimination and following the police killings of African Americans, and particularly the murder of George Floyd, make it clear that African Americans today continue to embrace and reflect, in many ways, the beliefs and values shared by protestors and activists of the civil rights movement. Much as Rev. Dr. Martin Luther King Jr. "sought to associate blacks' demands for freedom, equality and respect with the nation's founding principles,"[13] we can see how current protestors and activists, and African Americans more broadly, continue to embrace American values, such as patriotism and pride in being American, along with beliefs pertaining to respect and obedience for authority, even in the face of adversity and racial discrimination.

Moreover, a brief overview of the American Dream may offer additional insight as to why African Americans embrace other American values, such as the belief that one can succeed and accomplish anything as long as they work hard, and JHAC may play a key role. America is often described as being "a land of opportunity."[14] Thus, the American Dream is generally defined "as an ideology promoting the attainment of material and economic success . . . [or] as a steadfast optimism against adversity to achieve any opportunity and personal fulfillment through hard work."[15] This depiction of what the American Dream stands for is comparable to the theme of hard work and determination that is reflected in items used to measure JHAC; high-effort copers, unlike low-effort copers, embrace the belief "that just about any obstacle can be overcome through hard work and a strong determination to succeed."[16] It also echoes the individualistic nature of American society, which emphasizes that success is the result of individual hard work.[17] Importantly, the American Dream is an ideology reflective of American values that is embraced by both of the main political parties in the United States, and one that is generally supported across the board, "with minimal differences across gender or racial lines."[18]

However, research has also called into question whether the American Dream remains supported across the board, whether it is actually attainable, and whether people perceive it as attainable.[19] Given the nation's history and ongoing patterns of racial discrimination, African Americans in particular have faced and continue to face barriers to opportunities and economic advancement, which have made the attainment of and perceptions regarding the American Dream challenging and/or pessimistic.[20] Similarly, racial discrimination can affect individuals' life satisfaction, and both can affect whether one believes the American Dream is achievable or not.[21] Other factors that can shape beliefs in American values, and more specifically, the American Dream, include income, age, education level, changes in social mobility and income inequality, and perceptions of the economy.[22] Higher levels of racial discrimination are associated among African Americans with higher odds of believing they will never achieve the American Dream,[23] and increases in income inequality and decreases in social mobility are associated with decreased belief that the American Dream is attainable.[24]

While these lines of recent research help to explain why there may be variation in responses to statements concerning American values, we show in this chapter how JHAC plays a role in these ideological beliefs as well. Both Black nationalism and American values represent ideological views that have both historic and current relevance. Given how embedded these concepts (and those related to them) are within the nation's fabric, it is clear that these ideological beliefs will continue to play a critical role in shaping attitudes and behaviors in the United States in the future. In this chapter, we argue that JHAC plays a major role in shaping these ideological beliefs.

Expectations

JHAC provides an opportunity to explore whether a predisposition to be unrelenting in one's efforts to overcome structural vulnerability in race and social class predicts attitudes toward Black nationalism and American values among African Americans. Consequently, the objective in this chapter is to explore two major questions.

First, is there an association between the way one copes with adversity and support for Black nationalism? We expect to find that individuals who score high on JHAC will be more likely to score high (strongly agree) on Black nationalism than individuals who score low on JHAC. High-effort copers (individuals who score high on JHAC) tend to exhibit sustained cognitive effort; they are more likely to take action, and are more likely to believe that they can overcome or accomplish anything, than are low-effort copers. This leads us to expect that some of the ways in which high-effort copers might alleviate or address stress in their lives, such as daily encounters with racism, or injustices spanning a multitude of contexts (racial, social, economic, etc.), are by supporting members of their racial group—voting for Black candidates, forming a political party, shopping at Black-owned stores—and/or by embracing their racial identity and taking pride in it (for example, giving their kids African names).

Second, is there an association between the way one copes with adversity and support for American values? For national pride, we expect to find that individuals who score high on JHAC will be more likely to score high (agree or strongly agree) on national pride than individuals who score low on JHAC. In viewing coping as a process, scholars suggest that the ways in which people cope depend on multiple factors, including some that are situational (e.g., controllability) and some that are individual (e.g., self-confidence).[25] Given that high JHAC, much like high levels of internal efficacy, is reflective of one's own confidence and internal beliefs, we find it likely that high-effort copers will be more confident and prouder of their nationality (or the nation) than low-effort copers, who tend to lack confidence and belief in their own abilities and strengths.

For work ethic, we expect to find that individuals who score high on JHAC will be more likely to score high (strongly agree) on work ethic than individuals who score low on JHAC. High-effort copers, unlike low-effort copers, embrace the belief "that just about any obstacle can be overcome through hard work and a strong determination to succeed."[26] In addition, commitment to hard work, determination to succeed, and "efficacious mental and physical vigor" are three themes that Sherman James describes as being captured by the JHAC scale.[27] Therefore, we find strong support in the literature for our hypothesis.

For authoritarianism, we expect to find that individuals who score high on JHAC will be more likely to score high (strongly agree) on authoritarianism than individuals who score low on JHAC. High-effort copers reflect an internal locus of control, which is the belief that outcomes are dependent on one's own choices and actions.[28] Many African Americans teach their children from a young age what racism and racial discrimination are. To face, handle, and/or attempt to deescalate situations that may be hostile or even lead to conflict with persons of authority or otherwise—such as encounters with the police, or interactions in school or in the workplace—requires a certain level of knowledge and information regarding the ugly truths of living in a racist society and how to navigate it. That said, we recognize that obedience and respect for authority are not perfect solutions and will not prevent an individual from experiencing traumatic events attributable to racism. However, we do think there is reason to believe that teaching and applying these virtues is one way in which high-effort copers may feel a sense of control in terms of their own choices and actions. Generally speaking, obedience and respect for authority are virtues that may be beneficial in navigating any type of social interaction, especially at work or school, wherein there are certain norms regarding respect and obedience.

Finally, we explore interactions between coping and sociodemographic, political, racial, and psychosocial variables on ideological views. We do so since prior studies of JHAC and health outcomes underscore the importance of SES and context.[29] Based on what we already know from prior health-related studies, we hypothesize that there will be an interaction effect between JHAC and sociodemographic factors (such as age, education, and income), JHAC and psychosocial stressors (such as experiences with discrimination, race relations, and feelings toward whites), JHAC and race identity (public regard and linked fate), and JHAC and political ideology on ideological views.

Methods

Here the first dependent variable is Black nationalism. Black nationalism measures a "commitment to African culture and the degree to which blacks should confine their social relationships to other blacks."[30] It was assessed on the basis of responses to four questions: "Blacks should vote for Blacks"; "Blacks should form a political party"; "Blacks should shop Black-owned stores"; and "Blacks should give their kids African names." Each response was coded from 1 (strongly disagree) to 4 (strongly agree).[31] The responses were summed for participants who answered at least three of the four questions to provide a continuous measure of Black nationalism with values ranging from 3 to 16. The reliability coefficient (α) was .81. The mean score was 7.29 (SD = 2.92). Scores were then based on the median (7.00) to obtain quartiles: 3–4 (lowest), 5–6, 7–8, and 9–16 (highest).

Nearly 25.5 percent of the total sample reported high support for Black nationalism, while 30.5 percent had the highest degree of support. Support for Black nationalism, at the lowest level, was 21.7 percent. Chi-square tests were analyzed to compare differences between low and high coping in response to Black nationalism, and there was a significant relationship between coping and Black nationalism.

The second dependent variable is American values. To examine the relationship between coping and attitudes toward American values, we use three items: national pride, work ethic, and authoritarianism. Participants were asked whether they agreed or disagreed with each of the following statements: "I am very proud to be an American" (national pride); "America is the land of opportunity in which you only need to work hard to succeed" (work ethic); and "obedience and respect for authority are the most important virtues children should learn" (authoritarianism). Each item was coded using a four-point ordinal scale from 1 (strongly disagree) to 4 (strongly agree).

Table 4.1 presents the responses for the American values questions. Nearly 93 percent somewhat or strongly agreed that they were very proud to be an American, while 7 percent somewhat or strongly disagreed. Regarding work ethic, 78.3 percent somewhat or strongly agreed, while 21.7 percent said they somewhat or strongly disagreed, that America is the land of opportunity in which you only need to work hard to succeed. On the question of authoritarianism, 82.8 percent strongly or somewhat agreed with the statement that obedience and respect for authority are the most important virtues children should learn. On the other hand, 16.6 percent indicated a moderate or strong disagreement. Chi-square tests were analyzed to compare differences between low and high coping (i.e., JHAC) in response to American values (see table 4.1). The findings show that there is a significant relationship between coping and national pride (p = 0.000), work ethic (p = 0.000), and authoritarianism (p = 0.000).

Table 4.1. American Values by JHAC

	n (weighted %)		
	Low JHAC	High JHAC	p-value
National pride, n (wt. %)			0.000**
Strongly disagree	22 (2.1)	18 (2.4)	
Somewhat disagree	68 (6.6)	23 (2.7)	
Somewhat agree	276 (27.1)	112 (13.2)	
Strongly agree	718 (64.2)	750 (81.7)	
Work ethic, n (wt. %)			0.000**
Strongly disagree	80 (7.6)	42 (4.3)	
Somewhat disagree	224 (20.7)	87 (9.4)	
Somewhat agree	441 (40.4)	246 (26.7)	
Strongly agree	346 (31.3)	532 (59.6)	
Authoritarianism, n (wt. %)			0.000**
Strongly disagree	56 (6.4)	34 (4.0)	
Somewhat disagree	176 (15.9)	67 (7.6)	
Somewhat agree	401 (37.1)	236 (26.7)	
Strongly agree	458 (40.5)	567 (61.7)	

$^*p < 0.05; ^{**}p < 0.0001$
Source: Author created.

Analytical Strategy and Model Selection

Since the outcome variables, Black nationalism and American values, are ordinal in nature, we estimated models for each with ordered logistic regression. We then used the results from these models in a second set of estimates which calculate the marginal effect of independent variables under specific conditions, such as at a single level of the dependent variable. For significant interactions, we analyzed predicted probabilities for "strongly agree" responses to both Black nationalism and American values questions. Sample weights were created and used to account for nonresponse variations.

Results

BLACK NATIONALISM

Figure 4.1 shows the results from an ordered logit model for "Black nationalism." There is a statistically significant association between JHAC and Black nationalism. More specifically, examining each factor independently reveals that the odds of strongly agreeing with Black nationalism are 27 percent higher for those with high JHAC (OR: 1.27; 95% CI: 1.00, 1.61; p = 0.052). By contrast, the odds of strongly agreeing with Black nationalism are 29 percent lower for African American females (OR: 0.70; 95% CI: 0.55, 0.90; p = 0.005), 2 percent lower for those who hold higher feelings toward whites (OR: 0.99; 95% CI: 0.98, 0.99; p = 0.000), and 84 percent lower for those who perceive that whites view African Americans most positively (OR: 0.16; 95% CI: 0.09, 0.28; p = 0.000).

Figure 4.2 presents marginal effects of high JHAC on Black nationalism. The findings show that those who are high on JHAC are 5 percentage points more likely than those who are low on JHAC to have the highest level of support for Black nationalism. There is a significant difference between the low and high categories (p = 0.053) at this level of support. On the other hand, those who are high on JHAC are 2 percentage points less likely to have lower levels of support for Black nationalism (p = 0.056), and 4 percentage points less likely to have the lowest level of support for Black nationalism (p = 0.049). Additionally, there was an interaction between JHAC and linked fate on support for Black nationalism. Those who don't think what happens generally to Black people in this country will have something to do with what happens in their life and are low on JHAC are more likely to support Black nationalism. There were no other significant interactions.

NATIONAL PRIDE

Figure 4.3 shows results from an ordered logit model for "national pride." There is a statistically significant association between JHAC and national pride. More specifically, examining each factor independently reveals that the odds of strongly agreeing with national pride are 84 percent higher for those with high JHAC (OR: 1.84; 95% CI: 1.32, 2.56; p = 0.000), 2 percent higher with increasing age (OR: 1.02; 95% CI: 1.01, 1.03; p = 0.003), 81 percent higher for those residing in the South (OR: 1.81; 95% CI: 1.36, 2.43; p = 0.000), 2 percent higher for those who hold higher

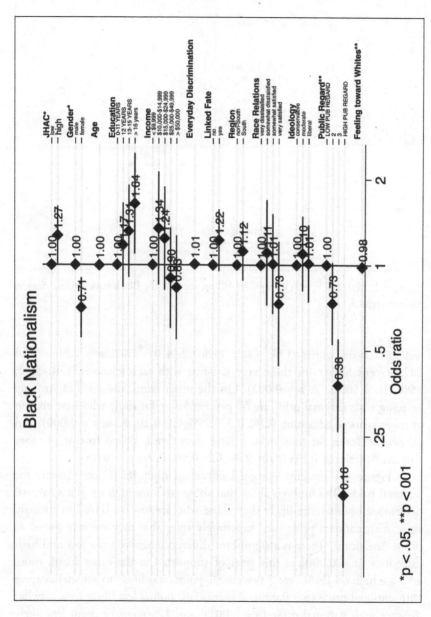

Figure 4.1. JHAC on Black nationalism. *Source:* Author created.

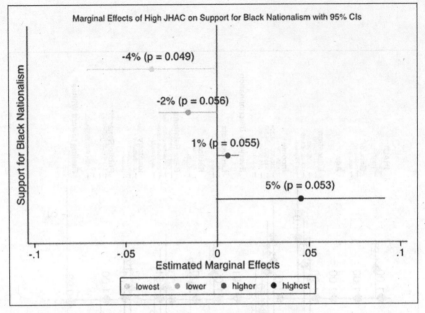

Figure 4.2. Marginal effects of high JHAC on support for Black nationalism. *Source:* Author created.

feelings toward whites (OR: 1.02; 95% CI: 1.01, 1.02; p = 0.000), and 222 percent higher for those very satisfied with race relations (OR: 3.22; 95% CI: 1.50, 6.72; p = 0.002). On the other hand, the odds of strongly agreeing with national pride are 67 percent lower for those who have sixteen or more years of education (OR: 0.33; 95% CI: 0.20, 0.56; p = 0.000), and 30 percent lower for those who believe their fate is linked to that of other African Americans (OR: 0.70; 95% CI: 0.50, 0.97; p = 0.033).

Figure 4.4 presents marginal effects of high JHAC on support for national pride. The findings show that those who are high on JHAC are 10 percentage points more likely than those who are low on JHAC to strongly agree with national pride (i.e., to strongly agree that they are very proud to be an American). There is a significant difference between the low and high categories (p = 0.000) at this level of support. On the other hand, those who are high on JHAC are 7 percentage points less likely to somewhat agree with national pride (p = 0.000), 2 percentage points less likely to somewhat disagree with national pride (p = 0.001), and 1 percentage point less likely to strongly disagree with national pride (p = 0.001).

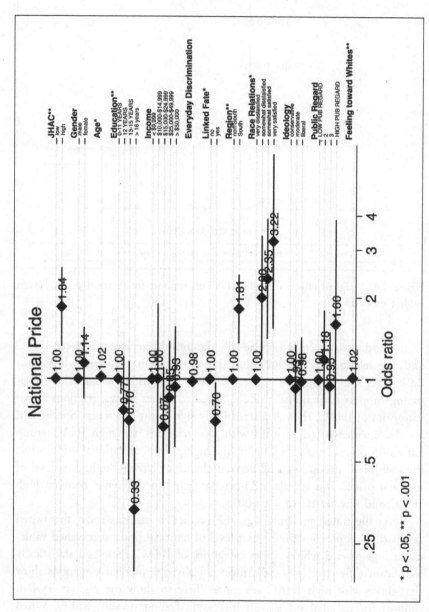

Figure 4.3. JHAC on national pride. *Source.* Author created.

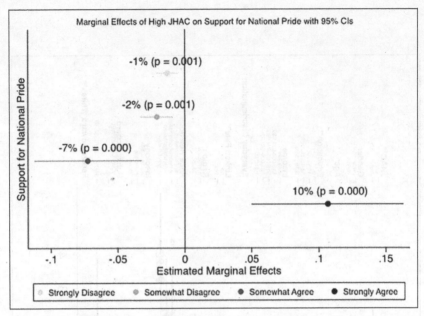

Figure 4.4. Marginal effects of high JHAC on support for national pride. *Source*: Author created.

In addition, there is a statistically significant interaction between JHAC and race relations (p = 0.042), and JHAC and feelings toward whites (p = 0.013). As seen in figure 4.5, the predictive margins show that when comparing support for national pride at specified values of race relations across categories of JHAC, there is a statistically significant difference. Specifically, for those somewhat dissatisfied with race relations, the high JHAC group has an 85 percent chance of having the highest level of national pride, while the low JHAC group has a 62 percent chance of having the highest level of national pride. This reveals a 23-percentage-point difference between high JHAC and low JHAC (p = 0.000).

As illustrated in figure 4.6, the predictive margins show that when comparing support for the highest level of national pride at specified values of feelings toward whites across categories of JHAC, there is a statistically significant difference (p = 0.013). Specifically, the predictive margins show that those with high JHAC are more likely to show the highest level of support for national pride with increasing feelings toward whites. When comparing support for the highest level of national pride at specified values of feelings toward whites across categories of JHAC, there are statistically

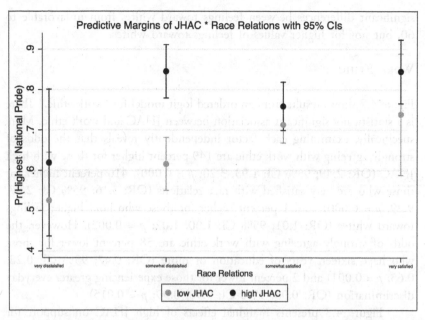

Figure 4.5. Interaction effect of JHAC and race relations on highest level of national pride. *Source*. Author created.

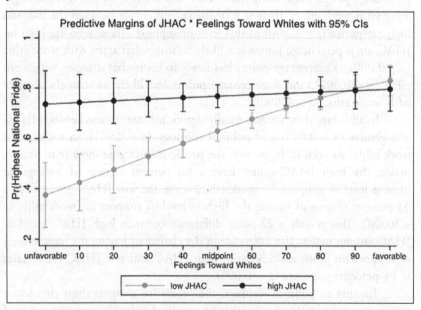

Figure 4.6. Interaction effect of JHAC and feeling toward Whites on highest level of national pride. *Source*: Author created.

significant differences between feelings toward whites from unfavorable to 60, but not for higher values of feelings toward whites.

WORK ETHIC

Figure 4.7 shows results from an ordered logit model for "work ethic." There is a statistically significant association between JHAC and work ethic. More specifically, examining each factor independently reveals that the odds of strongly agreeing with work ethic are 149 percent higher for those with high JHAC (OR: 2.49; 95% CI: 1.93, 3.20; p = 0.000), 416 percent higher for those who are very satisfied with race relations (OR: 5.16; 95% CI: 2.87, 9.29; p = 0.000), and 1 percent higher for those who hold higher feelings toward whites (OR: 1.01; 95% CI: 1.00, 1.02; p = 0.002). However, the odds of strongly agreeing with work ethic are 58 percent lower for those who have sixteen years of education or more (OR: 0.42; 95% CI: 0.28, 0.65; p = 0.001) and 2 percent lower for those experiencing greater everyday discrimination (OR: 0.98; 95% CI: 0.98, 0.99; p = 0.015)

Figure 4.8 presents marginal effects of high JHAC on support for work ethic. The findings show that those who are high on JHAC are 19 percentage points more likely than those who are low on JHAC to strongly agree with work ethic. There is a significant difference between the low and high categories (p = 0.000) at this level of support. Those who are high on JHAC are 6 percentage points less likely to somewhat agree with work ethic (p = 0.000), 9 percentage points less likely to somewhat disagree with work ethic (p = 0.000), and 4 percentage points less likely to strongly disagree with work ethic (p = 0.000).

In addition, there are statistically significant interactions between JHAC and gender (p = 0.013) and political ideology (p = 0.051) on support for work ethic. As seen in figure 4.9, the predictive margins show that, among males, the high JHAC group have a 60 percent chance of having the highest level of support for work ethic, while the low JHAC group have a 33 percent chance of having the highest level of support for work ethic (p = 0.000). This reveals a 27-point difference between high JHAC and low JHAC among males. The difference in the chance of having the highest level of support for work ethic between high JHAC and low JHAC for females is 14 percentage points (p = 0.000).

Turning to political ideology, the predictive margins show that when comparing support for work ethic at specified values across categories of

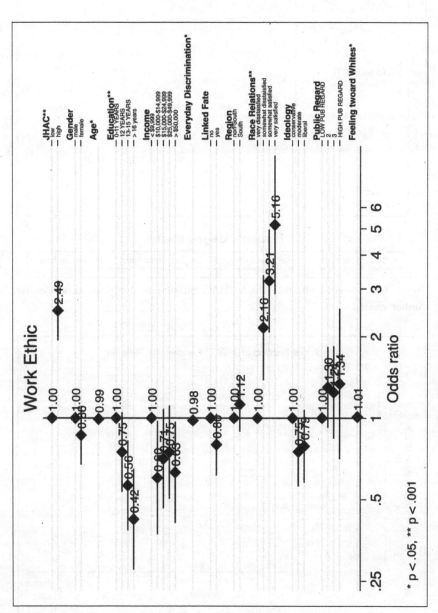

Figure 4.7. JHAC on work ethic. *Source:* Author created.

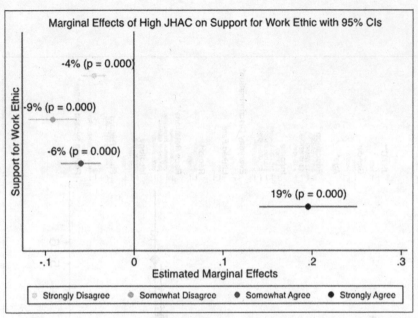

Figure 4.8. Marginal effects of high JHAC on support for work ethic. *Source*: Author created.

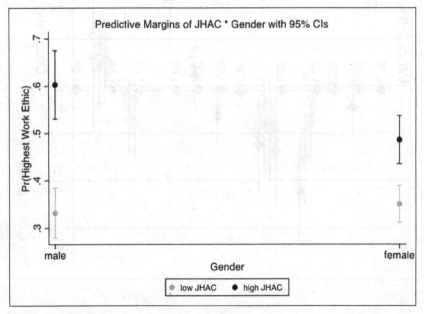

Figure 4.9. Interaction effect of JHAC and gender on highest level of work ethic. *Source*: Author created.

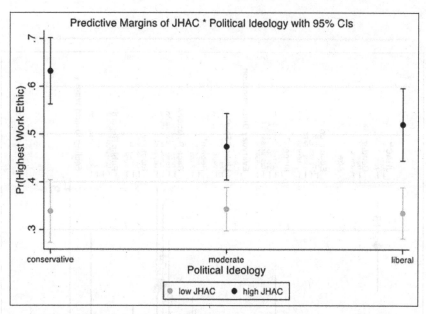

Figure 4.10. Interaction effect of JHAC and political ideology on highest level of work ethic. *Source*: Author created.

JHAC (see figure 4.10), there are statistically significant differences for all three affiliations, conservative (p = 0.000), moderate (p = 0.002), and liberal (p = 0.000). Specifically, among conservatives, the high JHAC group has a 63 percent chance of having the highest level of support for work ethic, while the low JHAC group has a 34 percent chance. This reveals a 29-point difference between high JHAC and low JHAC. The difference in the chance of having the highest level of support for work ethic between high JHAC and low JHAC for moderates is 13 points, and for liberals, it is 19 points.

Authoritarianism

Figure 4.11 shows results from an ordered logit model for "authoritarianism." There is a statistically significant association between JHAC and authoritarianism. More specifically, examining each factor independently reveals that the odds of strongly agreeing with authoritarianism are 118 percent higher for those with high JHAC (OR: 2.18; 95% CI: 1.67, 2.84; p = 0.000), and 27 percent higher for those residing in the South (OR: 1.27; 95% CI: 1.00, 1.62; p = 0.056). However, the odds of strongly agreeing with

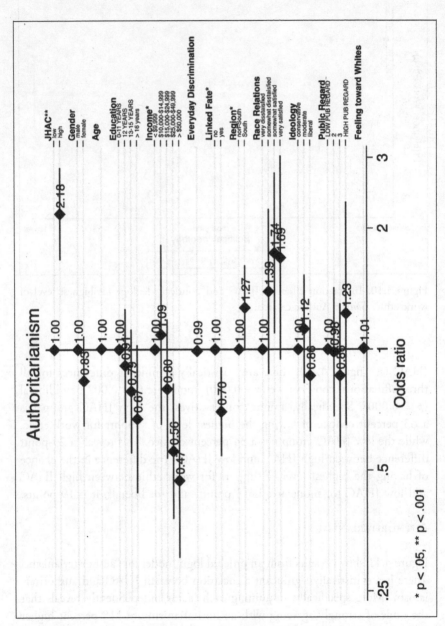

Figure 4.11. JHAC on authoritarianism. *Source:* Author created.

authoritarianism are 53 percent lower for those whose income is greater than $50,000 (OR: 0.47; 95% CI: 0.30, 0.73; p = 0.001), and 30 percent lower for those who believe their fate is linked to that of other African Americans (OR: 0.70; 95% CI: 0.54, 0.90; p = 0.006).

Figure 4.12 presents marginal effects of high JHAC on support for authoritarianism. The findings show that those who are high on JHAC are 18 percentage points more likely than those who are low on JHAC to strongly agree with authoritarianism. There is a significant difference between the low and high categories (p = 0.000) at this level of support. On the other hand, those who are high on JHAC are 8 percentage points less likely to somewhat agree with authoritarianism (p = 0.000), 7 percentage points less likely to somewhat disagree with authoritarianism (p = 0.000), and 3 percentage points less likely to strongly disagree with authoritarianism (p = 0.000). There were no significant interactions.

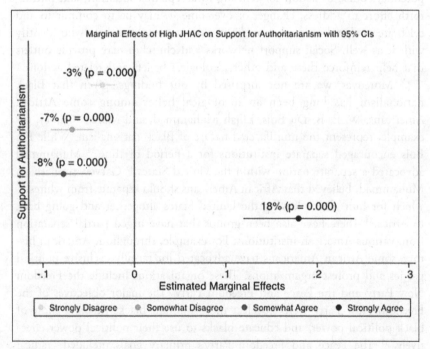

Figure 4.12. Marginal effects of high JHAC on support for authoritarianism. *Source*: Author created.

Conclusion

The findings show that JHAC has an impact on measures of both Black nationalism and American values. Specifically, those high on JHAC are more supportive of Black nationalism. As we stated in our expectations, high-effort copers are more likely than low-effort copers to believe that they can overcome or accomplish anything and are constantly figuring out ways to alleviate stress in their lives. Based on our findings, one way of doing that, among those who score high on JHAC, is through Black nationalism, by supporting members of their racial group (voting for African American candidates, forming a political party, shopping at African American–owned stores) and/or by embracing their racial identity and taking pride in it (giving their kids African names). In a society wherein individuals constantly face stressors, challenges, and barriers on account of systemic racism, a potential course of action for refusing to accept this situation, and putting forth effort to address, change, or overcome it, may be to commit to and celebrate one's culture and to make it a point to uplift others who identify with it as well. Social support networks and churches may provide outlets that help reinforce these and other ideological beliefs and related actions.

Moreover, we are not surprised by our findings, given that Black nationalism has long been an ideological belief among some African Americans. W. E. B. Du Bois, Elijah Muhammad, and Marcus Garvey, for example, represent the multifaceted nature of Black nationalism. While Du Bois encouraged separate institutions for a period of time,[32] Muhammad advocated a separate nation within the United States.[33] Garvey, similarly to Muhammad, believed that African Americans should separate from whites—which for him meant leaving the United States altogether and going back to Africa.[34] There have also been groups that have urged partial separation from various American institutions. For example, throughout American history, some African Americans have advocated for racially exclusive political parties and protest organizations. These organizations include the Freedom Now Party and the Peace and Freedom Party. The major objectives of the Freedom Now Party were "to elect more militant blacks, make a show of black political power, and educate blacks to use their political power effectively."[35] The Peace and Freedom Party's primary goals included "radical economic programs, black freedom, and peace in Vietnam."[36] Additionally, others feeling disenfranchised by the traditional Democratic Party formed their own political parties, such as the Mississippi Freedom Democratic Party and the United Citizens Party of South Carolina.[37] Their primary objective was to elect African American candidates.

Prior research shows that those who are more likely to support Black nationalism are: "younger,"[38] "males,"[39] "higher income earners,"[40] "middle class,"[41] "black working-class or poor,"[42] "more liberal,"[43] "religious,"[44] "those who believe Christ was black,"[45] Muslims,[46] "those exposed to higher levels of black media,"[47] "those who are disillusioned,"[48] "members of black organizations,"[49] and "those who are high on racial centrality."[50] Our findings, then, add another dimension to the research on Black nationalism—a psychological dimension. Specifically, the degree to which one copes with psychosocial stressors affects support for Black nationalism.

American values represent ideological views that many individuals, regardless of race or gender, embrace. As noted, though, American values can take many forms and their meanings may differ from person to person. For this reason, among others, ideological views reflecting American values can be challenging to define and measure. For example, scholars have pointed out that the terms *patriotism, nationalism,* and *national identity* are at times used inconsistently and/or conflated, and there is not a consensus for one particular measure.[51] However, to understand these concepts, it is useful to look at the ways in which they are conceptualized and measured in the literature. Scholars have analyzed affective aspects, which reflect how one feels about one's country, and have found that "affective attachment to one's nation is primarily associated with the emotions of love and pride. While love of the nation is found equally across the political ideological spectrum, pride appears to manifest differently."[52]

In an overview of the literature on and approaches to studying national pride, Rui De Figueiredo and Zachary Elkins[53] point out that concepts such as patriotism and nationalism can be (and have been) differentiated based on their point of reference—with one dimension of national identity, patriotism, having a more positive connotation, and the other dimension, nationalism, a more negative connotation.[54] In this line of thinking, "national pride (patriotism) is self-referential, a positive regard for one's country, while *chauvinism* (nationalism) stems from comparison between one's own and other countries and is almost exclusively downward."[55] In other words, patriotism "refers to an attachment to the nation, its institutions, and its founding principles, [while] nationalism refers to a belief in national superiority and dominance—that is, a commitment to the denigration of the alternatives to the nation's institutions and principles."[56] In our examination of American values, national pride, or agreement with the statement, "I am very proud to be an American," is tapping into affective attachment and pride in one's country, which aligns more with the concept of patriotism based on the literature overviewed here.

Beyond American/national pride, ideological views reflecting American values that tap into the notion of the American Dream are captured in our measure "work ethic": the notion that "America is the land of opportunity in which you only need to work hard to succeed." Research on American values as they relate to the American Dream illustrates the long-standing association between the nation's democratic principles and hard work.[57] The American Dream and American values pertaining to work ethic are a common ideology that continues to be embraced by Americans regardless of partisan identification, political ideology, gender, or race.[58] In fact, a majority of Americans believe in it, and data from public opinion polls exemplify this: In the General Social Survey (GSS), between 1985 to 2006, a majority of respondents "reported that hard work (rather than luck) matters most in getting ahead," and between 1999 and 2007, in each of six surveys, over 60 percent of respondents agreed with the statement that "most people who want to get ahead can make it if they're willing to work hard."[59] In the context of the American Dream, Republicans and Democrats alike, as well as liberals and conservatives, generally embrace it.[60] However, in a slightly different context, polling data also show that some Americans do associate particular political parties in the United States with the American Dream: "Respondents were consistently more likely to say that the Democratic Party (in contrast to the Republican Party) will do a better job of helping more people achieve the American Dream, although the Republican Party has made some gains."[61]

In terms of the American values we explored, the findings show that those high on JHAC demonstrate more support for American/national pride, work ethic, and authoritarianism. We are not surprised by these findings, given what we know about JHAC. Perhaps the most obvious finding is that individuals who score high on JHAC are more likely to score high on our measure of work ethic. This finding aligns with the research on JHAC, which makes it clear that individuals who score high on JHAC view themselves as being in control of outcomes, are strongly determined to succeed, and believe that just about anything can be overcome if one works hard.[62]

Much of the research on American values has focused on white respondents. On the question of American pride, research has shown that white respondents who are ideologically conservative are much more likely to support the notion of American pride.[63] Scholars have found that beyond ideology and partisan identification, age, gender, education, income, region, religion, and race have been associated with high levels of American pride.[64] For example, in a recent study using GSS data, the average respondents classified as "ardent nationalists," who (among other things) were most likely to score high on items concerning national/American pride, were older (mean age = 51), white, religious males with relatively little formal education and moderately low incomes, living in the South, and identifying as Republicans.[65] Having said that, it is clear that the wording of items concerning nationalism, national identity, patriotism, and American/national pride can and often does capture different ideas and beliefs, and can therefore contribute to varying results across studies.

For example, "pride, chauvinism, symbolic patriotism, and blind patriotism have been found to be more common in conservatives,[66] and constructive patriotism has been more often attributed to liberals."[67] Moreover, scholars have shown how national identity differs from other measures of patriotism and nationalism by using data from two undergraduate student samples and the 1996 GSS, wherein they found that "national pride was not ideological in nature and was no stronger among conservatives than liberals."[68] Setting the varying results and wording of measures concerning American pride in previous studies aside, we are not surprised by our finding that high scores on JHAC are associated with more support for American pride, given that African Americans in particular have long stood up for and fought for democratic principles, an attitude that goes hand in hand with themes often represented by JHAC: strong determination, physical and mental vigor, commitment to success and hard work, and self-confidence.[69]

When we turn to the American value concerning authoritarianism, we can again see a connection between it and patriotism or American pride. "Uncritical patriotism," or blind patriotism, in particular "is linked to authoritarianism, which is characterized, in turn, by a tendency to defer to authority figures and support them unconditionally. And authoritarians are typically conservative (although not all conservatives are authoritarians)."[70] However, similar to the literature on concepts related to American pride, authoritarianism may be conceptualized and measured differently depending on the context. Our measure of authoritarianism, which is in agreement with the statement "Obedience and respect for authority are the most important virtues children should learn," clearly taps into individual beliefs/American values concerning what is important for children to learn. With regard to JHAC, it makes sense that those who score high on JHAC are more likely to support this measure of authoritarianism when we consider the connection between authoritarian parenting and JHAC. In research on authoritarian parenting, scholars explain that it is embraced by "demanding" parents who place heavy emphasis on psychological control.[71]

Scholars have also found that authoritarian parenting is relatively common among African Americans.[72] Drawing from the work of Hyeon-Ju Cha and Hee-Sun Cho,[73] and L. S. Vygotsky,[74] Veronica Smith explains that "African American authoritarianism can be a human process of learning and mastery, as it directly correlates with human culture group assimilation, the learning process, and ongoing routine interactions in one's social environment."[75] This understanding of authoritarian parenting embraced by African Americans illustrates its relation to JHAC: both reflect an emphasis on mastery/control, and the environment plays a role in shaping the attitudes and behaviors affiliated with each. Moreover, given the frequency at which African Americans experience racial discrimination in their everyday lives and in various social interactions, the notion that these stressors and events would shape what they instill in their children, or what they find important for children to learn more broadly, makes it clear why the American value of authoritarianism is associated with high levels of JHAC in our findings.

Recent events, such as the duration and scope of protests associated with the Black Lives Matter movement, as well as the calls to "Buy Black," are illustrative of the ideological views embraced by the African American community. While research shows a number of factors correlated with ideological views such as Black nationalism and American values, our goal in this chapter is to expand that body of literature to include a psychological factor: coping. It is our belief and expectation that coping could help predict and/or explain behaviors and attitudes that manifest in the participation of BLM protests and/or shopping at Black-owned businesses (among other activities) in recent years, but due to data limitations, we can only speculate that such a relationship exists. However, using the data we do have available, our findings suggest that John Henryism Active Coping is associated with ideological views such as Black nationalism and American values. The lack of data available to explore the connection between JHAC and ideological views in recent years is indicative of a gap that future scholars could fill, and based on our findings, we believe this is a promising area for future research.

In conclusion, we argue in this chapter that future research should not ignore psychological influences on questions of ideological beliefs. How much one experiences psychosocial stressors is a factor shaping ideological beliefs, but so is the degree to which one copes with such stressors. The cognitive and emotional engagement that affects social, psychological, and health outcomes is also at work in shaping ideological beliefs and behaviors associated with them. These outcomes vary as a function of the type of cognitive and emotional engagement and the degree of effort an individual puts forth, which is indicative of the type of coping the individual embraces and reflects.

In this chapter, we have explored how the type of effort, whether it is low or high, that an individual exerts to overcome psychosocial and environmental stressors is associated with ideological beliefs encompassing Black nationalism and American values. More specifically, individuals who put forth a high degree of effort to overcome stressors—that is, those who score high on JHAC ("high-effort copers")—are more likely to score high on measures of ideological beliefs relating to Black nationalism, American pride, work ethic, and authoritarianism. Conversely, individuals who score low on JHAC, otherwise known as "low-effort copers" or "passive copers," are less likely to score high on measures of ideological beliefs relating to these variables.

Thus, our empirical results align with our theoretical expectations for ideological views and provide further support for the book's central argument that an underlying mechanism driving a host of outcomes—both those previously explored, and those we are exploring at length in this book—is an individual's coping style, and the degree of effort one puts forth in order to overcome a variety of stressors, as reflected in our measure of JHAC. The qualities reflected in JHAC and the literature on it, including self-confidence, a degree of mastery, the role of the environment and interactions within it, sustained cognitive and mental engagement, physical and mental vigor, a commitment to succeed, and a strong drive and determination, make it clear that there are many similarities between active copers and those who agree with Black nationalism and American values. In a subsequent chapter, we continue building this argument concerning the role of JHAC in shaping outcomes by applying it to Black information consumption—an action or activity that reflects some of the same qualities and beliefs underlying those that form the connections between JHAC and ideological views.

CHAPTER 5

Coping and Policy Preferences

The protestors in Lafayette Park on June 1 may have been galvanized by the disturbing video of the murder of George Floyd, suffocated to death beneath the knee of a Minneapolis police officer just a week prior. But at the core of their movement is much more than the outrage over the latest instances of police brutality. Centuries of racist policy, both explicit and implicit, have left black Americans in the dust, physically, emotionally and economically.[1]

—Justin Worland, "America's Long Overdue Awakening to Systemic Racism"

While racism is certainly not new to the United States, recent increases in police brutality, racial discrimination, and cases wherein police officers have killed African Americans have inspired discussions concerning race-specific policies and the need to address issues that unjustly make the lives of African Americans far more difficult and challenging, and even at serious risk of danger or harm, including death. Though the prominent cases we highlight in the introduction to this book, and throughout the rest of it, range in severity from blatant discrimination to outright murder, they all sparked outrage, protests, and calls for change—along with movements consisting of individuals from an array of backgrounds.[2] Just a few years ago, in 2015, only half of Americans (in a Monmouth University poll) said racial discrimination was a "big problem," and a year later, only one-third of Americans believed African Americans (in comparison to non–African Americans) were "more likely to suffer from police brutality."[3] However, a 2020 Monmouth poll shows that today "more than 75 percent of Americans say discrimination is a big problem and 57 percent understand that African Americans are more likely to suffer from police violence than other demographic groups are."[4] Though this awakening of the larger US population is long overdue, recent events have made it clear to the majority that such injustices can no longer be ignored. As a result, more policies are being discussed now, and people are advocating for serious change.

Many of these calls for change are targeted toward law enforcement agencies and particular institutions, but there have also been calls for change in our society at large.[5] Take, for example, the case of Christian Cooper and his encounter with Amy Cooper while bird-watching in the Ramble, as described in chapter 3.[6] What could and should have been a simple exchange turned into a case of racial profiling and a white woman calling 911, falsely claiming an African American man was threatening her and her dog.[7] This case illustrates how embedded racism is in America: it is not limited to law enforcement officers, or those involved in the criminal justice system; it is also found and on display in our parks, streets, and neighborhoods. Technology (especially social media) has helped, in part, to bring attention to the racial discrimination and everyday psychosocial stressors that African Americans in particular face.

While the viral exchange that was recorded by Christian Cooper showed Amy Cooper calling 911 the first time, it was revealed in court in October 2020 that Amy Cooper made a second call to 911, during which she also accused Christian Cooper of assaulting her (though she later admitted to police that he did not).[8] Following this event, and considering the rate at which similar situations have transpired, "Governor Cuomo signed into law State Senate Bill 8492, which imposes a civil penalty for calling the cops on a black person, or any other member of a 'protected class,' when there's 'no reason to believe a crime or offense, or imminent threat to person or property, is occurring.' "[9] While this is one example of a policy reaction to particular cases of racial discrimination, whether it will lead to actual change or not remains to be seen, and only time will tell whether it has any meaningful effect or not. It also raises the question why such a bill was only just now, in 2020, signed into law. On the one hand, it is an unfortunate reality that the need for such a law exists, but on the other, it seems that the viral nature of many of these—and related—cases may be what it has taken to get such a dialogue started, and to get at least one state's lawmakers to listen to people and take action. Yet it is also clear that more needs to be done.

"The U.S. may think it has brushed chattel slavery into the dustbin of history after the Civil War, but the country never did a very good job incinerating its traumatic remains, instead leaving embers that still burn today: an education system that fails black Americans, substandard health care that makes them more vulnerable to death and disease, and an economy that leaves millions without access to a living wage."[10] While this is a very short list that illustrates just a few of the ways in which systemic racism is embedded in the US, it speaks to the conversations more and more people are having in light of recent events and realizations. Beyond the push for police and criminal justice reform, policy debates concerning reparations have also received increasing attention throughout 2020 and 2021, in particular.[11]

We use the cases of racial discrimination documented in the introduction as an illustration of recent events that have inspired conversations surrounding, and protests demanding, change in the form of policies, but we recognize that not everyone will agree with certain policies. Thus, we turn our attention to the following question: What else might affect policy positions for African Americans? In this chapter, we argue and show that John Henryism Active Coping can affect African Americans' policy positions and preferences.

Much of the debate about African American support for race-specific policies centers on two major explanations. The first, a class argument, suggests that economic dispersion within the African American community creates less cohesive support for certain race-specific policies such as redistribution of wealth, government aid to Blacks, welfare benefits, reducing inequality, Black autonomy, and affirmative action.[12] Works by William Julius Wilson[13] and E. Franklin Frazier[14] began to disentangle this class argument. Their major theory was that as economic class distribution increased among African Americans, there would be greater intragroup disagreement on race-specific policies. In other words, high-status African Americans would have less of a reason to support such policies than poor African Americans. As evidence of this declining relationship among African Americans, Frazier wrote, "The Black bourgeoisie has tended to break completely with the traditions of the Negro. As the system of rigid racial segregation has broken down, the Black bourgeoisie has lost much of its feeling of racial solidarity with the Negro masses."[15]

The second explanation, a race argument, suggests that mere membership within the African American group increases support for race-specific policies—a direct rebuttal of sorts to the class argument. For the scholars behind this argument, there is an acknowledgment that members of the African American community are bound together by a unique set of experiences, even in the midst of varying economic successes within the community. For example, "Black utility heuristic," a term coined by Michael Dawson,[16] describes a group consciousness among African Americans due to a shared history, which has "resulted in group interests serving as a useful proxy for self-interest."[17] Although Dawson measures group consciousness as "common fate or linked fate,"[18] others have conceptualized it as "racial salience," "closeness," "Black separatism," "racial self-esteem," "Africentrism," "racial solidarity," and "racial awareness and consciousness."[19] Regardless of how group connectedness is measured, research shows that economic success among African Americans doesn't create a schism between higher- and lower-status individuals when it comes to certain race-specific policies. Specifically, African Americans who are high income earners remain strong supporters of race-specific policies.[20] For example, African Americans who feel a "linked fate" with the larger African American community are more likely (than those who do not feel a "linked fate") to support welfare spending.[21] Others have found a relationship between racial consciousness and African Americans' support for affirmative action,[22] social welfare programs,[23] and reparations for slavery.[24]

While class and race have received the bulk of the attention, we know much less about the psychological determinants on attitudes toward race-specific policies. The little we do know shows that experiences with racial discrimination lead to support for race-specific policies.[25] However, we are unaware of any research that has investigated the relationship between the way one copes with adversity (such as discrimination, unemployment, job insecurity, chronic financial strain, and so forth) and support for race-specific policies. In other words, it is important to explore experiences of adversity and their role in shaping policy preferences, and this has received scholarly attention; it is equally important, however, to explore how one internalizes those experiences and its influence on policy preferences. Thus, our primary contribution is to begin a dialogue on the importance of including psychological determinants (specifically, coping) in studies concerning policy preferences.

Expectations

JHAC provides an opportunity to explore whether a predisposition to be unrelenting in one's efforts to overcome race and social class structural vulnerability predicts race-specific policy preferences among African Americans. Therefore, the objective in this chapter is to explore two questions.

First, is there an association between the way one copes with adversity and support for race-specific policies (for example, creations of political districts to help minorities, policies to help African Americans, and the government paying African Americans reparations)? Second, do moderating factors (e.g., sociodemographic, political, and psychosocial factors) interact with coping on race-specific policy attitudes? Since this is one of few research studies that explores the association between coping and nonhealth outcomes, our expectations about the role of coping in support for race-specific policies remain unclear. In this respect, we are cautious in our hypotheses.

Our general hypothesis is that there will be an association between support for race-specific policies and coping. Specifically, we expect those who score high on JHAC (high-effort copers) to be more likely to support race-specific policies, because prior research in health-related studies shows that high-effort copers do not give up and are constantly trying to figure out ways to succeed. In other words, high-effort copers "are characterized by their persistent, prolonged efforts to cope with the blocked opportunities put in place by racism and buttressed by acts of discrimination."[26] Consequently, their support for race-specific policies may constitute an avenue to success. On the other hand, we predict that individuals who score low on JHAC (low-effort copers) will be less supportive of race-specific policies. Research on JHAC shows that those who score low on JHAC are not as relentless in their efforts to overcome social and economic stressors, because they are often discouraged and burned out from dealing with daily confrontations with psychosocial stressors. This constant struggle could lead to a diminished faith in race-specific policies and in government institutions that aid in alleviating psychosocial stressors.

We also explore the interaction between coping and sociodemographic, political, racial, and psychosocial variables. Previous studies of JHAC and health outcomes underscore the importance of SES and context.[27] Based on what we already know from prior health-related studies, we hypothesize that there will be an interaction effect between JHAC and sociodemographic factors (such as age, education, and income), JHAC and psychosocial stressors (for example, experiences with discrimination), JHAC and race identity, and JHAC and political party on race-specific policy preferences. Specifically, education and income are reasonable indicators of the adequacy of individual-level coping resources to deal with structural adversity. Consequently, both background factors may affect how persons scoring high, as opposed to low, on JHAC view the responsibility of government to help alleviate the chronic stress African Americans face because of historical disadvantages.

As for age, we hypothesize that those who are older and high on JHAC will show a higher degree of support for race-specific policies. Older age groups have not only lived through an era that included government-sanctioned and overt forms of discrimination (such as segregation), but they have also witnessed a change in the very institutional systems that allowed discrimination to exist, and for this reason, our expectation is that they will be supportive of success by any means necessary, even if it relies on governmental institutions to create aid in that success. We also expect to find that experiences with discrimination will interact with JHAC on race-specific policy support. Specifically, as experiences with discrimination increase, those who score high on JHAC will be more supportive of race-specific policies.

Methods

Here the dependent variables are race-specific policy beliefs. To examine the relationship between coping and race-specific policy beliefs, we use three race-specific policy items: (1) the need for more political districts, so as to elect more racial minorities (majority minority districts); (2) a general view that the government should enact policies to help Blacks; and (3) a general view that the government should pay reparations to Blacks for slavery. The exact wording of these items is as follows: political districts need to be formed so that more racial minority candidates can be elected; the government should make every effort to improve the social and economic position of Blacks living in the United States; and the government should give reparations (compensation, payback) to African Americans for historical injustices and slavery. Each item is coded using a four-point ordinal scale from 1 (strongly disagree) to 4 (strongly agree). Each of the three items will be considered a dependent variable in the analysis.

Nearly 75.1 percent of respondents somewhat or strongly agreed on the need for majority minority districts, while 24.9 percent somewhat or strongly disagreed. On the statement that the government should help Blacks, 88.4 percent of respondents somewhat or strongly agreed, while 11.6 percent said they somewhat or strongly disagreed with such a policy. On the policy question concerning whether the government should pay reparations, 76 percent of respondents strongly or somewhat agreed. On the other hand, 24 percent of respondents indicated a moderate or strong disagreement. Chi-square tests were analyzed to compare differences between low and high coping (i.e., JHAC) in response to race-specific policy questions (see table 5.1). The findings show a significant relationship between coping and

Table 5.1. Racial Policy Beliefs by JHAC

	n (weighted %)		
	Low JHAC	High JHAC	p-value
Need new political districts to elect minorities, n (wt. %)			0.001**
Strongly disagree	76 (7.3)	65 (8.3)	
Somewhat disagree	192 (19.3)	123 (14.5)	
Somewhat agree	526 (51.5)	373 (45.5)	
Strongly agree	233 (21.8)	296 (31.7)	
Government should help Blacks, n (wt. %)			0.000**
Strongly disagree	28 (2.9)	29 (3.1)	
Somewhat disagree	101 (9.3)	63 (7.5)	
Somewhat agree	475 (45.0)	286 (34.4)	
Strongly agree	450 (42.8)	510 (55.0)	
Government should pay reparations, n (wt. %)			0.102
Strongly disagree	84 (7.3)	86 (9.8)	
Somewhat disagree	174 (17.1)	113 (14.1)	
Somewhat agree	333 (32.2)	230 (29.0)	
Strongly agree	454 (43.5)	441 (47.1)	

*p < 0.05; **p < 0.0001
Source: Author created.

support for majority minority districts ($p = 0.001$) and coping and support for policies to help Blacks ($p = 0.000$). However, there was not a significant relationship between coping and support for reparations ($p = 0.102$).

Analytical Strategy and Model Selection

Since the outcome variables for race-specific policy beliefs are ordinal in nature (from "strongly disagree" to "strongly agree"), we estimated models for each with ordered logistic regression. We then used the results from these models in a second set of estimates that calculate the marginal effect of independent variables under specific conditions, such as at a single level of the dependent variable. For significant interactions, we analyzed predicted probabilities for the "strongly agree" response to the race-specific policy questions. Sample weights were created and used to account for nonresponse variations.

Results

MAJORITY MINORITY DISTRICTS

Figure 5.1 shows results from an ordered logit model for supporting "majority minority districts." There is a statistically significant association between JHAC and support for majority minority districts. More specifically, examining each factor independently reveals that the odds of strongly agreeing with majority minority districts are 54 percent higher for those with high JHAC (OR: 1.54; 95% CI: 1.17, 2.01; p = 0.002), 84 percent higher for those who earn between $10,000 and $14,999 (OR: 1.84; 95% CI: 1.18, 2.89; p = 0.008), and 51 percent higher for Democrats (OR: 1.51; 95% CI: 1.00, 2.29; p = 0.050).

Figure 5.2 presents marginal effects of high JHAC on support for majority-minority districts. The findings show that those who are high on JHAC are 8 percentage points more likely than those who are low on JHAC to strongly agree with majority-minority districts. There is a significant difference between the low and high categories (p = 0.002) at this level of support. On the other hand, those who are high on JHAC are 1 percentage point less likely to somewhat agree with majority minority districts (p = 0.106), 4 percentage points less likely to somewhat disagree with majority minority districts (p = 0.004), and 3 percentage points less likely to strongly disagree with majority minority districts (p = 0.001). There was not a statistically significant interaction between JHAC and our independent variables.

POLICIES TO HELP BLACKS

Figure 5.3 shows results from an ordered logit model for supporting "policies to help Blacks." There is a statistically significant association between JHAC and support for policies to help Black individuals. More specifically, examining each factor independently reveals that the odds of strongly agreeing with enacting policies to help Black individuals are 64 percent higher for those with high JHAC (OR: 1.64; 95% CI: 1.27, 2.13; p = 0.000), 10 percent higher for those who experience greater amounts of lifetime discrimination

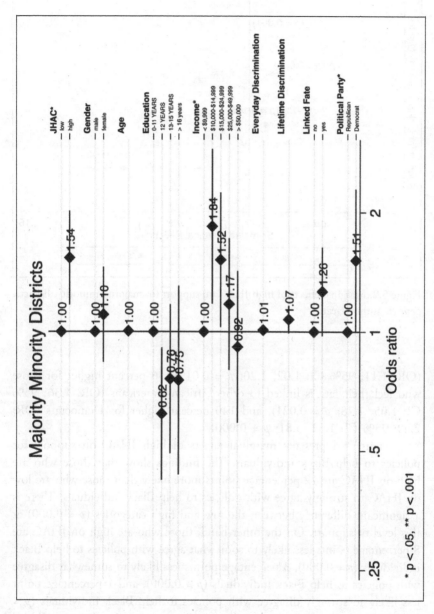

Figure 5.1. JHAC on support for majority minority districts. *Source:* Author created.

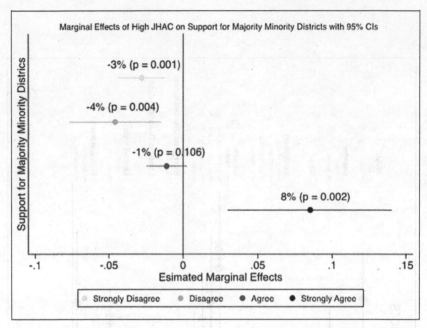

Figure 5.2. Marginal effects of high JHAC on support for majority minority districts. *Source:* Author created.

(OR: 1.11; 95% CI: 1.02, 1.20; p = 0.019), 36 percent higher for those who feel their fate is linked to other African Americans (OR: 1.36; 95% CI: 1.05, 1.78; p = 0.021), and 140 percent higher for Democrats (OR: 2.40; 95% CI: 1.52, 3.81; p = 0.000).

Figure 5.4 presents marginal effects of high JHAC on support for policies to help Black individuals. The findings show that those who are high on JHAC are 12 percentage points more likely than those who are low on JHAC to strongly agree with policies to help Black individuals. There is a significant difference between the low and high categories (p = 0.000) at this level of support. On the other hand, those who are high on JHAC are 8 percentage points less likely to somewhat agree with policies to help Black individuals (p = 0.000), 3 percentage points less likely to somewhat disagree with policies to help Black individuals (p = 0.000), and 1 percentage point less likely to strongly disagree with policies to help Black individuals (p = 0.000). There was not a statistically significant interaction between JHAC and our independent variables.

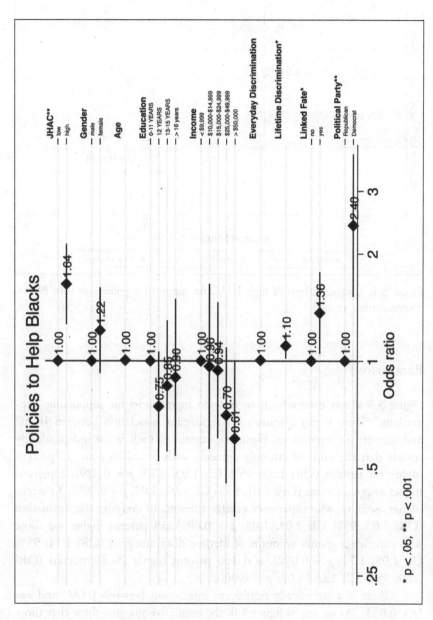

Figure 5.3. JHAC on support for policies to help Blacks. *Source:* Author created.

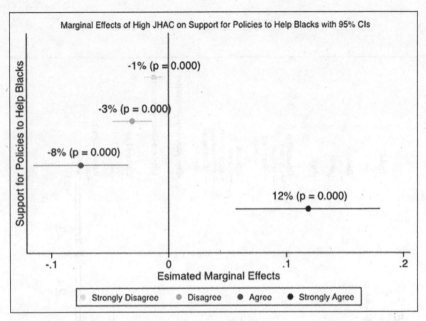

Figure 5.4. Marginal effects of high JHAC on support for policies to help Blacks. *Source*: Author created.

Reparations

Figure 5.5 shows results from an ordered logit model for supporting "reparations." There is not a statistically significant association between JHAC and support for reparations. However, examining each factor independently reveals that the odds of strongly agreeing with reparations are 33 percent higher for females (OR: 1.33; 95% CI: 1.03, 1.73; $p = 0.029$), 1 percent higher as age increases (OR: 1.01; 95% CI: 1.00, 1.02; $p = 0.005$), 3 percent higher for those who experience greater amounts of everyday discrimination (OR: 1.03; 95% CI: 1.01, 1.05; $p = 0.003$), 14 percent higher for those who experience greater amounts of lifetime discrimination (OR: 1.14; 95% CI: 1.05, 1.24; $p = 0.002$), and 160 percent higher for Democrats (OR: 2.60; 95% CI: 1.65, 4.09; $p = 0.000$).

There is a statistically significant interaction between JHAC and age ($p < 0.045$). As we see in figure 5.6, the predictive margins show that those

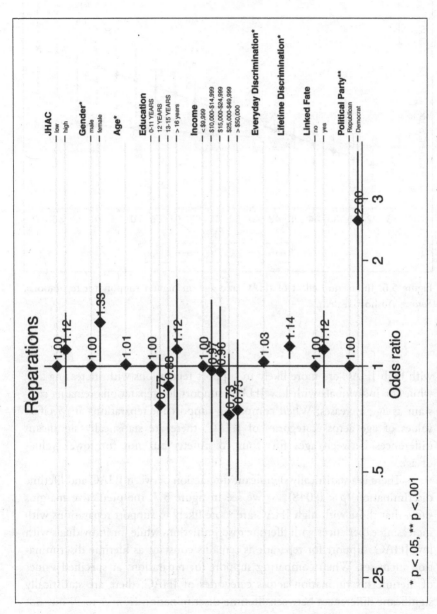

Figure 5.5. JHAC on support for reparations. *Source:* Author created.

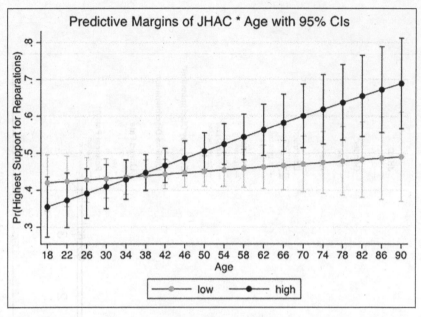

Figure 5.6. Interaction effect of JHAC and age on highest support for reparations. *Source*: Author created.

with high JHAC are more likely to support reparations with increasing age, while for individuals with low JHAC, support for reparations remains constant as age increases. When comparing support for reparations at specified values of age across categories of JHAC, there are statistically significant differences between ages fifty-four to ninety, but not for lower values of age.

There is a statistically significant interaction between JHAC and lifetime discrimination ($p < 0.048$). As we see in figure 5.7, the predictive margins show that those with high JHAC are more likely to support reparations with increasing experiences with lifetime discrimination, while for individuals with low JHAC, support for reparations remains constant as lifetime discrimination increases. When comparing support for reparations at specified values of lifetime discrimination across categories of JHAC, there are statistically significant differences between lifetime discrimination from 4 to 9, but not for lower values of lifetime discrimination.

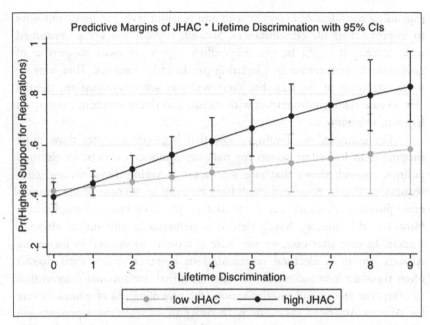

Figure 5.7. Interaction effect of JHAC and lifetime discrimination on highest support for reparations. *Source*: Author created.

Conclusion

Our primary objective in this chapter was to investigate whether coping (i.e., the manner in which one copes with adversity) predicts support for race-specific policies among African Americans and whether SES (for example, education and income), life experiences (for example, age cohort, experiences with discrimination, linked fate), and political affiliation would modify these policy preferences. Our general working hypothesis was that there would be an association between JHAC scores and race-specific policy preferences. The findings show that African Americans who are strongly predisposed to engage difficult life stressors with high-effort coping display the strongest agreement with majority-minority districts and policies that help Black individuals. We are not surprised by this finding, for two notable reasons. First, high-effort copers may see any intervention that brings some aid to them as a positive, because they are the ones, after all, who are expending considerable energy year-in and year-out trying to figure out ways to improve their life circumstances. Second, beyond just being concerned with success, it might be that high-effort copers are more supportive of government intervention in alleviating psychosocial stressors. They may be more cognizant of the fact that sheer will and self-determination, though able to ease one's confrontation with racism and discrimination, cannot, on its own, overcome it.

For example, our findings show that high-effort copers show more support than low-effort copers for majority-minority districts. In electoral politics, research shows that race is a factor in voting decisions, and consequently, African American candidates running in majority white districts often pursue a "de-racial" campaign strategy, in which race is deemphasized. However, this strategy hasn't yielded a tremendous amount of electoral success. In case after case, we see there is a desire to succeed in increasing African American electoral representation; however, desire itself doesn't often translate into success. It has often required institutional intervention to overcome racism and discrimination (the unwillingness of whites to vote for African American candidates). In order to increase the representation of African Americans, the Supreme Court (as an institution) mandated in *Thornburgh v. Gingles*[28] "the creation of a maximum number of minority districts whenever a geographical area contains a large, politically cohesive minority group."[29] Consequently, government intervention in this case alleviates (and may eliminate) the psychosocial stressors an African American candidate would otherwise face. Thus, those scoring high on JHAC may see success for minority political candidates as ultimately a success for themselves, at least in terms of policy outputs (that is, programs and policies) that benefit their everyday lives.

Those who score low on JHAC show lower levels of support for race-specific policies. There are several possible explanations. Due to constant encounters with psychosocial stressors, this group may not have a positive outlook on any interventions offered. Another possible explanation is that high-effort copers might understand that race-specific policies have a direct association with the life of the African American group. In other words, it could be that those who score low on JHAC think individualistically, with a "what's in it for me?" mentality, whereas high-effort copers may have a collectivistic mentality.

Our findings also show a significant interaction between coping and age on two of the race-specific policies. Specifically, the older age group and those high on JHAC have higher levels of support for race-specific policies. The importance of lived experiences interacting with the way one copes with psychosocial stressors seems to play an important role in shaping support for race-specific policies. The older generation of African Americans has lived through Jim Crow laws, but it has also witnessed a change in the very institutional systems that allowed discrimination to exist, including the election of the first African American president. Therefore, the older generation might be more hopeful than the younger generation.

This chapter moves us beyond the current policy research, which primarily accounts for class and race arguments. Our work adds a psychological component, which we think is equally important and should be accounted for in future policy research. For example, policy researchers currently account for discrimination, unemployment, job insecurity, and financial strain, but (to our knowledge) do not account for how one copes with these adversities. We believe accounting for this is important, since reactions to these difficulties will differ, and as this research has shown, coping affects support for race-specific policies.

The implication beyond race-specific policies is that it may be that the way one copes affects civic participation and social activism (that is, willingness to participate in African American social organizations or engage in protests). It may be that those who actively cope with social and economic adversity are also more willing to protest the inequalities that exist in society and/or participate in social organizations, among other activities.

Reflecting on the increase in police brutality and racial discrimination in recent years, we cannot directly claim that the increases in protests in response to these events are reflective of individual protestors' coping processes, nor can we claim that recent revelations (in the form of changes in public opinion) of the frequency and severity of racial discrimination and police brutality in the United States are tied to coping patterns. However, we do know that these issues have become more widely discussed and led to increased protest participation and recognition in public opinion polls and on social media networks, and we suspect that coping could help predict and/or explain changes in race-specific policy preferences in recent and coming years. Due to data limitations, we are unable to explore the relationship between race-specific policy preferences and coping in recent years, but we believe it would be a worthwhile endeavor for future scholars if and when data that incorporate measures such as JHAC are collected and/or made available.

CHAPTER 6

Coping and Black Information Consumption

Individuals who identify as Black or African American may take or show pride in their racial identity in a variety of ways, including through the support of businesses, networks, programs, and organizations that are Black-owned or those presenting perspectives or messages by, for, or through Black individuals. The types (and frequency) of information individuals are exposed to and process in this pursuit, and in their daily lives more broadly, may not only shape their beliefs, but also lead to discussions and actions. For example, the countless cases of police brutality and racial discrimination that made news (and went viral) far and wide throughout 2020 in particular, demonstrate how the consumption of information can spark outrage, calls for justice, broaden movements, and drive political action. The protests that broke out all over the world following George Floyd's murder have been well documented,[1] and the diversity of the protestors seems to be directly connected to the ease of access to information, the type of information consumed, and the fact that this injustice went viral; many individuals involved in these protests had never protested before, but they were inspired to do so after seeing the video and reading the news about it.[2]

One protestor, Wengfay Ho, who was already a supporter of the Black Lives Matter movement, explained to the BBC that "George Floyd's death was a particular 'catalyst' that prompted her to take to the streets for the first time. It 'prompted a lot more emotion, and the call for change is so much more urgent right now.'"[3] At the same time, the COVID-19 pandemic may have played a role; with people constantly consuming social media, it has become harder to look away from what has been going on and the desire to speak out and mobilize has increased.[4] Others echo this idea, explaining that during the height of the lockdown, more people were paying attention than ever before to the news and what was on TV, and some felt that during an election year, politicians would be more inclined to respond to protests and calls for change.[5]

Similar to the rise in actions and discussions relating to and/or inspired by information consumption, we have seen a rise in individuals promoting and shopping at Black-owned businesses in recent years, for example, through the Buy Black movement, and the creation of businesses that mainly or solely sell products by or from Black creators.[6] "The rise of apps like the Official Black Wall Street and I Am Black Business create easy access to information about African American owned businesses, and their creation is impacting African Americans' ability to support black-owned businesses with their purchasing power."[7] Financial decisions such as these emphasize but also go beyond race and ethnicity, as they make social, political, and economic statements as well. Kristian Henderson, founder of BLK + GRN (a Washington, DC, marketplace that sells all-natural Black-created products), equates spending one's money with voting: "You're voting on what companies are successful and what companies aren't. . . . Dollars are that powerful."[8] In addition to supporting one's own community and those who share the same or similar identities, these actions also serve as a way to stand up to the systemic racism African Americans experience on a regular, if not daily, basis. " 'Racism is inherent to the fabric that is America, and there's really nothing we can do to change that,' [Henderson] said. 'But what we can do is be really, really conscientious about how we spend our money.' "[9] Going beyond the more traditional physical goods bought at brick-and-mortar shops or online, individuals also have a choice in the sorts of platforms and networks they pay for and/or view in terms of entertainment and news.

The support, solidarity, and pride reflected by African Americans' increasing call for buying and promoting Black-owned businesses and products is also seen in other areas and actions relating to them. For example, when it comes to television consumption, "the TV shows African Americans are watching don't always match that of the general population as Black viewers gravitate more towards content that reflect[s] their images and storylines—particularly among younger viewers."[10] The development, launch, and existence of television channels, newspapers, programs, and so on, that are geared toward serving the needs and desires (informational, social, and otherwise) of this specific community is critical; these platforms and other mediums serve a multitude of purposes. We can reflect on the launch of Black Entertainment Television (BET) in 1980, which at the time was "the only national channel targeted for the black audience,"[11] and see a similarity four decades later: in June 2020, there was the launch of "BIN: Black Information Network, the first and only 24/7 national and local all news audio service dedicated to providing an objective, accurate and trusted source of continual news coverage with a Black voice and perspective."[12]

Much like the launch of BET in 1980, the launch of BIN represents efforts to provide sources of entertainment and news that are designed with African American viewers in mind. While individuals' racial identity can play a role in the information they prefer to consume and/or the type of media they select,[13] media and information consumption can also play a role in shaping or influencing their attitudes, behavior, and identity.[14] Moreover, with notes of Black nationalism, actions such as these make it clear that representation matters, and African Americans champion one another and their racial identity in ways that shape a variety of outcomes, including those relating to politics.

In this chapter, we offer a brief overview of Black information consumption. We draw from studies concerning identity, racial orientation, and socialization, as well as from those concerning media consumption and information sources. In doing so, we further expand our argument that John Henryism Active Coping plays a role in a multitude of contexts; in this case, in the information individuals consume. We build this argument by drawing connections between what we know from the literature on Black information consumption and the literature on JHAC. Then, we posit that individuals who score high on JHAC will be more likely to consume Black information than individuals who score low on JHAC before presenting empirical results testing this hypothesis.

Black Information Consumption

Some individuals "use consumption to express and transform their collective identity and acquire social membership, that is, to signify and claim that they are full and equal members in their society."[15] In this light, consumption can be viewed as individual affirmation of one's identity and membership, as well as an effort to have these attributes recognized by others; thus, both "group identification" and "social categorization" are at play.[16] In a similar vein, other aspects of the self may shape attitudes and behaviors. Racial orientation is one example, which "refers to an individual's desire to maintain his or her race's cultural values. Most studies define the construct as an individual's level of racial identification as measured by racial pride and perceptions of racial distinctiveness."[17] In the previous chapter, we explored how JHAC may influence a similar construct, Black nationalism, or a "commitment to African culture and the degree to which blacks should confine their social relationships to other blacks."[18] We found that individuals who score high on JHAC are more likely to score high on Black nationalism than individuals who score low on JHAC. Given that we recognize Black information consumption as sharing some aspects of Black nationalism, in that both tap into attitudes and actions concerning identity, racial orientation, and socialization, we hypothesize that one's coping style, particularly JHAC, may be associated with Black information consumption in a similar way. "The enjoyment and appreciation of one's own people and culture"[19] may lead individuals to consume information that is designed with their own racial identity in mind.

When we think about the socialization process ("the process by which one learns information, cognitive processes, values, attitudes, social roles, self-concepts, and behaviors that are generally accepted within American society"[20]), agents such as the family, school, workplace, and church may first come to mind, but studies show how other institutions and various media, including television, also play a role.[21] Thus, there is a complex relationship at play: while individual preferences and choices shaped by identity and other factors influence our choice of media to get information and entertainment from, a socialization process occurs during media consumption, which in turn can influence beliefs and behaviors.[22] For example, recent research on Black identity development explains, "While Black-oriented networks such as Black Entertainment Television and TV One explicitly deliver 'real life and entertainment programming from the Black point-of-view,'[23] mainstream networks with programs featuring Blacks also contribute to notions of 'basic Black' behavior and mind-sets."[24]

As for the ways in which media content is "processed, stored, and put to routine use,"[25] a number of factors play a role, including "those associated with our identities as members of groups."[26] In a similar light, "television content can even be assumed to provide a form of parasocial interaction, which suggests that people who are favorably oriented toward people of their own race would tend to prefer content that enables such an interaction, even if it is indirect."[27] Previous research[28] has shown that "the black audience prefers to watch television programs that feature black characters or performers and themes emphasizing the black experience."[29] The importance of this representation can be seen in studies concerning the effects of watching specific programs on individual beliefs and behavior. In a study concerning multiracial identity theory, scholars point out "an emergent cultural space where mixed-race people who identify as 'multiracial' are visible in the media and 'multiracial' identity is increasingly viewed as a legitimate racial identity."[30] Such an example illustrates the ability of media to influence the socialization process. A program that features story lines or characters that individuals can relate to influences those individuals, as well as societal norms. With regard to "the impact of Black media messages on racial identity, findings show the media as a teacher, media consumers as students and racial identity development as the lesson."[31]

Information and media consumption has a relationship not only with social and psychological factors, but with health factors as well. Research shows that "mass media are powerful socializing agents regarding health."[32] Some studies show "adolescents acquire some attitudes and employ some modeling behaviors related to sexual activities from entertainment television";[33] meanwhile, young individuals are particularly responsive to advertising for tobacco products such as cigarettes, and the use of smoking in films (and elsewhere) sends a message that "smoking is an accepted behavior."[34] The process of socialization that takes place via media consumption can thus influence health attitudes and behaviors, positively or negatively depending on the context. Newspapers offer another example of this, and how Black information consumption can be advantageous when it comes to information regarding health. For example, studies have found that "black newspapers are more likely than are the mainstream press to publish health and cancer stories that include personally relevant and localized information for their readership . . . [such as] stories about specific cancers in line with the higher mortality rates experienced by blacks."[35] This form of Black information consumption may tap into one element of JHAC, which is an individual's sense of control. By reading health information from a trusted source, such as Black newspapers, African Americans may be more likely to adopt healthy behaviors that provide a sense of control over their life and health based on the knowledge gained from them and the credibility of the source.

Scholars have also found that "black newspapers' stories include more prevention and community resource information,"[36] which is yet another way that Black information consumption can be beneficial and tap into the beliefs high-effort copers usually embrace, which is that outcomes are dependent on one's own actions and choices. In this case, again, knowledge derived from Black information sources can instill a sense of control and power for individuals with regard to actions that can be taken concerning preventive health measures, and resources that are available. In this light, we can see how individuals who prefer Black information sources, and who score high on Black information consumption, may very well also score high on JHAC.

Just as we can see some overlap in ideological views concerning Black nationalism and Black information consumption, we can also see some overlap in ideological views regarding American values, the American Dream, and Black information consumption, which further contributes, in part, to our expectation that Black information consumption will be related to JHAC. For example, scholars have found that "marketing specialists believe that blacks use consumption to signify and acquire equality, respect, acceptance and status,"[37] which leads some Black individuals to purchase more expensive products than whites do, and "as the chairman and chief executive officer of one of the main national Black marketing firms put it: 'We have more money, or disposable income, for attainable status symbols. It is how we acquire the American dream.'"[38] In this light, we can again see how consumption is a way for individuals to express themselves and send a signal. The type of products or media individuals consume may also encourage them to embrace their identity that much more, and/or to make political, social, and economic statements.

Importantly, though, like many things, media consumption can have a negative or a positive effect, depending on the context. For example, a recent study found that "Black information sources positively affect racial identity development, elevating race to a more important level of the individuals' definitions of self. On the other hand, greater consumption of Black information decreases public regard, leading Blacks to believe other groups have more negative feelings toward them."[39] In addition, while representation is important in media, "not all representations of Black people and African American culture in American media are favorable."[40] While positive lessons can come from media consumption, so too can negative lessons, based on stereotypes.[41] Though we recognize the importance of this point, our takeaway from these literatures is that choice and identity, among other things, play a role in the types of information individuals prefer and consume. Similarly, choice plays a role in JHAC in that high-effort copers tend to embrace a sense of control that puts the consequence (of outcomes) on their own choices and actions.

Expectations

John Henryism Active Coping offers us an opportunity to test whether Black information consumption is predicted by the predisposition to overcome challenges often stemming from racial, social, and economic disparities through a commitment to hard work, determination to succeed, an emphasis on mastery, and "efficacious mental and physical vigor."[42] Thus, in this chapter, we explore one main research question: Is there an association between the way one copes with adversity (i.e., JHAC) and Black information consumption?

We expect to find that individuals who score high on JHAC will be more likely to score high on Black information consumption than individuals who score low on JHAC. High-effort copers (individuals who score high on JHAC) emphasize hard work and the idea that outcomes are dependent on their own choices and actions. They also tend to put forth high levels of sustained cognitive effort, and are determined to succeed, believing that through hard work and perseverance, anything can be overcome. Given that some stress in daily life comes from encounters with racism and racial discrimination, we expect that high-effort copers may tap into their sense of control by choosing which type of information they consume (for example, which networks and programs, and from which perspective), much as they choose what they spend their money on and which businesses and organizations they support—financially, socially, and politically.

In a country where many groups are marginalized, one way to overcome or address this may be by choosing to consume information that reflects one's own life story, values, and ideas. In tapping into their sense of control by choosing to consume information produced by or through the lens of Black individuals or organizations, high effort copers may be both taking pride in their identity and supporting members of their racial group in a way that stands up to systemic injustices rooted in racism. In other words, Black information consumption may be an action that high-effort copers engage in that gives power to the voices of African Americans who share their stories, including both the struggles and successes, in a way that reaffirms their sense of control and ability to affect outcomes.

Methods

Here the dependent variable is Black information consumption. For the Black information measure, we created an additive index from responses to the following six questions: In an average week, how often do you listen to Black radio, watch Black TV shows, read Black newspapers, read Black magazines, read Black literature, and watch Black movies? Responses were coded using a four-point Likert-type scale ranging from 1 (never) to 4 (very often). The scale reliability coefficient (α) was .84.

Table 6.1. Black Information Consumption by JHAC

	Low JHAC	High JHAC	p-value
Black information consumption, wt. mean (SD)	2.9 (0.65)	3.1 (0.67)	0.000**
Black radio, n (wt. %)			0.000**
Never	43 (3.3)	28 (3.0)	
Not too often	171 (15.3)	117 (12.5)	
Fairly often	304 (28.4)	160 (17.6)	
Very often	569 (53.0)	605 (66.9)	
Black TV, n (wt. %)			0.000**
Never	23 (2.3)	13 (1.1)	
Not too often	206 (18.4)	115 (13.8)	
Fairly often	432 (41.8)	285 (30.6)	
Very often	419 (37.5)	492 (54.5)	
Black newspapers, n (wt. %)			0.000**
Never	223 (19.3)	176 (18.3)	
Not too often	463 (44.0)	273 (32.1)	
Fairly often	240 (22.9)	216 (24.8)	
Very often	150 (13.9)	236 (24.8)	
Black magazines, n (wt. %)			0.000**
Never	63 (5.4)	60 (6.9)	
Not too often	309 (29.1)	202 (23.4)	
Fairly often	416 (39.3)	273 (31.2)	
Very often	295 (26.2)	369 (38.6)	
Black literature, n (wt. %)			0.000**
Never	96 (8.9)	87 (9.2)	
Not too often	375 (37.2)	215 (24.5)	
Fairly often	356 (32.2)	279 (32.7)	
Very often	251 (21.8)	319 (33.5)	
Black movies, n (wt. %)			0.000**
Never	21 (2.0)	19 (1.9)	
Not too often	232 (20.4)	120 (13.4)	
Fairly often	452 (43.9)	267 (30.1)	
Very often	375 (33.7)	487 (54.5)	

$*p < 0.05$; $**p < 0.0001$

Source: Author created.

Table 6.1 presents the responses for the overall measure, as well for each of the six Black information items. The mean score shows that those who are high on JHAC consume more Black information. Chi-square tests were analyzed to compare differences between low and high coping in response to Black information consumption (see table 6.1). The findings show a significant relationship between coping and the overall Black information consumption measure (p = 0.000).

Table 6.1 also presents the responses for each of the six Black information consumption items. Nearly 82.4 percent of respondents agreed that they listen to Black radio fairly often or very often, 81.8 percent agreed that they watch Black TV fairly often or very often, 67.2 percent agreed that they read Black magazines fairly often or very often, 59.4 percent agreed that they read Black literature fairly often or very often, and 80.5 percent agreed that they watch Black movies fairly often or very often. However, less than half (42.5 percent) of the respondents indicated that they read Black newspapers never or not too often. Chi-square tests were analyzed to compare differences between low and high coping (i.e., JHAC) and Black information consumption items (see table 6.1). The findings show a significant relationship between coping and the consumption of Black radio (p = 0.000), Black TV (p = 0.000), Black newspapers (p = 0.000), Black magazines (p = 0.000), Black literature (p = 0.000), and Black movies (p = 0.000).

Analytical Strategy and Model Selection

In the first analysis, we estimated the model with linear regression, since the outcome variable (Black information consumption) is continuous in nature. We present the linear regression results in figure 6.1. We also tested whether coping interacts with a series of demographic, political, race identity, and psychosocial control variables in influencing the consumption of Black information. We present predicted margins for Black information consumption.

In addition, we ran separate models for each of the six different types of Black information sources. Since the outcome variables are ordinal in nature (ranging from "never" to "very often"), we estimated models for each with ordered logistic regression. We then used the results from these models in a second set of estimates that calculate the marginal effect of independent variables under specific conditions, such as at a single level of the dependent variable. For significant interactions, we analyzed predicted probabilities for consuming Black information from the various sources "very often." Sample weights were created and used to account for nonresponse variations.

Results for Overall Black Information Consumption

Linear regression was used to analyze the relationship between JHAC and Black information consumption. The results show a significant positive relationship between JHAC and Black information consumption (β = 0.16, p = 0.000; see figure 6.1). In other words, those high on JHAC consumed more Black information than those low on JHAC. In addition, those who scored high on racial centrality (β = 0.15, p = 0.000), members of Black organizations (β = 0.16, p = 0.006), females (β = 0.11, p = 0.003), and those who hold higher levels of social dominance (β = 0.04, p = 0.000) consume more Black information. By contrast, older respondents (β = -0.01, p = 0.000) consumed less Black information. Income is also a significant predictor of Black information consumption (p = 0.028).

Figure 6.2 presents predicted margins for consuming Black information. These predicted margins were estimated from the model presented, while setting all variables at their modal category or mean value. This allowed us to isolate the association of JHAC for the average respondent. The predicted margins show that higher levels of JHAC are associated with higher levels of Black information consumption. There is a significant difference between the low and high categories (p = 0.000). There are statistically significant interactions between JHAC by education (p < 0.042), JHAC by political ideology (p < 0.026), and JHAC by Black organizational membership (p < 0.052) on Black information consumption.

Specifically, there were higher levels of Black information consumption among those in the high JHAC category (compared to low JHAC) across three of the four categories of education. The statistically significant differences for JHAC across the three categories of education are: 0–11 years (p = 0.020), 12 years (p = 0.003), and 13–15 years (p = 0.000).

For political ideology, the predictive margins show there was an increase in Black information consumption among those in the high JHAC category (compared to low JHAC) across the three categories of political ideology. Additionally, there were statistically significant differences for JHAC across two of the categories of political ideology: conservative (p = 0.002) and liberal (p = 0.000).

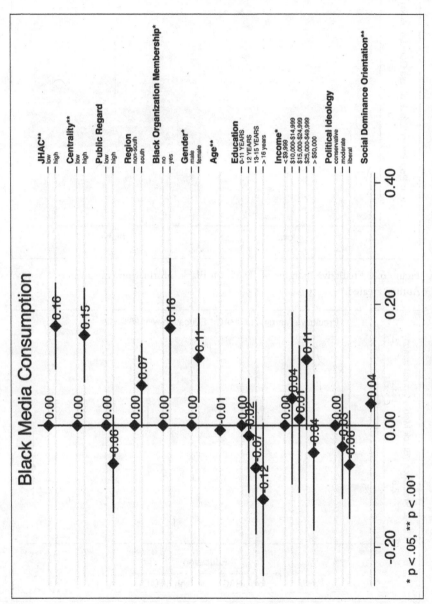

Figure 6.1. JHAC on Black information consumption. *Source:* Author created.

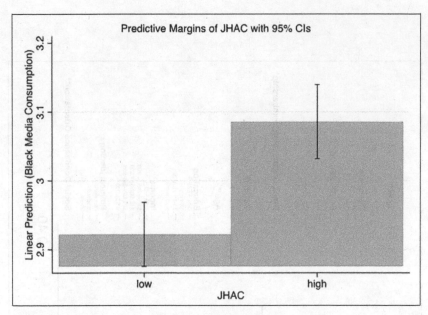

Figure 6.2. Predictive margins of JHAC on Black information consumption. *Source*: Author created.

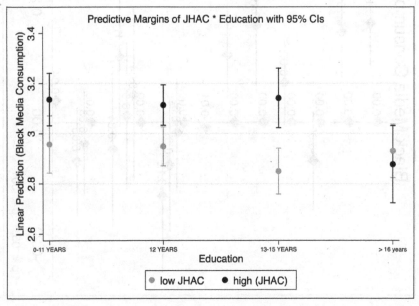

Figure 6.3. Interaction effect of JHAC and Education on Black information consumption. *Source*: Author created.

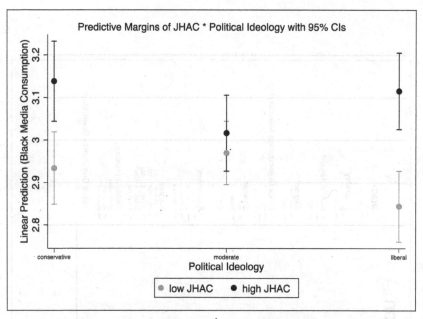

Figure 6.4. Interaction effect of JHAC and Political Ideology on Black information consumption. *Source*: Author created.

Results for Each Black Information Source

BLACK RADIO

In figure 6.5, we present results from an ordered logit model for consuming "Black radio." We found a statistically significant association between JHAC and Black radio consumption. More specifically, examining each factor independently reveals that the odds of consuming Black radio very often are: 46 percent higher for those with high JHAC (OR: 1.46; 95% CI: 1.13, 1.90; $p = 0.004$), 77 percent higher for those high on racial centrality (OR: 1.77; 95% CI: 1.37, 2.30; $p = 0.000$), 70 percent higher for those residing in the South (OR: 1.70; 95% CI: 33, 2.16; $p = 0.000$), and 7 percent higher for those high on social dominance (OR: 1.07; 95% CI: 1.02, 1.11; $p = 0.007$). On the other hand, the odds of consuming Black radio very often are 4 percent lower as age increases (OR: 0.96; 95% CI: 0.96, 0.97; $p = 0.000$), and 54 percent lower for those who have earned greater than 16 years of education (OR: 0.46; 95% CI: 0.30, 0.71; $p = 0.000$).

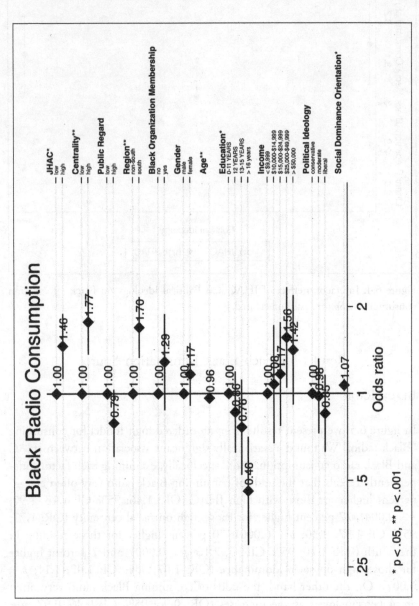

Figure 6.5. JHAC on Black radio consumption. *Source.* Author created.

Figure 6.6 presents marginal effects of high JHAC on Black radio consumption. The findings show that those who are high on JHAC are 8 percentage points more likely than those who are low on JHAC to consume Black radio very often. There is a significant difference between the low and high categories (p = 0.004) at this level of consumption. On the other hand, those who are high on JHAC are 3 percentage points less likely to consume Black radio fairly often (p = 0.007), 4 percentage points less likely to consume Black radio not too often (p = 0.003), and 1 percentage point less likely to never consume Black radio (p = 0.005).

In addition, there is a statistically significant interaction between JHAC and education (p = 0.013). In figure 6.7, the predictive margins show that, when comparing the highest level of Black radio consumption at specified values of education levels across categories of JHAC, there are statistically significant differences for 0–11 years of education (p = 0.000) and 12 years of education (p = 0.021), but not for 13–15 years education (p = 0.134) or for 16 or more years of education (p = 0.188). Specifically, among those

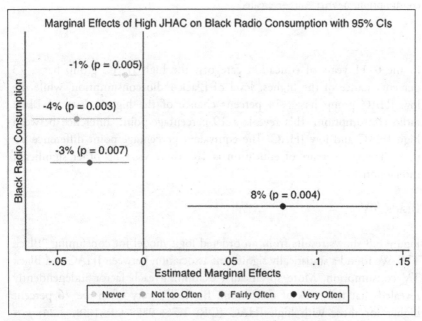

Figure 6.6. Marginal effects of high JHAC on Black radio consumption. *Source*: Author created.

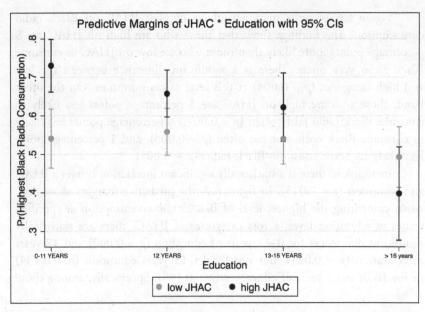

Figure 6.7. Interaction effect of JHAC and education on highest level of Black radio consumption. *Source*: Author created.

in the 0–11 years of education category, the high JHAC group has a 73 percent chance of the highest level of Black radio consumption, while the low JHAC group has a 54 percent chance of the highest level of Black radio consumption. This reveals a 19-percentage-point difference between high JHAC and low JHAC. The equivalent percentage point difference for those having 12 years of education is 10. There were no other significant interactions.

Black TV

Figure 6.8 shows results from an ordered logit model for consuming "Black TV." We found a statistically significant association between JHAC and Black TV consumption. More specifically, examining each factor independently revealed that the odds of consuming Black TV very often are 76 percent higher for those with high JHAC (OR: 1.76; 95% CI: 1.38, 2.24; p = 0.000), 43 percent higher for those high on racial centrality (OR: 1.43; 95% CI: 1.11, 1.83; p = 0.005), 30 percent higher for those residing in

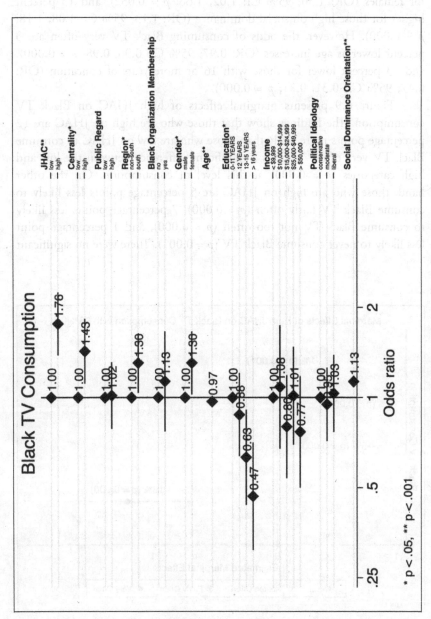

Figure 6.8. JHAC on Black TV consumption. *Source.* Author created.

the South (OR: 1.30; 95% CI: 1.04, 1.64; p = 0.023), 30 percent higher for females (OR: 1.30; 95% CI: 1.02, 1.66; p = 0.032), and 13 percent higher for those high on social dominance (OR: 1.13; 95% CI: 1.08, 1.18; p = 0.000). However, the odds of consuming Black TV very often are 3 percent lower as age increases (OR: 0.97; 95% CI: 0.96, 0.98; p = 0.000), and 53 percent lower for those with 16 or more years of education (OR: 0.47; 95% CI: 0.31, 0.71; p = 0.000).

Figure 6.9 presents marginal effects of high JHAC on Black TV consumption. The findings show that those who are high on JHAC are 12 percentage points more likely than those who are low on JHAC to consume Black TV very often. There is a significant difference between the low and high categories (p = 0.000) at this level of consumption. On the other hand, those who are high on JHAC are 5 percentage points less likely to consume Black TV fairly often (p = 0.000), 7 percentage points less likely to consume Black TV not too often (p = 0.000), and 1 percentage point less likely to never consume Black TV (p = 0.001). There were no significant

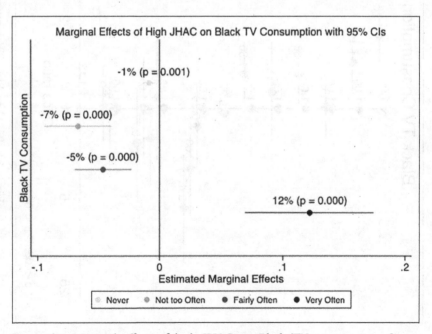

Figure 6.9. Marginal effects of high JHAC on Black TV consumption. *Source*: Author created.

interactions between JHAC and other independent variables on Black TV consumption.

Black Newspapers

Figure 6.10 shows results from an ordered logit model for consuming "Black newspapers." There is a statistically significant association between JHAC and Black newspaper consumption. More specifically, examining each factor independently reveals that the odds of consuming Black newspapers very often are 40 percent higher for those with high JHAC (OR: 1.40; 95% CI: 1.13, 1.174; $p = 0.003$), 28 percent higher for those high on racial centrality (OR: 1.28; 95% CI: 1.01, 1.63; $p = 0.040$), 42 percent higher for those with membership in a Black organization (OR: 1.42; 95% CI: 1.06, 1.91; $p = 0.020$), and 15 percent higher for those high on social dominance (OR: 1.15; 95% CI: 1.10, 1.20; $p = 0.000$).

Figure 6.11 presents marginal effects of high JHAC on Black newspaper consumption. The findings show that those who are high on JHAC are 5 percentage points more likely than those who are low on JHAC to consume Black newspapers very often. There is a significant difference between the low and high categories ($p = 0.003$) at this level of consumption, and those who are high on JHAC are 3 percentage points more likely to consume Black newspapers fairly often ($p = 0.003$). On the other hand, those who are high on JHAC are 3 percentage points less likely to consume Black newspapers not too often ($p = 0.005$), and 5 percentage points less likely to never consume Black newspapers ($p = 0.002$).

In addition, there is a statistically significant interaction between JHAC and political ideology ($p = 0.040$) on Black newspaper consumption. The predictive margins show that when comparing consumption of Black newspapers at specified values across categories of JHAC (see figure 6.12), there are statistically significant differences for two of the three ideological affiliations, conservative ($p = 0.043$) and liberal ($p = 0.002$). Specifically, among conservatives, the high JHAC group has a 24 percent chance of having the highest level of Black newspaper consumption, while the low JHAC group has a 17 percent chance. This reveals a 7-percentage point difference between high JHAC and low JHAC. The difference in the chance of having the highest level of Black newspaper consumption between high JHAC and low JHAC for liberals is 10 percentage points.

In addition, there is a statistically significant interaction between JHAC and Black organizational membership ($p = 0.006$) on Black newspaper con-

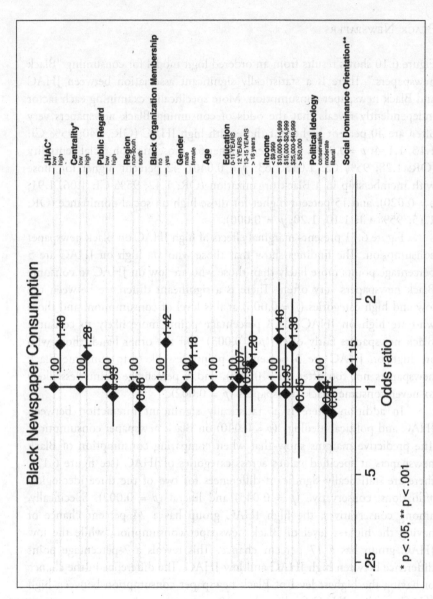

Figure 6.10. JHAC on Black newspaper consumption. *Source.* Author created.

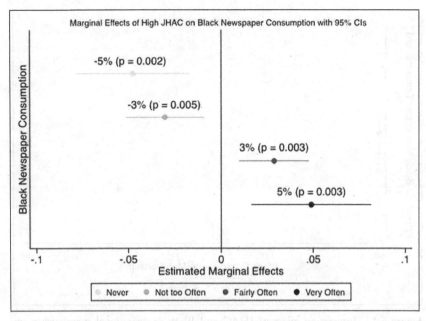

Figure 6.11. Marginal effects of high JHAC on Black newspaper consumption. *Source*: Author created.

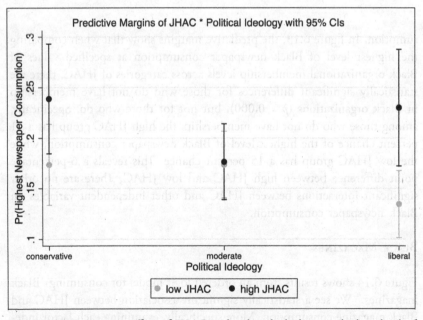

Figure 6.12. Interaction effect of JHAC and political ideology on highest level of Black newspaper consumption. *Source*: Author created.

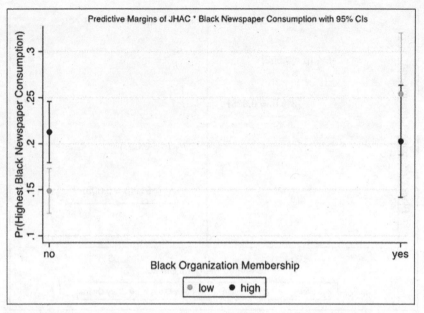

Figure 6.13. Interaction effect of JHAC and Black organizational membership on highest level of Black newspaper consumption. *Source*: Author created.

sumption. In figure 6.13, the predictive margins show that when comparing the highest level of Black newspaper consumption at specified values of Black organizational membership levels across categories of JHAC, there are statistically significant differences for those who do not have membership in Black organizations (p = 0.000), but not for those who do. Specifically, among those who do not have membership, the high JHAC group has a 21 percent chance of the highest level of Black newspaper consumption, while the low JHAC group has a 15 percent chance. This reveals a 6-percentage point difference between high JHAC and low JHAC. There are no other significant interactions between JHAC and other independent variables on Black newspaper consumption.

BLACK MAGAZINES

Figure 6.14 shows results from an ordered logit model for consuming "Black magazines." We see a statistically significant association between JHAC and Black magazine consumption. More specifically, examining each factor inde-

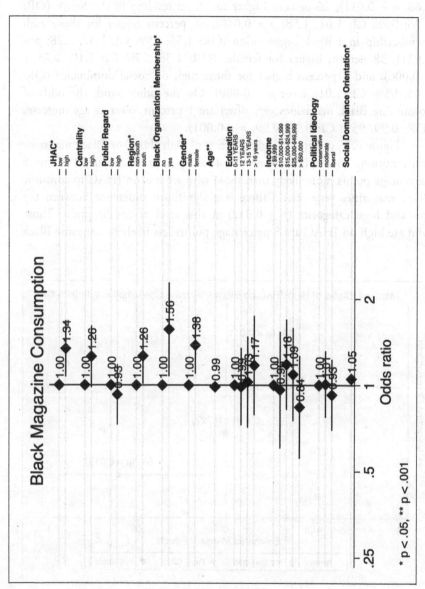

Figure 6.14. JHAC on Black magazine consumption. *Source.* Author created.

pendently reveals that the odds of consuming Black magazines very often are 34 percent higher for those with high JHAC (OR: 1.34; 95% CI: 1.07, 1.68; p = 0.011), 26 percent higher for those residing in the South (OR: 1.26; 95% CI: 1.01, 1.58; p = 0.040), 56 percent higher for those with membership in a Black organization (OR: 1.56; 95% CI: 1.07, 2.28; p = 0.021), 38 percent higher for females (OR: 1.38; 95% CI: 1.10, 1.73; p = 0.006), and 5 percent higher for those high on social dominance (OR: 1.05; 95% CI: 1.01, 1.10; p = 0.000). On the other hand, the odds of consuming Black magazines very often are 1 percent lower as age increases (OR: 0.99; 95% CI: 0.98, 0.99; p = 0.001).

Figure 6.15 presents marginal effects of high JHAC on Black magazine consumption. The findings show that those who are high on JHAC are 6 percentage points more likely than those who are low on JHAC to consume Black magazines very often. There is a significant difference between the low and high categories (p = 0.012) at this level of consumption. Those who are high on JHAC are 5 percentage points less likely to consume Black

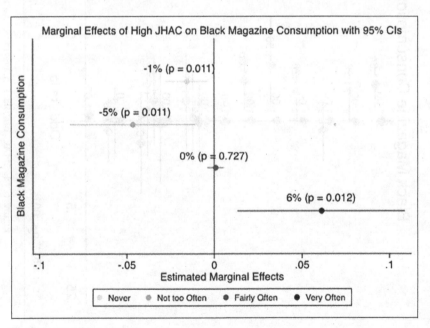

Figure 6.15. Marginal effects of high JHAC on Black magazine consumption. *Source:* Author created.

magazines not too often (p = 0.011), and 1 percentage point less likely to never consume Black magazines (p = 0.011).

In addition, there is a statistically significant interaction between JHAC and political ideology (p = 0.002). In figure 6.16, the predictive margins show that when comparing the highest level of Black magazine consumption at specified values of political ideology across categories of JHAC, there are statistically significant differences for those who are conservative (p = 0.043) and for those who are liberal (p = 0.002). However, there is no statistical difference between high JHAC and low JHAC among political moderates (p = 0.901). Specifically, among conservatives, the high JHAC group has a 24 percent chance of the highest level of Black magazine consumption, while the low JHAC group has a 17 percent chance. This reveals a 7-percentage-point difference between high JHAC and low JHAC. Among liberals, the high JHAC group has a 29 percent chance of the highest level of Black magazine consumption, while the low JHAC group has a 13 percent chance. This reveals a 16-percentage-point difference

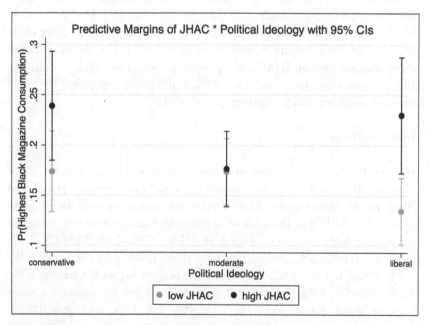

Figure 6.16. Interaction effect of JHAC and ideology on highest level of Black magazine consumption. *Source*: Author created.

between high JHAC and low JHAC. There are no other significant inter-actions between JHAC and other independent variables on Black magazine consumption.

BLACK LITERATURE

Figure 6.17 shows results from an ordered logit model for consuming "Black literature." There is a statistically significant association between JHAC and Black literature consumption. More specifically, examining each factor independently reveals that the odds of consuming Black literature very often are 55 percent higher for those with high JHAC (OR: 1.55; 95% CI: 1.24, 1.94; p = 0.000), 43 percent higher for those high on racial centrality (OR: 1.43; 95% CI: 1.13, 1.82; p = 0.003), 79 percent higher for those with membership in a Black organization (OR: 1.79; 95% CI: 1.29, 2.48; p = 0.001), and 47 percent higher for females (OR: 1.47; 95% CI: 1.18, 1.84; p = 0.001).

Figure 6.18 presents marginal effects of high JHAC on Black literature consumption. The findings show that those who are high on JHAC are 8 percentage points more likely than those who are low on JHAC to consume Black literature very often (p = 0.000), and 2 percentage points more likely to consume Black literature fairly often (p = 0.001). On the other hand, those who are high on JHAC are 7 percentage points less likely to consume Black literature not too often (p = 0.000), and 3 percentage points less likely to never consume Black literature (p = 0.000).

BLACK MOVIES

Figure 6.19 shows results from an ordered logit model for consuming "Black movies." There is a statistically significant association between JHAC and Black movie consumption. More specifically, examining each factor inde-pendently reveals that the odds of consuming Black movies very often are 81 percent higher for those with high JHAC (OR: 1.81; 95% CI: 1.41, 2.32; p = 0.000), 28 percent higher for those residing in the South (OR: 1.28; 95% CI: 1.01, 1.62; p = 0.040), 30 percent higher for females (OR: 1.30; 95% CI: 1.02, 1.67; p = 0.037), and 10 percent higher for those high on social dominance (OR: 1.10; 95% CI: 1.06, 1.15; p = 0.000). On the other hand, the odds of consuming Black movies very often are 4 percent lower as age increases (OR: 0.96; 95% CI: 0.96, 0.97; p = 0.000),

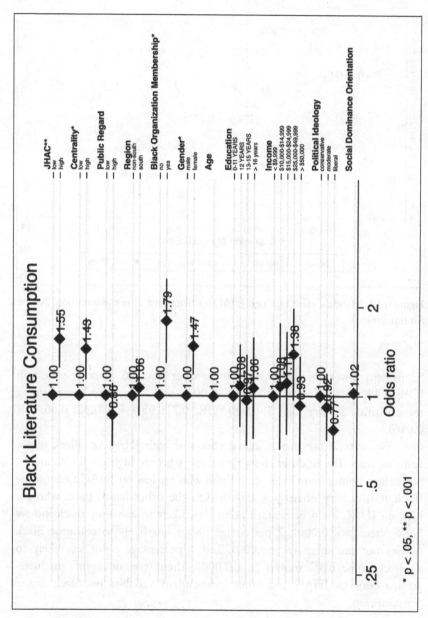

Figure 6.17. JHAC on Black literature consumption. *Source.* Author created.

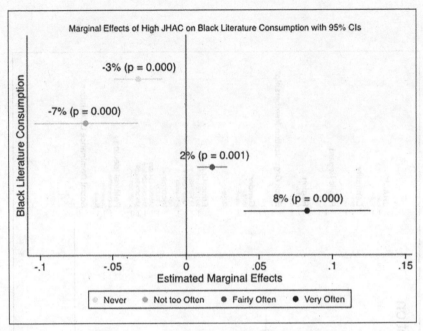

Figure 6.18. Marginal effects of high JHAC on Black literature consumption. *Source*: Author created.

52 percent lower among those having greater than 16 years of education (OR: 0.48; 95% CI: 0.31, 0.74; p = 0.003), and 29 percent lower among those earning greater than \$50,000 (OR: 0.71; 95% CI: 0.32, 0.66; p = 0.016).

Figure 6.20 presents marginal effects of high JHAC on Black movie consumption. The findings show that those who are high on JHAC are 12 percentage points more likely than those who are low on JHAC to consume Black movies very often (p = 0.000). On the other hand, those who are high on JHAC are 4 percentage points less likely to consume Black movies fairly often (p = 0.000), 7 percentage points less likely to consume Black movies not too often (p = 0.000), and 1 percentage point less likely to never consume Black movies (p = 0.000). There were no significant interactions between JHAC and other independent variables on Black movie consumption.

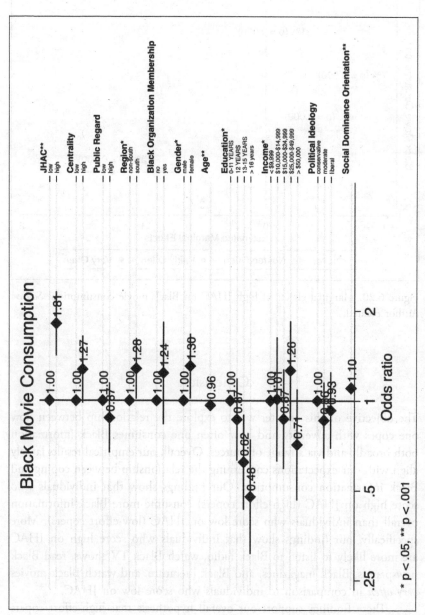

Figure 6.19. JHAC on Black movie consumption. *Source.* Author created.

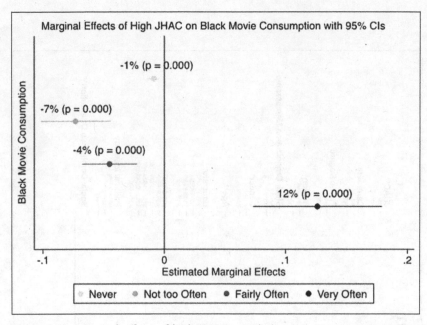

Figure 6.20. Marginal effects of high JHAC on Black movie consumption. *Source*: Author created.

Conclusion

The objective of this chapter was to explore the relationship between how one copes with adversity and how often one consumes Black information both broadly and via a range of sources. Overall, our empirical results largely align with our expectations concerning the relationship between coping and Black information consumption. Our findings show that individuals who score high on JHAC (high-effort copers) consume more Black information overall than individuals who score low on JHAC (low-effort copers). More specifically, our findings show that individuals who score high on JHAC are more likely to listen to Black radio, watch Black TV shows, read Black newspapers, Black magazines, and Black literature, and watch Black movies *very often* in comparison to individuals who score low on JHAC.

These findings support our overall hypothesis that high-effort copers are more likely to consume Black information (and to do so more often) than low-effort copers. We know that high-effort copers tend to embrace a stronger sense of personal control and self-confidence, and are more likely than low-effort copers, on average, to put forth a high degree of effort in order to address and/or overcome stressors and accomplish goals. As we illustrate in chapter 4, high-effort copers are also more likely to embrace views concerning Black nationalism and partake in activities that reflect a commitment to their racial identity and values. In thinking about Black nationalism as "the philosophy that African Americans should be both self-defining and self-determined vis-à-vis the remainder of American society,"[43] and/or as a "commitment to African culture and the degree to which blacks should confine their social relationships to other blacks,"[44] it makes sense that it is associated with high levels of JHAC. The themes of internal control, commitment, degree of effort, self-confidence and empowerment, taking action to alleviate stressors, and so on, that are typically reflected in those with high levels of JHAC are similar to some of the beliefs and behaviors captured in both Black nationalism and Black information consumption.

In addition, both Black nationalism and Black information consumption tap into attitudes and behaviors relating to one's identity and orientation, as well as socialization. For example, consumption may be used to express one's identity and/or to acquire social membership,[45] and in some sense, outlets such as television may even offer a form of indirect social interaction.[46] Choosing to consume information produced by and/or for African Americans not only offers one the ability to express and take pride in one's racial identity and orientation, but also offers a sense of community and membership, a reinforcement of social and cultural norms, a resource that can be trusted, and the power to choose what one reads, watches, and listens to. At the same time, individuals may simply have preferences for shows, movies, music, literature, and so on that present story lines and/or characters they can relate to and identify with,[47] on account of both connection and representation.

Moreover, it is possible that when it comes to agreeing with and/or embracing Black nationalism and consuming Black information, another commonality for high-effort copers is the power to decide, and the power to push back against a system that is rooted in racism. In other words, believing in and/or partaking in activities that reflect Black nationalism (for instance, believing Blacks should vote for Black candidates, or shop at Black-owned stores) and consuming Black information (whether it is Black radio, TV shows, newspapers, magazines, literature, or movies) may give individuals who frequently encounter racism and racial discrimination a sense of control and a way to alleviate stressors in their lives. It may be

that these factors, along with JHAC, are also connected to protest participation. As protestors who attended demonstrations following George Floyd's
murder acknowledged, the viral video and discussions concerning it were
motivating, anger-inducing, and inspired many to do something about it
in the form of protest. It would be interesting, if data were available, to
explore the relationship between Black information consumption, ideological
views, protest participation, and coping. We suspect, though we do not have
the data to test it ourselves, that coping is associated with these attitudes
and behaviors. This area of research has plenty of room to grow, and its
significance cannot be overstated. The decisions individuals make, whether
financial, social, psychological or health-oriented, or relating to entertainment or information consumption, have power (including, but not limited
to, political power) and offer individuals some control over their lives.[48]

While additional factors such as high centrality, high social dominance,
and membership in Black organizations are also associated with Black information consumption, we argue the connections between these are similar
to those between Black nationalism and Black information consumption.
Choosing to consume Black information may be a reflection of one's group
consciousness, membership, and/or support for Black nationalism; one's racial
identity, orientation, racial and/or cultural pride; the sources one trusts; one's
commitment to pushing back against racism; and/or one's efforts to alleviate
stressors. As our results suggest, Black information consumption may also be
a reflection of one's coping style (more specifically, whether an individual is a
low- or high-effort coper). In the overall measure and in the separate items,
JHAC is consistently associated with Black information consumption, and
similarly to actions reflecting Black nationalism, the decisions individuals
make (in this case, what type of information to consume and how often)
are in and of themselves powerful statements. An understanding of JHAC
enables us to better understand these actions and their associated statements,
which are often political as much as they are social and psychological. In
the next chapter, we explore the relationship between JHAC and more
direct political statements in the form of measures of political participation.

CHAPTER 7

Coping and Political Participation

The US presidential election is significant to and has consequences for people and politics, not only in the US, but also throughout the world.[1] In a year of heightened social and political divisions and countless cases of police brutality and racial discrimination, and in the midst of a global pandemic, the significance of and pressures surrounding the 2020 election were particularly clear for the African American community, whose commitment to mobilization and standing up for justice is undeniable.[2] "We've spent the past 100 years mobilizing Black people across the country to get out the vote," Derrick Johnson, president and CEO of the NAACP, explained, "but this movement started long before. Throughout the history of the United States, Black people have always led the charge to make this country live up to its ideals of fairness and equality."[3]

While African Americans have been disproportionately targeted in cases of police brutality and racial discrimination,[4] the African American community's ongoing commitment to stand up and fight for the nation's core values is a reflection of its ideological views and activism.[5] It may, however, also reflect differences in how individuals cope with adversity. For some, frequent if not daily encounters with racism may leave them feeling resigned to accept it as a part of life and/or believing that it is beyond their control, while others may be unrelenting in their efforts to alleviate such stressors and committed to doing something about it. The former would generally meet our understanding of what it means to be a low-effort coper (coping passively), while the latter would generally meet our understanding of what it means to be a high-effort coper (coping actively).

141

Speaking to Clive Myrie of BBC News, Percy Christian of Phoenix, Arizona, who was arrested and jailed for a week after attending a peaceful civil rights march, explained, "I'm willing to do whatever it takes. I'm willing to put my life on the line to raise awareness about the issue that police brutality is real . . . that the system is set up and designed to hold a certain group of individuals back and that's my people."[6] Christian's overall statement, and particularly his commitment to doing "whatever it takes," is an illustration of the degree of effort and the qualities (such as the belief that individual actions can and do make a difference in outcomes) often exhibited by high-effort copers, or individuals who score high on John Henryism Active Coping. While raising awareness about issues such as police brutality is not the most conventional form of political participation, unlike, say, voting in federal, state, or local elections, it is one form of political participation, and we can see how it may be reflective of and/or connected to JHAC.

In this chapter, we explore how JHAC may be related to and/or influence a variety of actions that fall under the umbrella of political participation. We begin with a brief overview of the literature on political participation (with a focus on political participation among African Americans), which often includes discussions about political efficacy. Then, we present our expectations by connecting what the literature says about political participation with what we know about JHAC. Thereafter, we present our data and methods, our empirical results, a discussion of our findings (including limitations), and suggestions for future research.

Political Participation

Political participation is viewed as an important component of democratic government, a reflection of governmental legitimacy and a citizenry's acceptance of the government, as well as a civic duty.[7] It has been argued via the civic voluntarism model that citizens participate in politics for three main reasons: (1) they have resources that offset the costs of voting; (2) they are interested in the election, believe there are important differences between the political parties, and believe government responds to public actions; and (3) they are encouraged to participate either by people in their social networks or by those in the political parties.[8] It is worth noting that *political participation* is an umbrella term for myriad political activities. While voting is one form of political participation, other actions include contacting government officials; working or volunteering for a political party; donating to a political campaign or party; running for office; attending political events (such as strikes, protests, or demonstrations); signing petitions; joining and/or maintaining membership in political parties, groups, clubs, or organizations; lobbying; and participating in boycotts.[9] These activities can be split into different types of political participation: more traditional actions such as voting, being involved in a campaign, and joining a political organization are typically referred to as conventional[10] or institutional[11] forms of political participation, while actions such as protesting, signing petitions, attending demonstrations, and boycotting are referred to as unconventional or less institutionalized forms of political participation.[12]

There has been an increase in recent years in less conventional, more "citizen-initiated and policy-oriented ([or] 'activist') forms of political activity."[13] Thus, studying political participation requires a consideration of the various forms of activities that come under the umbrella of the broad term, as well as consideration of the differences in resources required and meanings attributed to each type of political participation.[14] In its various forms, political participation offers ways for individuals to be either indirectly or directly involved in politics and to exert some level of influence over the policy-making process.[15] Yet research shows some individuals and groups are more likely, while others are less likely, to engage in political participation.[16]

What factors play a role in shaping political participation? For starters, scholars typically incorporate traditional control variables such as education, gender, age, income, and employment status in models of political participation.[17] Age is generally positively related to increased political participation in more of the conventional activities such as voting.[18] In addition, education, employment status, and income are often associated with higher levels of political participation for both men and women in these studies,[19] although employment status (particularly as hours on the job increase) can have a negative effect on women's political participation.[20] On the one hand, the positive effect of employment on participation (for men) may be reflective of advantages and opportunities that men have in the US, while the sometimes negative effect of employment on participation (for women) may be the result of indirect disadvantages associated with women spending no less time on housework or domestic duties, even as their time at work increases, thereby lowering the amount of time they have to devote to other activities, including those that are considered forms of political participation.[21] However, while there used to be a sizable gender gap in voting across countries, with men voting at higher rates than women, this gap has been shrinking in recent years and has even reversed in some countries.[22]

Political knowledge, political efficacy, political interest, and/or trust in government are incorporated in many models of political participation, with research finding that on average, individuals with higher levels of these political attitude variables are generally more likely to participate in politics.[23] Women, on average, tend to have lower levels of these political attitude variables than men,[24] but it is worth noting that women who do engage in political participation may have higher levels of political knowledge than men who engage in political participation, and among those with high levels of political knowledge, women are, on average, more likely than men to vote, work for political campaigns, and/or wear a political button.[25] In explorations of political participation among African Americans, scholars have found mixed results:[26] some show African American women are roughly as likely as African American men to engage in political participation,[27] while others show that the likelihood is higher among African American women.[28]

Some studies have found an association between participation, gender, and race and ethnicity;[29] for example, "white women and Latinas are significantly less likely than men to engage in private activism (making campaign contributions and working informally in the community)."[30] Other studies suggest that African Americans and Latinos are, on average, less likely to vote than whites.[31] Yet when differences in SES are controlled for, some studies show that Black political participation rates are actually higher than white political participation rates,[32] and it has been hypothesized that one explanation for this may be greater levels of group consciousness, or a stronger sense of group identity/community, among Black individuals.[33] For example, prior work by Verba and Nie, Gamson, Gurin et al., and Shingles, highlights the importance of Black consciousness in the study of political participation.[34]

Given the United States' history, it is perhaps unsurprising that an awareness (Black consciousness) among Black Americans of a shared status as an oppressed group,[35] in combination with the injustices and challenges that come with navigating an unfair system, is associated with and contributes to political distrust, as well as motivates political activity. One way of dealing with unfair circumstances is to become involved and attempt to change the system by having your voice heard, running for office, and/

or supporting candidates who share your vision. African Americans have a long history of standing up and speaking out against unjust circumstances, and the African American community's political activism reflects both the awareness of oppression and attempts to overcome injustices. Indeed, prior works, especially that of Verba and Nie, suggest that this awareness (Black consciousness) motivates Black individuals to be more politically active than Black individuals who are unaware of their shared status as an oppressed group, as well as to be more active than white individuals of a similar SES.[36]

However, as previously noted, *political participation* is a broad umbrella term capturing numerous activities. The effects of political efficacy and political trust vary depending on the type of political activity; high political efficacy and high political trust are linked to conventional forms of political participation, while high political efficacy and low political trust are linked to more unconventional forms of political participation.[37] Moreover, individuals lacking a sense of political efficacy are less likely to be politically active than those who have a strong sense of political efficacy, which contributes to our expectations of a similar relationship between political participation and JHAC. While we expect to find a similar relationship (as exists between internal political efficacy and political participation) between political participation and JHAC, we cannot currently compare the two factors (efficacy and JHAC) due to data limitations. However, future research may benefit from exploring whether JHAC has an additional, interactive effect between these political attitudinal measures (efficacy, trust, Black consciousness) and behavioral measures (various forms of political participation). A strong sense in one's ability to affect change (e.g., high internal efficacy, and/or high JHAC) should serve as confidence and motivation to act, and Gamson argues that a lack of political trust serves as the "need to act."[38] Thus, even cynical, mistrusting individuals may be motivated to actively participate in politics if their mistrust is coupled with a strong sense of internal political efficacy.[39]

Gurin et al. essentially expand on Gamson's mistrust-efficacy work by bringing in the Protestant work ethic, which essentially attributes one's lot in life to a person's own actions or inaction, a belief that no doubt weighs heavier on some groups (such as low SES groups) than others.[40] Yet, when deprived groups come to see their misfortune as the product of the system (rather than of their own, individual actions), this externalization of guilt and transfer of responsibility—from the individual to the system—both improves their own self-confidence while increasing their political cynicism and mistrust.[41] Building on the work of Gurin and Gamson,[42] and resulting in the Gamson-Gurin thesis, Shingles (1981) argues that "Black consciousness contributes to political mistrust and a sense of internal political efficacy which in turn encourages policy-related participation" among Black Americans.[43] This literature, then, suggests that political participation rates may vary by activity, efficacy, trust, and Black consciousness.

Additional factors have been explored that may explain racial disparities in political participation, including but not limited to the aforementioned SES,[44] neighborhood contexts,[45] and discriminatory laws.[46] Moreover, scholars have looked at the role various factors may play in increasing the political participation of certain groups. For example, it has been argued that "Black empowerment derived from the presence of African Americans in public office increases political trust, efficacy, and knowledge among Blacks,"[47] which may in turn increase political participation.[48] However, it is worth pointing out again that there are different forms of political participation requiring different types and amounts of resources, and people may assign different meanings to each activity. Furthermore, a recent study shows how issues and issue-specific motivators may even better explain racial and ethnic differences than traditional factors such as access to economic or social resources.[49] For example, this research reveals the following:

> The effect of race and ethnicity on participation varied significantly across issues such that members of racial and ethnic groups were more likely to engage in participation to express opinions about issues that were more relevant to their racial or ethnic group (e.g., Blacks were more likely to engage in activism to express opinions about affirmative action than were Whites or Latinos and Latinos were more likely to engage in activism to express opinions about immigration than were Whites or Blacks).[50]

Thus, it may be that individuals feel more compelled to engage in certain forms of political participation and to get involved in politics when issues they feel connected to or are affected by are particularly salient.

Furthermore, studies have examined the relationship between political participation and a number of factors relating to religion (such as religiosity, religious affiliation, and religious service attendance).[51] Religiosity, religious affiliation, and participating in religious organizations can have a positive effect on political participation by increasing an individual's likelihood of learning and applying civic skills, appealing to a sense of duty, and fostering networks that promote political discussions and involvement.[52] While women are on average more likely to be religiously affiliated and religious, the effect of religion may matter more for men who are religious; for example, some studies have found that the positive effect of religious service attendance on political engagement is stronger for men.[53] This may be explained by differences in the positions some men and women hold in churches or differences in their respective duties; for instance, "women may have less access to the civic skills, networks, and political information acquired through church leadership, because such leadership is inherently gendered."[54]

Thus, from the literature it is clear that a host of variables, including but not limited to age, gender, race, income, education, employment status, trust in government, political efficacy, political interest, political knowledge, religiosity and/or church attendance, and involvement in certain organizations, are or may be related to political participation in its various forms. Based on the literature on political participation and coping, we argue that JHAC may be yet another variable related to political participation.

Expectations

JHAC allows us to explore whether a predisposition to exert sustained mental and cognitive effort in order to confront and alleviate one's stressors predicts political participation. Thus, the main objective in this chapter is to first explore the broad question: Is there an association between the way one copes with adversity and political participation? We then explore additional questions regarding more specific measures of political participation. We first expect to find that individuals who score high on JHAC will be more likely to engage in political participation than individuals who score low on JHAC. Individuals who score high on JHAC (high-effort copers) tend to be more likely than low-effort copers to take action, believe that they can accomplish or overcome anything, and put forth a high degree of sustained effort. The sense of control and mastery associated with high-effort copers, which reflects an internal locus of control, suggests that they are empowered and unrelenting in their efforts to alleviate stressors in their lives. Thus, we expect that political participation may offer unique ways for high-effort copers to alleviate or address stressors in their lives.

Next, we break political participation down to explore more specific measures. Thus, our second question asks: Is there an association between the way one copes with adversity and voting in the last presidential election, or in state and local elections in the past year (referring to the year prior to the study)? We expect to find that individuals who score high on JHAC will be more likely to have voted (whether in the last presidential election or in state and local elections in the past year) than individuals who score low on JHAC. Third, we ask: Is there an association between the way one copes with adversity and working for a political party? We expect to find that individuals who score high on JHAC will be more likely to work for a political party than individuals who score low on JHAC. Fourth, we ask: Is there an association between the way one copes with adversity and contacting the government about a problem? We expect to find that individuals who score high on JHAC will be more likely to contact the government about a problem than individuals who score low on JHAC.

The expectations for the second, third, and fourth research questions are driven by the same rationale as our expectations for the first, broad question: individuals who score high on JHAC are more likely to take action, more likely to view outcomes as dependent on their own choices and actions, and more likely to be unrelenting in their efforts to alleviate stressors. These political participation measures (voting, working for a political party, and contacting government officials about a problem) offer direct and hands-on ways for individuals to get involved in politics, and thus may provide them with a sense of control and/or empowerment.

For our fifth question, we ask: Is there an association between the way one copes with adversity and membership in Black national advancement organizations? We expect to find that individuals who score high on JHAC will be more likely to be members of Black national advancement organizations than individuals who score low on it. Finally, we ask: Is there an association between the way one copes with adversity and involvement in Black clubs, associations, or groups in the neighborhood? We expect to find that individuals who score high on JHAC will be more likely to be involved in Black clubs, associations, or groups in the neighborhood than individuals who score low on JHAC.

The expectations for our fifth and sixth research questions are based on similar logic with regard to the characteristics and themes reflected by JHAC, but extend to the research on Black nationalism as well. We know from chapter 4 that individuals who score high on JHAC are more likely to score high on items measuring Black Nationalism via their agreement with statements such as "Blacks should vote for Black candidates," "Blacks should shop Black-owned stores," "Blacks should form their own political party," and "Blacks should give their kids African names." While other underlying factors likely play a role, we argue that it is the qualities reflected in JHAC, such as the tendency to believe that anything can be overcome or accomplished, and that individuals have control over outcomes and are thus more confident and likely to take action, which leads to the association between JHAC and Black nationalism. Actions such as joining and being involved in social and/or political groups wherein racial identity plays an important or even key role are very similar in that they may serve as ways in which high-effort copers can take control and alleviate stressors in their lives while embracing and taking pride in their racial identity.

Methods

Here the dependent variables are forms of political participation. The NSAL queried African American respondents on their participation in politics. The six various political participation questions are as follows: (1) Did the respondent vote in the last presidential election? (2) Did they vote in state and local elections in the year prior to the study? (3) Have they ever worked for a political party? (4) Have they ever contacted the government about problems? (5) Are they involved in Black clubs, associations, or groups in the neighborhood? and (6) Are they a member of any Black national advancement organizations? Responses were "no" or "yes" for each item. Each of the six questions will be considered a dependent variable in the analysis.

Descriptive statistics indicate that 66 percent of respondents voted in the past presidential election, while 34 percent did not; 62 percent voted in past state or local elections, while 38 percent did not; 85 percent have never worked for a political party, while 15 percent have; 75 percent have never contacted the government about a problem, while 25 percent said they have; 73 percent are not involved in any African American clubs, associations, or groups in their neighborhood, while 27 percent are involved; and 88 percent are not members of Black national advancement organizations, while 12 percent indicated they are members of Black national advancement organizations.

Chi-square tests were analyzed to compare differences between low-and high-effort coping in response to political participation (see table 7.1). The findings show that there is a significant relationship between coping and contacting government about problems (p = 0.028). The remaining relationships between JHAC and political participation were not statistically significant.

Table 7.1. Political Participation by JHAC

	n (weighted %)		
	Low JHAC	High JHAC	p-value
Vote in presidential election			0.245
No	324 (32.67)	273 (35.89)	
Yes	715 (67.33)	575 (64.11)	
Vote in state and local elections			0.204
No	376 (36.21)	327 (39.68)	
Yes	708 (63.79)	579 (60.32)	
Ever worked for a political party			0.069
No	893 (83.61)	774 (86.96)	
Yes	191 (16.39)	130 (13.04)	
Ever contacted government about problems			0.028*
No	774 (71.99)	695 (77.13)	
Yes	311 (28.01)	212 (22.87)	
Involved in neighborhood Black organizations			0.284
No	334 (74.49)	233 (70.49)	
Yes	136 (25.51)	107 (29.51)	
Member of national Black organization			0.831
No	968 (87.82)	812 (87.40)	
Yes	133 (12.18)	108 (12.60)	

*p < 0.05; **p < 0.0001
Source: Author created.

Analytical Strategy and Model Selection

Since the outcome variables are binary (two response options, "no" and "yes"), we estimated models for each of the six political participation variables with logistic regression. For each type of political participation, six separate models were analyzed—that is, voting in the last presidential election; voting in state and local elections; working for a political party; contacting the government about problems; involvement in Black clubs, associations, or groups in the neighborhood; and membership in Black national advancement organizations. In addition, we included demographic, political, race identity, and psychosocial controls. We tested whether coping interacts with these control variables in influencing political participation. We also analyzed predicted probabilities for the political participation questions. Sample weights were created and used to account for nonresponse variations.

Results

Voting in Presidential Election

There is not a statistically significant association between coping and "vote in presidential election" (see figure 7.1). However, other variables in the model were significant. More specifically, examining each factor independently reveals that the odds of voting in the presidential election are 58 percent higher for females (OR: 1.58; 95% CI: 1.13, 2.21; p = 0.008), 4 percent higher as age increases (OR: 1.04; 95% CI: 1.03, 1.06; p = 0.000), and 133 percent higher for those having 13 to 15 years of education (OR: 2.33; 95% CI: 1.47, 3.69; p = 0.000). There were no significant interactions.

Voting in State and Local Elections

There is not a statistically significant association between coping and "vote in state and local elections" (see figure 7.2). However, there are other variables in the model that are significant. Specifically, the odds of voting in state and local elections are 33 percent higher for those consuming higher levels of Black information (OR: 1.33; 95% CI: 1.05, 1.67; p = 0.016), 93 percent higher for those attending church at least once a week (OR: 1.93; 95% CI: 1.15, 3.23; p = 0.050), 62 percent higher for females (OR: 1.62; 95% CI: 1.18, 2.23; p = 0.003), 4 percent higher as age increases (OR: 1.04; 95%

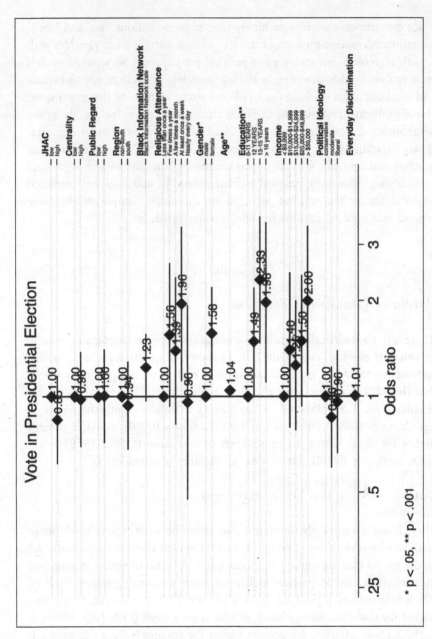

Figure 7.1. JHAC on voting in presidential election. *Source.* Author created.

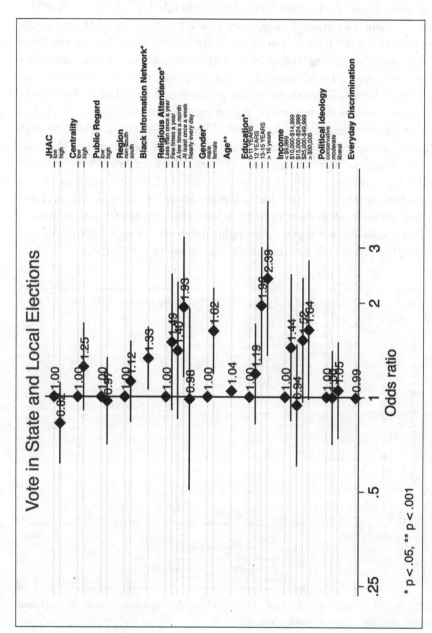

Figure 7.2. JHAC on voting in state and local elections. *Source:* Author created.

CI: 1.03, 1.05; p = 0.000), and 139 percent higher for those with sixteen or more years of education (OR: 2.39; 95% CI: 1.35, 4.22; p = 0.001).

There is a statistically significant interaction between JHAC and public regard (p = 0.027). As we can see in figure 7.3, the predictive margins show that, when comparing voting in local and state elections at specified values of public regard levels across categories of JHAC, there are statistically significant differences for those low on public regard (p = 0.029). Specifically, among those in the low public regard category, the low JHAC group had a 69 percent chance of voting in local and state elections, while the high JHAC group had a 61 percent chance of voting in local and state elections. This reveals an 8-percentage-point difference between low JHAC and high JHAC. However, among those in the high public regard category, it was the high JHAC group that had a higher chance of voting in the local and state elections: 68 percent against the low JHAC group's 62 percent chance. This reveals another 6-percentage-point difference between high JHAC and low JHAC, but it is not statistically significant (p = 0.240).

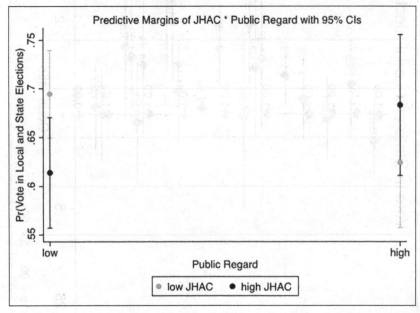

Figure 7.3. Interaction effect of JHAC and public regard on voting in local and state elections. *Source*: Author created.

Working for a Political Party

There is not a statistically significant association between coping and "ever worked for a political party" (see figure 7.4), although other variables in the model are significant. Specifically, the odds of working for a political party are 37 percent higher for those consuming higher levels of Black information (OR: 1.37; 95% CI: 1.04, 1.80; p = 0.027), 3 percent higher as age increases (OR: 1.03; 95% CI: 1.02, 1.04; p = 0.000), and 271 percent higher for those with sixteen or more years of education (OR: 3.71; 95% CI: 2.04, 6.76; p = 0.000).

There is a statistically significant interaction between JHAC and Black information (p = 0.011). As we can see in figure 7.5, the predictive margins show that, when comparing working for a political party at specified values of Black information levels across categories of JHAC, there are statistically significant differences for the four lowest levels of Black information, 1 (p = 0.009), 1.5 (p = 0.005), 2 (p = 0.005), and 2.5 (p = 0.011). As Black information consumption increases above a 2.5, there isn't a significant difference between high and low JHAC groups on working for a political party.

Contacting Government about Problems

There is not a statistically significant association between coping and "ever contacted government about problems" (see figure 7.6), although other variables in the model are significant. Specifically, the odds of ever having contacted the government about problems are 50 percent higher for those high on centrality (OR: 1.50; 95% CI: 1.08, 2.09; p = 0.015), 5 percent higher as age increases (OR: 1.05; 95% CI: 1.04, 1.06; p = 0.000), 39 percent higher for females (OR: 1.39; 95% CI: 1.00, 1.91; p = 0.047), 330 percent higher for those with sixteen or more years of education (OR: 4.30; 95% CI: 2.50, 7.42; p = 0.000), and 3 percent higher for those experiencing higher levels of everyday discrimination (OR: 1.03; 95% CI: 1.01, 1.05; p = 0.001). On the other hand, the odds of ever having contacted the government about problems are 38 percent lower for those from the South (OR: 0.62; 95% CI: 0.46, 0.84; p = 0.002). There were no significant interactions between JHAC and the independent variables.

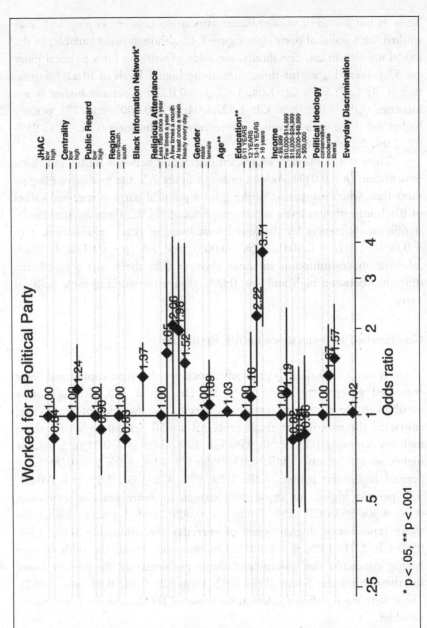

Figure 7.4. JHAC on working for a political party. *Source*: Author created.

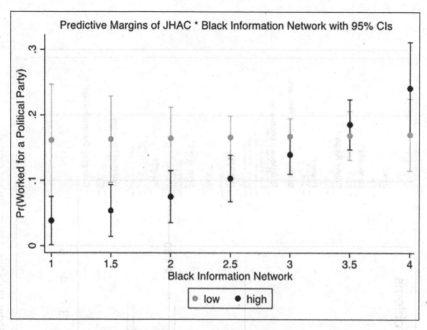

Figure 7.5. Interaction effect of JHAC and Black information on working for political party. *Source*: Author created.

Involvement in Neighborhood Black Organizations

There is not a statistically significant association between coping and "involved in neighborhood Black organizations" (see figure 7.7). However, there are other variables in the model that are significant. Specifically, the odds of being involved in neighborhood Black organizations are 4 percent higher as age increases (OR: 1.04; 95% CI: 1.02, 1.05; p = 0.000). No other variables were significant on involvement in neighborhood Black organizations.

Membership in National Black Organizations

There is not a statistically significant association between coping and "member of national Black organization" (see figure 7.8). However, there were other variables in the model that were significant. Specifically, the odds of being a member of a national Black organization are 54 percent higher for those

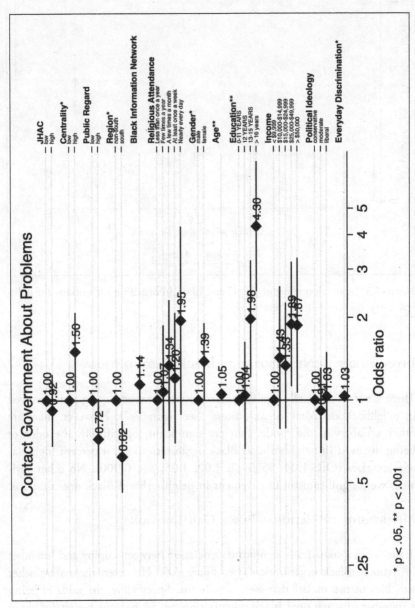

Figure 7.6. JHAC on contacting government about problems. *Source:* Author created.

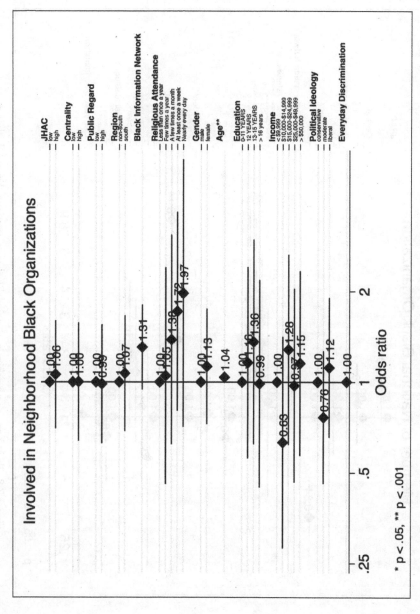

Figure 7.7. JHAC on involvement in neighborhood Black organizations. *Source:* Author created.

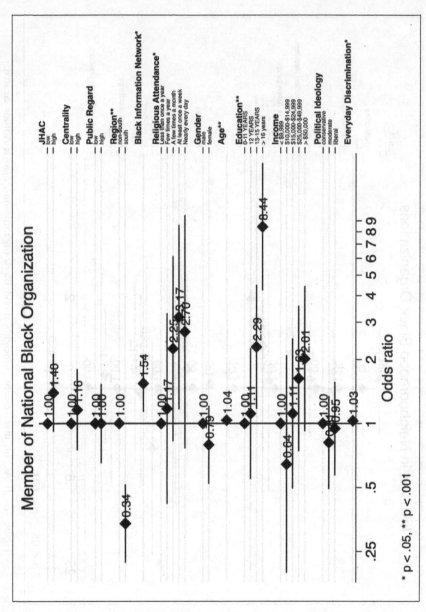

Figure 7.8. JHAC on membership in national Black organizations. *Source:* Author created.

consuming higher levels of Black information (OR: 1.54; 95% CI: 1.13, 2.10; p = 0.006), 217 percent higher for those attending church at least once a week (OR: 3.17; 95% CI: 1.17, 8.60; p = 0.011), 4 percent higher as age increases (OR: 1.04; 95% CI: 1.02, 1.05; p = 0.000), 744 percent higher for those having sixteen or more years of education (OR: 8.44; 95% CI: 4.23, 16.84; p = 0.000), and 3 percent higher for those experiencing higher levels of everyday discrimination (OR: 1.03; 95% CI: 1.00, 1.05; p = 0.019). On the other hand, the odds of being a member of a national Black organization are 66 percent lower for those from the South (OR: 0.34; 95% CI: 0.22, 0.52; p = 0.000).

There is a statistically significant interaction between JHAC and Black information consumption (p = 0.028). As we see in figure 7.9, the predictive margins show, when comparing membership in a national Black organization at specified values of Black information consumption levels across categories of JHAC, that there are statistically significant differences for those whose Black information consumption is lowest (p = 0.036). More specifically,

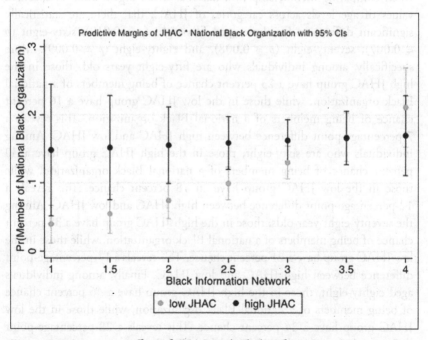

Figure 7.9. Interaction effect of JHAC and Black information consumption on membership in national Black organizations. *Source*: Author created.

among individuals in the lowest Black information consumption category, those in the high JHAC group have a 15 percent chance of being members of a national Black organization, while those in the low JHAC group have a 4 percent chance of being members of a national Black organization. This reveals an 11-percentage-point difference between high JHAC and low JHAC. There is also a significant difference between high JHAC and low JHAC in the second lowest category of Black information consumption (p = 0.021). Specifically, among individuals in this category, those in the high JHAC group have a 15 percent chance of being members of a national Black organization, while those in the low JHAC group have a 5 percent chance of being a member of a national Black organization. This gives a 10-percentage-point difference between high JHAC and low JHAC. There is also a significant difference between high JHAC and low JHAC in the third (p = 0.012) and fourth (p = 0.011) categories of Black information consumption.

Finally, there is a statistically significant interaction between JHAC and age (p = 0.053). As we see in figure 7.10, the predictive margins show, when comparing membership in a national Black organization at specified values of age levels across categories of JHAC, that there are statistically significant differences for those aged fifty-eight (p = 0.012), sixty-eight (p = 0.007), seventy-eight (p = 0.008), and eighty-eight (p = 0.009). More specifically, among individuals who are fifty-eight years old, those in the high JHAC group have a 23 percent chance of being members of a national Black organization, while those in the low JHAC group have a 16 percent chance of being members of a national Black organization. This reveals a 7-percentage-point difference between high JHAC and low JHAC. Among individuals who are sixty-eight, those in the high JHAC group have a 30 percent chance of being members of a national Black organization, while those in the low JHAC group have an 18 percent chance. This reveals a 12-percentage-point difference between high JHAC and low JHAC. Among the seventy-eight-year-olds, those in the high JHAC group have a 38 percent chance of being members of a national Black organization, while those in the low JHAC group have a 21 percent chance. This reveals a 17-percentage-point difference between high JHAC and low JHAC. Finally, among individuals aged eighty-eight, those in the high JHAC group have a 46 percent chance of being members of a national Black organization, while those in the low JHAC group have a 24 percent chance. This reveals a 22-percentage-point difference between high JHAC and low JHAC.

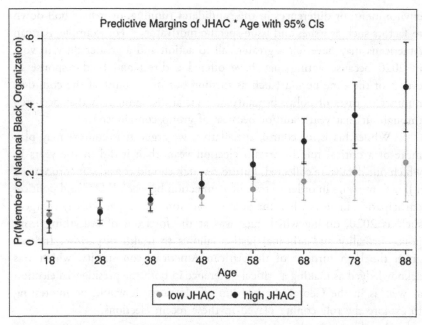

Figure 7.10. Interaction effect of JHAC and age on membership in national Black organizations. *Source:* Author created.

Conclusion

We do not find empirical support for our theoretical argument and expectations concerning the connection between JHAC and political participation, but we argue that this may be explained by data limitations. Unlike other beliefs and behaviors, we argue that political participation is unique in that context plays a significant role. While we do not have data to test this, we would expect to find that political participation among African Americans in particular ebbs and flows depending on the political environment and time period. Representation may also play a role. For example, between 1964 and 2016, the highest turnout among Black voters occurred in the 2008 and 2012 presidential elections, both of which featured Barack Obama, the first African American president of the United States.[55] In comparison, overall turnout among African Americans was lower in the 1996, 2000, and 2004 presidential elections.[56] This could be because of differences in the political environment, or differences in the candidates running, or it may boil down to factors such as issues and issue-specific motivators.[57] For example, African Americans may have felt a greater call to action and a greater duty to vote in 2020 because voting may have offered a direct and bold response to events of the time period (such as turning out on account of the countless number of cases of police brutality and racial discrimination that occurred throughout that year), and/or because of group consciousness.

While this is, of course, speculative, we argue that context may play more of a critical role in certain election years than it did in the years in which our data were collected. Future research should consider incorporating a JHAC measure in order to test the connection between JHAC and political participation in years when the political environment is particularly charged, such as 2020, during which race was at the forefront of everything from police brutality and criminal justice failures to health disparities. Indeed, given the high turnout of the African American community, which was acknowledged as making a critical difference in both the presidential election as well as in the Georgia Senate run-off elections, it would be interesting to explore the role coping played in these recent elections.

Another reason the results go against our expectations may be geographical location; the majority (65 percent) of respondents in our data set live in the South, and more specifically, in Southern states that are overwhelmingly conservative and Republican. For example, in looking at measures such as working for a political party, contacting the government about problems, and membership in Black national organizations, we see that living in the South decreases one's odds of participation. Previous research has shown that the region in which an individual lives can affect beliefs and behaviors.[58] Thus, living in a region wherein the dominant political ideology and party (among other things) is at odds with one's own beliefs and values may lead an individual to feel like involvement in politics is a lost cause.

Moreover, we must consider that even if the political environment is charged, it does not necessarily mean that high-effort copers will participate in politics, for example, through voting, because there are barriers to political participation. Voter registration laws and policies designed to disenfranchise certain voters not only make it more difficult for African Americans to vote, they are also demoralizing and serve as further examples of racial discrimination and the stressors associated with it. Following the high turnout among the African American community in the 2020 presidential election and Georgia Senate run-offs, hundreds of registration- and voting-related bills were introduced throughout state legislatures that may make voting harder; many of these bills have been criticized as directly targeting minority voters.

On the other hand, experiences with racial discrimination may motivate some individuals to get involved politically. We found a statistically significant interaction between everyday discrimination and JHAC; individuals who experience high levels of everyday discrimination, and who score high on JHAC, are more likely to have voted in the last presidential election. Moreover, controlling for the effects of other variables, individuals with higher levels of everyday discrimination are also more likely to contact the government about problems and belong to national Black organizations. Thus, everyday discrimination can either bolster or hamper political participation, and its effects vary across the type of activities. We suspect that data from recent years would capture similar findings, and potentially show more of a relationship between coping and political participation than our data show, given the changes in the political environment in recent years.

In previous chapters, we found a strong and statistically significant effect of JHAC on measures concerning individual will (such as reactions to discrimination), and it may be that the difference between those findings and our findings related to political participation also boil down to the level of difficulty and/or the degree to which one believes an action will make a difference. For example, thinking, talking, and praying about a situation wherein one experienced racial discrimination is arguably easier than actually doing something about it, much like thinking and talking about politics requires less effort (and fewer structural barriers) than voting or working for a political party does. In addition, encountering racial discrimination and doing something about it may be viewed as time-consuming and draining, but it may feel more rewarding or more likely to make a difference than certain forms of political participation, particularly in areas such as the South.

It is also worth noting that again in this chapter, we see the importance of Black information consumption and the role it plays in politics. Individuals who consume high levels of Black information are more likely (than individuals who consume lower levels of Black information) to participate in five out of the six political participation measures (all except contacting the government about problems). This may tie into the mobilization and get-out-the-vote efforts of the African American community, as well as the types of information that are featured.

The overall, unexpected findings in this chapter may be attributable to any number of reasons, proposed herein or otherwise. However, it is our hope that future research will consider these factors and the role JHAC plays, whether in a direct or indirect manner, in political participation. We continue to argue that the incorporation of JHAC in political science offers promising contributions and insight for the study of political outcomes, though we acknowledge that coping may play a greater or lesser role depending on, among other things, the time period, the political and media environment, and region.

Conclusion

The goal of this book is to highlight the importance of coping in studying, exploring, and explaining human behavior. Individuals experience a myriad of stressors in their everyday lives, and while many people experience some of the same types of stressors, responses and reactions to stressful life events, interactions, and situations often vary. Moreover, we know that some groups experience more psychosocial stressors (and do so more often) than other groups. Thus, the way one copes with psychosocial stressors is important for explaining human behavior and variations across and within groups.

While 2020 offers numerous cases that illustrate the importance of exploring and explaining human behavior, all of which could benefit from an analysis incorporating coping and politics, we begin this chapter with two more cases that are particularly notable: a new wave of legislation targeting voting access following the high turnout rate (particularly among African Americans) in the 2020 elections, and the global COVID-19 pandemic. Both of these recent (and at the time of writing, ongoing) cases highlight the relevance of coping in studying human behavior. They each illustrate real-life stressors, how and why coping matters in the political sphere and beyond, and the role coping plays (or can play) in social, economic, political, psychological, and health outcomes.

Following these final two examples, we summarize the specific purpose of the book, highlight key implications and findings, and close with a discussion of limitations and future research.

Curtailing the Vote?

Following the 2020 presidential election, which saw high voter turnout among minorities, and Georgia flipping blue for the first time in decades,

Republicans across the United States "introduced hundreds of proposals to change voting laws."[1] As of mid-February 2021, "more than 250 bills to curb or complicate access to polls have been introduced in state legislatures."[2] These include bills restricting voter access in forty-three states.[3] In one such state, Georgia, Nick Corasaniti and Jim Rutenberg report the following:

> Republicans are proposing new restrictions on weekend voting that could severely curtail one of the Black church's central roles in civic engagement and elections. Stung by losses in the presidential race and two Senate contests, the state party is moving quickly to push through these limits and a raft of other measures aimed directly at suppressing the Black turn-out that helped Democrats prevail in the critical battleground state. . . . The push for new restrictions in Georgia comes amid a national effort by Republican-controlled state legislatures to impose harsh restrictions on voting access, in states like Iowa, Arizona and Texas. But the targeting of Sunday voting in new bills that are moving through Georgia's Legislature has stirred the most passionate reaction, with critics saying it recalls some of the racist voting laws from the state's past.[4]

These proposals, if enacted, will limit access to voting in a variety of ways (including but not limited to the following): they will restrict early and absentee voting, purge voters from rolls, add voter identification require-ments, and "eliminate automatic and same-day voter registration."[5] Bishop Reginald T. Jackson, of Georgia, argues, "The only reason you have these bills is because they lost. . . . What makes it even more troubling than that is there is no other way you can describe this other than racism, and we just need to call it what it is."[6]

By limiting access and opportunity to vote, these proposals present yet another stressor that individuals may face in their attempts to participate in the political process. Given that voting plays a major role in the demo-cratic process, such proposals may strain trust in government and serve as additional barriers to participation. In addition, legislation of this sort calls into question matters of fairness and equality and offers an age-old outlet for racial discrimination to continue to present itself. Subsequently, some groups (particularly African Americans) may bear the brunt of it, but there may be differences in response to it. Coping can help explain why and how some individuals may be discouraged by legislation curtailing voter access, while others may be emboldened to mobilize in the face of threats to their participation.

Importantly, while we have focused and continue to focus on how active coping among African Americans shapes their attitudes and behaviors in the political sphere, we believe active coping can and will serve future research that goes beyond our focus here. Meanwhile, in yet another example of how anything, even a public health crisis, can be political, we turn to the example of the COVID-19 pandemic to further demonstrate the relevance of coping and why it is important to continue studying it in the future.

COVID-19: How a Global Pandemic Reveals Political, Social, Economic, and Health Cleavages

An outbreak of a novel coronavirus, COVID-19, first linked to wet food markets in Wuhan, China, in December 2019, rapidly spread to other countries, with confirmed cases reported in Japan, South Korea, and Thailand, as well as the United States, in January 2020.[7] By late January, it was apparent COVID-19 was spreading rampantly, with serious implications, and the World Health Organization (WHO) declared it a global health emergency.[8] In the months that followed, it became abundantly clear that COVID-19 was being spread from person to person at alarming rates, the illness was resulting in rapidly increasing deaths, and following the acknowledgment of worldwide spread, the WHO declared it a pandemic in March 2020.[9]

Throughout 2020, the pandemic ushered in a variety of responses across countries and governments, from restricted air travel, limited group gatherings, and closure of nonessential businesses and schools, to complete lockdowns. In the United States alone, responses varied significantly, as some states took more drastic measures than others (and earlier), as the federal government failed all the while to present a united front and response plan.[10] Though full coverage of it is beyond the scope of this chapter, the pandemic offers a clear example of how often politics and coping are intertwined in social, economic, psychological, and health outcomes.

For example, in the same vein that some individuals and groups experience more psychosocial stressors than others, COVID-19 has made it increasingly clear how disadvantaged individuals become even more disadvantaged on account of social, economic, health, and political issues. "Long-standing systemic health and social inequities have put many people from racial and ethnic minority groups at increased risk of getting sick and dying from COVID-19."[11] Discrimination in its various forms, from health care to housing, education, and criminal justice, has a negative impact on individuals beyond the stress it brings; it also puts them in social and economic disadvantage, at greater risk of developing mental and physical health issues, and as we have seen during this pandemic, at increased risk of getting sick or dying from COVID-19.[12] The pandemic brought health disparities to the forefront, with minority groups at greater risk of getting and dying from COVID-19 (and suffering major social and/or economic losses). A variety of factors play a role in this, from the type of job an individual works (which is often associated with their level of education, and which affects their income level), the form of transportation an individual uses, and the local and state government's response, to the access (or a lack thereof) to childcare, and so on.

While physical health, financial, economic, and political concerns have been front and center in many government responses, another major concern throughout the pandemic has been mental health. Social isolation, loneliness, job loss, worry and stress, among other things, have led many individuals to report that the pandemic has negatively affected their mental health.[13] In addition, some individuals have increased their consumption of (or started consuming) alcohol and/or illicit drugs throughout the pandemic as a way to deal with or cope with their emotions and the current circumstances.[14] As a result, numerous organizations have released information relating to mental health and coping (with tips, guides, and resources), including but not limited to the US Department of Health and Human Services,[15] the Centers for Disease Control and Prevention,[16] the WHO,[17] Massachusetts General Hospital,[18] The Harvard T. H. Chan School of Public Health,[19] and the American Psychiatric Association.[20] Various emotions and challenges are expected and a part of an infectious disease outbreak, and how individuals respond in such a situation matters. An understanding of coping and the role it plays stands to benefit scholars, practitioners, and policy makers alike.

Unsurprisingly, scholars have already started exploring how coping has played a role in the pandemic,[21] particularly among nurses and students. While studies relating to the pandemic (and beyond) will continue to focus on the role coping plays in social, psychological, and health outcomes, we see a fruitful area of opportunity to expand this literature to political attitudes, behaviors, and outcomes (in relation to the pandemic, and in other contexts). An example of this is demonstrated in *Anxious Politics: Democratic Citizenship in a Threatening World* by Bethany Albertson and Shana Kushner Gadarian.[22] *Anxious Politics* focuses on the role anxiety plays in politics in terms of the coping mechanisms it can lead individuals to embrace when faced with a threat (for example, a public health crisis, which they refer to as an "unframed threat"). The coping mechanisms they explore across four policy areas (public health, immigration, terrorism, and climate change) are seeking information (often threatening information), trusting political actors and/or experts, and supporting protective policies on account of increased anxiety.[23] While *Anxious Politics* shows how anxiety is connected to three coping mechanisms, and differs from this book in numerous ways, it similarly reinforces how multidisciplinary research enriches our understanding of human behavior and attitudes.

In our breakdown of the areas explored throughout this book, we will point out additional connections between coping and politics. Importantly, while this book is peppered with recent, relevant cases, we argue that an understanding and application of coping in the political sphere (and beyond) will continue to be fruitful for future research, both in similar and in different contexts.

Specific Purpose of the Book

The role of coping in social, psychological, and health outcomes is well documented, but the role coping plays in political outcomes has not been sufficiently explored. Throughout this book, we have laid the groundwork for ways that scholars in political science and related disciplines can think about and incorporate coping into research concerning the political sphere and beyond. We have highlighted several ways in which coping is relevant to and associated with a number of beliefs and behaviors, including those that are political in nature. Consistent with prior research, we have incorporated several traditional sociodemographic variables as controls throughout our analyses in this book, and while the findings vary with regard to their significance within certain contexts, we have consistently found that psychosocial factors play a key, and often overlapping, role in these outcomes.

This book is, to our knowledge, the first to explore active coping in the political sphere, and more specifically, active coping among African Americans in the political sphere. Under this umbrella, we have explored several topics that make it increasingly clear that psychosocial variables are important to include in studies concerning human behavior and politics. While scholars often come close to incorporating coping in political science studies through their use of measures such as internal political efficacy, we argue that these measures fall short of capturing the full complexity and importance of coping. Coping is more than just the internal beliefs about one's own ability or inability to do something and/or make a difference in doing so (which most measures of internal political efficacy capture in terms of beliefs about one's own political abilities); it is also about the degree of effort an individual is willing to put forth. Importantly, the environment and one's interactions within that environment play a role in coping as well. John Henryism Active Coping (JHAC) captures the complexity of coping and illustrates the significance of it in politics, in both a direct and an indirect manner.

Topics Explored

The data we used allowed us to explore five main topics: reactions to discrimination, ideological views, support for race-specific policies, information consumption, and political participation. Broadly speaking, we hypothesized that high-effort copers (individuals known to cope actively or who score high on JHAC) would be more likely to react to discrimination, embrace ideological views that fall under the categories of Black nationalism and American values, support race-specific policies, and consume Black information (and more often), as well as participate in politics, than low-effort copers (individuals known to cope passively or who score low on JHAC). Our overall findings are presented in table C.1, which indicates whether the relationship between each measure and JHAC was statistically significant (+) or not (-).

Overall, our empirical results largely align with our theoretical expectations. The manner in which one copes with adversity does, indeed, shape a variety of beliefs and behaviors within the political sphere. We found a statistically significant relationship between JHAC and reactions to discrimination, JHAC and ideological views, JHAC and support for race-specific policies, and JHAC and Black information consumption. While our empirical results do not align with our theoretical expectations for political participation, we argue that many factors may explain why that is. To offer a synopsis of our key results and why they matter, we break down each finding and what it means, in the subsequent sections.

Reactions to Discrimination

The manner in which one copes with adversity has a statistically significant relationship with reactions to discrimination. More specifically, we found that,

Table C.1. JHAC Findings

	high JHAC (vs. low JHAC)
Coping in Reactions to Discrimination	
Prayed about it	+
Tried to do something about it	+
Worked harder to prove others wrong	+
Coping and Ideological Views	
Black nationalism	+
National pride	+
Authoritarianism	+
Work ethic	+
Coping and Policy Preferences	
Need political districts to elect minorities	+
Government should help Blacks	+
Government should pay reparations	−
Coping and Black Information Consumption	
Overall measure of Black information consumption	+
Black radio	+
Black TV	+
Black newspapers	+
Black magazines	+
Black literature	+
Black movies	+
Coping and Political Participation	
Vote in presidential election	−
Vote in state and local elections	−
Ever worked for a political party	−
Ever contacted government about problems	−
Involved in neighborhood Black organizations	−
Member of a national Black organization	−

(+) = significant; (−) = not significant
Source: Author created.

controlling for the effects of other variables, individuals who score high on JHAC are more likely than those who score low on JHAC to pray about it, and more likely to work harder to prove others wrong. While individuals who score high on JHAC are also more likely than those who score low on JHAC to try to do something about the discrimination experience, this relationship is not statistically significant. Taken together, these findings suggest that coping should be considered when studying how individuals respond to discrimination. In 2020 alone, countless cases of racial discrimination went viral and sparked protests both within and outside of the United States.[24] Coping offers a promising lens through which we can better understand how and why some individuals react differently to discrimination, as well as the extent and degree to which individuals respond to it.

To expand on the example of the COVID-19 pandemic, within the context of discrimination, we can reflect on the case of Dr. Susan Moore, an African American internist who died of COVID-19 "weeks after she shared a video in which she accused a doctor at Indiana University Health North Hospital (IU North) of ignoring her complaints of pain and requests for medication because she was Black."[25] Dr. Moore's story is sadly not an isolated event, but it is an example of racial discrimination during the pandemic. While some individuals feel resigned to the fact that racial bias is a problem in health care, others find ways to fight against it. Dr. Moore's son, Henry Muhammed, spoke about her time receiving treatment for an inflammatory disease: "Nearly every time she went to the hospital, she had to advocate for herself, fight for something in some way, shape or form, just to get baseline, proper care."[26] As a physician, Dr. Moore knew how she should be treated as a COVID-19 patient, and she advocated for that treatment. As a patient, she knew that she had to fight for herself. In recording her experience and calling the racist treatment out for what it was, Dr. Moore did just that, and reflected qualities of active coping in the process.

IDEOLOGICAL VIEWS

Active coping has a statistically significant relationship with ideological views that fall under Black nationalism and American values (national pride, work ethic, and authoritarianism). More specifically, we found that, controlling for the effects of other variables, individuals who score high on JHAC are more likely than individuals who score low on JHAC to strongly agree with Black nationalism and all three of our American values measures. These findings align with our theoretical expectations and suggest that one's way of coping with adversity is associated with one's level of support for certain ideological views. Among African Americans, it is not surprising that high-effort copers, who put forth high degrees of effort to alleviate stress in their lives, are more likely than low-effort copers to strongly support Black nationalism. After all, Black nationalism, broadly speaking, is an ideology that reflects a commitment to one's racial identity and group, and advocates for supporting members of the African American community, an action that may go hand-in-hand with working to alleviate stressors in their daily lives.

Similarly, it is not surprising that high-effort copers strongly agree with the three American values we tested: national pride, hard work, and authoritarianism. African Americans have long advocated and fought for democratic principles, showing a determination and commitment to American values that is arguably unparalleled. Moreover, with forms of authoritarianism (such as authoritarian parenting) emphasizing mastery, these findings align with what we know about JHAC. Given the role ideological views play in society, from the news sources we trust to the parties we vote for and the companies we take our business to, these findings suggest it is important to include coping in political studies spanning a variety of topics.

RACE-SPECIFIC POLICIES

The way one copes with adversity has a statistically significant relationship with race-specific policy beliefs. More specifically, we found that controlling for the effects of other variables, individuals who score high on JHAC are more likely than those who score low on JHAC to strongly support/agree with majority-minority districts and policies to help Black individuals. These findings align with our expectations. Individuals who actively cope with adversity know full well the amount of effort it requires, and while active coping emphasizes individual action, high-effort copers may recognize that overcoming obstacles and alleviating stressors would be more feasible (for themselves and others) if policies such as these were put into place.

Thus, recognizing that there is an association between coping and support for race-specific policies provides insight not only for scholars, but for policy makers as well. Other factors can and do play a role in shaping support for certain policies, but coping warrants a space in these considerations. We can and should go beyond the traditional sociodemographic considerations, and measures such as JHAC offer additional nuance that may serve as predictors for other policy beliefs and the degree to which individuals support (or oppose) them.

BLACK INFORMATION CONSUMPTION

Coping also has a statistically significant relationship with Black information consumption. More specifically, we found that, controlling for the effects of other variables, individuals who score high on JHAC are more likely than individuals who score low on JHAC to consume Black information very often, via radio, TV shows, newspapers, magazines, literature, and movies. These findings align with our theoretical expectations. One of the ways individuals can alleviate stress in their lives is by being informed. By consuming Black information in particular, which is designed with the African American community in mind (and therefore tends to provide information most relevant to them) and generally viewed as trustworthy, African Americans who score high on JHAC are not only supporting members of their community but are also putting forth a high degree of effort to be informed. This means that an understanding of the way in which someone copes with adversity provides insight into their information consumption habits, which can shape a variety of attitudes and behaviors.

In the context of the pandemic, this finding is important because "the media play an important role in shaping Americans' views about the crisis."[27] A recent report shows how the TV network an individual watches is associated with their views of COVID-19: for example, individuals who identify as Republican and do not watch Fox News are far more likely than Republicans who do watch Fox News to report that COVID-19 "was worse than they expected."[28] The type of information individuals consume, and the source it comes from, influences the way they think about the world, not only in the context of the pandemic, but beyond it as well. This is important because our beliefs often shape our behaviors. Therefore, an understanding of coping is important because it can offer an additional insight into information consumption, and the role it plays in shaping beliefs and behaviors.

POLITICAL PARTICIPATION

Active coping does not have the statistically significant relationship with political participation that we thought it would. Contrary to our theoretical expectations, our findings show that African Americans who are high on JHAC are less likely than those low on JHAC to have ever worked for a political party or to have ever contacted the government about a problem. These findings may be explained by a number of factors, including data limitations, and more specifically, the years in which the data were collected. In addition, factors such as political interest, political knowledge, and trust in government, among others, play a role in political participation that we were not able to account for. We did find some JHAC interaction effects that suggest JHAC may indirectly affect political participation. For example, we found that, controlling for the effects of other variables, individuals who score high on JHAC and who report high levels of everyday discrimination are more likely to have voted in the last presidential election.

Given the rise in cases of racial discrimination in 2020, as well as the politically charged environment, it would be interesting to explore the direct and indirect effects of JHAC on political participation with more recent data. For example, we suspect that JHAC would have a statistically significant effect on variations in political participation between 2008 and 2020. Beyond the politically charged environment and countless cases of racial discrimination that brought race to the forefront of numerous social, political, economic, and health issues throughout this time period, we know that African Americans' turnout rates in presidential elections between 1964 and 2016 were at their highest in the 2008 and 2012 presidential elections, which featured Barack Obama.[29] We also know that African American turnout in 2020 was particularly high and had a critical outcome on the presidential election as well as Georgia Senate contests.

We recognize that a number of factors play a role in political partici-pation, from the traditional variables such as age, gender, education, income, partisan identification, and political ideology, to political interest and polit-ical knowledge, but we argue that future models should incorporate coping as well. While internal (political) efficacy may capture a small component of coping (e.g., beliefs in one's own ability or inability to affect change), JHAC captures this component as well as the degree of effort an individual puts forth. Thus, it would be interesting to test the effects of both JHAC and internal political efficacy on political participation in recent years. We suspect that results would show that individuals have been more motivated to put forth higher degrees of effort in order to alleviate daily stressors and to affect political change in recent years.

Limitations and Future Research

It would be remiss to conclude this book without acknowledging its limita-tions, some of which offer ideas for future research. For starters, we recognize that this study has data limitations. The data come from the 2001–2003 National Survey of American Life, with the majority of respondents completing interviews face to face, though a small proportion (less than 15 percent) of interviews were completed either partially or entirely over the telephone. Regardless of the format, we recognize there is no such thing as a perfect process—all data have limitations, including those we use in this book.

In addition, our analyses are solely based on responses from individuals who identify as African Americans. In terms of future research, it would be enlightening if more recent data were available (to test the relationship between coping and the variables we have explored in this book, as well as the relationship between coping and recent behaviors and attitudes), if our sample size were larger and nationally representative, and if data with these measures were available for a multitude of countries to test whether the relationships between JHAC and these factors vary across and/or within racial and ethnic categories, regions (within the US, and throughout the world), forms of government, and so on. Scholars spanning multiple disciplines (for example, psychology and public health) have explored the role JHAC plays in a variety of settings and with differing sample populations, suggesting its reliability and applicability in different contexts. It is our hope that JHAC will become a more commonly used measure in political science, thus expanding the opportunity to study it and its relationship with a variety of political outcomes in the future.

Moreover, we did not have a measure of internal political efficacy to compare our JHAC results to. Future research would benefit from an examination of both factors, which we expect would have similar but slightly different results in that JHAC arguably captures more (and slightly different beliefs and behaviors) than internal political efficacy does. We also recognize that there are several other variables, which are or may be relevant to our study, that we were not able to include in our analyses. These include (but surely are not limited to) trust in government, political knowledge, political interest, attending a protest, boycotting a product, signing a petition, and so on. Future research could expand on this study by incorporating any number of these variables (and/or others we were not able to include).

Another idea for future research would be to look at the relationship between JHAC and support for a range of policy preferences. While this study offers a starting point, our exploration into the relationship between JHAC and policy preferences is limited to support for race-specific policies (and only three of them). It would be interesting to examine the role coping plays in one's level of support for (or opposition to) social welfare policy, economic policy, education policy, environmental policy, health-care policy, foreign policy, and so on, as well as additional race-specific policies.

Furthermore, some of our measures are vague, especially the items in our chapter on reactions to discrimination and Black information consumption. For example, one of the reactions to discrimination is "tried to do something about it." One way to improve on measures such as this would be to make them more straightforward and specific; instead of leaving it open to interpretation, it would be more informative if the item outlined a specific action, such as "participated in a protest," that an individual could engage in as an effort to do something about an experience with discrimination. Similarly, while the Black information consumption measures break the sources of information down into six types (radio, TV, newspapers, magazines, literature, and movies), it may be more useful to ask about specific radio channels, TV shows, newspapers, magazines, literature, and movies. Not all sources offer the same type of information and identifying specific sources would enable us to better understand the type of information that is being consumed, whether it has an ideological or partisan skew, what the average audience demographics are, and so on. Knowing which media individuals and/or groups prefer is insightful to the extent that such preferences can be catered to, but knowing what kind of information a specific source is providing would paint a fuller picture and broaden our understanding of the role information consumption plays not just in politics, but in social, economic, and health outcomes as well. The media often shape our views, and our views play a role in shaping our actions. Further insight into coping and its association with information consumption would broaden this line of research. Finally, future research should consider exploring the role of coping in other areas within the political sphere, both within and outside of the United States.

Overall Implications

Taken together, the arguments we advance in this book, as well as the findings that largely support them, come with a range of implications. Coping plays a role in political outcomes just as it does in social, economic, psychological, and health outcomes. Incorporating coping into political science research would strengthen our understanding of the role psychosocial factors play in shaping and explaining human behavior. In addition, our empirical chapters suggest that coping is important in studies concerning public opinion and policy. Coping offers insight into why some individuals believe and behave in the ways that they do. Understanding and further exploring the various psychosocial factors, including coping, that shape political beliefs and behaviors offers a perspective and approach that has been largely underdeveloped in political science. Reflecting on the events and political environment in 2020 alone, we argue that studies exploring social, political, economic, and health outcomes should all consider the role coping played in how individuals reacted to experiences of racial discrimination, cases of police brutality, political divisions, protests, and boycotts, and how individuals navigated a global pandemic.

As we have shown throughout this book, the manner in which one copes with adversity is associated with how one reacts to discrimination, ideological views, policy beliefs and support for certain policies, and with the type of information one consumes (as well as how often one consumes it). Thus, scholars studying a range of topics (for example, political behavior, political and/or social psychology, public opinion and affairs, media studies, race and ethnicity, and so on) within political science and related fields may benefit from this work and expand on it. Through coping, we can better understand why and how people think about a range of topics and policies in the ways they do, as well as the actions individuals carry out and the degree of effort that they put forth in order to do so. We can also better understand which media individuals prefer and rely on, which is important in a world wherein so much information is instantly at our fingertips. Thus, coping is important for understanding and exploring the why and how of many factors, but it is also important for individuals, organizations, and policy makers wishing to usher in change and/or progress, or even to appeal to or better understand their audience.

Notes

Introduction

1. Susan B. King Distinguished Professor Emeritus, Sanford School of Public Policy, Duke University.

2. W. E. B. Du Bois [1903] (1993), *The Souls of Black Folk*, New York: Alfred A. Knopf, 9.

3. John Henryism, and its potential health consequences, are not unique to African Americans. The construct and associated measurement tool, the John Henryism Active Coping scale, has been successfully used in a variety of populations and cultures.

4. See Sherman A. James (1993), "The Narrative of John Henry Martin," *Southern Cultures*, Inaugural Issue, 83–106.

5. Historian Scott Nelson suggests that the legendary John Henry was most likely a convict laborer underscoring the reasonable notion that one's social location in the political economy shapes both one's personality and life chances. See Scott R. Nelson (2006), *Steel-Drivin' Man: The Untold Story of an American Legend*, New York: Oxford University Press.

6. In the NSAL, "conservative," "moderate," and "liberal" signify political ideologies, but the complex, unspecified cultural, economic, and political values inhering within these ideologies are not easily disentangled, especially for African Americans.

7. For more on this point, see Sherman A. James (1994), "John Henryism and the Health of African Americans," *Culture, Medicine and Psychiatry*, esp. 178–80.

8. Amelia Thomson-DeVeaux and Conroy Meredith (2020), "Women Won the Right to Vote 100 Years Ago. They Didn't Start Voting Differently from Men until 1980," *FiveThirtyEight*.

9. Michelle Obama (2020), "The Gift of Girlfriends with Denielle, Sharon, and Kelly," Spotify.

10. Michelle Obama, "Gift of Girlfriends."

11. Michelle Obama, "Gift of Girlfriends."

12. Sherman James, "John Henryism and the Health," 166–67; Sherman A. James, Sue A. Hartnett, and William D. Kalsbeek (1983), "John Henryism and Blood Pressure Differences among Black Men," *Journal of Behavioral Medicine* 6: 259–78.

13. James, "John Henryism and the Health," 166–67.

14. James, "John Henryism and the Health," 163–82.

15. James, "John Henryism and the Health," 163; Sherman A. James et al. (1992), "Socioeconomic Status, John Henryism, and Blood Pressure in Black Adults: The Pitt County Study," *American Journal of Epidemiology* 135 (1): 59–67; James et al., "Socioeconomic Status, John Henryism," 664–73; James, Hartnett, and Alsek, "John Henryism and Blood Pressure," 259–78.

16. Harold W. Neighbors, Rashid Njai, and James S. Jackson (2007), "Race, Ethnicity, John Henryism, and Depressive Symptoms: The National Survey of American Life Adult Reinterview," *Research in Human Development* 4: 71–87.

17. Anita F. Fernander et al. (2003), "Assessing the Reliability and Validity of the John Henry Active Coping Scale in an Urban Sample of African Americans and White Americans," *Ethnicity & Health* 8 (2): 151.

18. Michael Deegan-McCree (2020), "An Anti-lynching Law Would Not Get Rid of Bad Cops, but It Would Go a Long Way toward Acknowledging America's Troubled History on Race, Abuse," *USA Today*.

19. Richard Faussett (2020), "What We Know about the Shooting Death of Ahmaud Arbery," *New York Times*.

20. J. Brandeberry (2020), "Glynn County Police Department Public Release Incident Report for G20-11303," *New York Times*.

21. Bill Hutchison and Rachel Katz. (2020), "Ahmaud Arbery Was Struck by Vehicle before He Was Shot Dead; Suspect Yelled Racial Slur: Investigator, *ABC News*.

22. Barajas, Angela. (2020). "Man Who Recorded Ahmaud Arbery's Killing Tried to 'Confine and Detain' Him with His Vehicle, Warrant Says," *CNN*.

23. Laura Italiano (2020), "William Roddie Bryan Tried to 'Confine and Detain' Ahmaud Arbery, Warrant Says," *New York Post*.

24. Minyvonne Burke (2020). "White Man Accused of Killing Ahmaud Arbery Allegedly Used Racial Slur after Shooting, Investigator Says," *NBC News*.

25. Melanie Eversley (2020), "Running while Black: Ahmaud Arbery's Killing Reveals Runners' Shared Fears of Profiling," *Undefeated*.

26. Eversley, "Running while Black."

27. Eversley, "Running while Black."

28. Eversley, "Running while Black."

29. Vanessa Taylor (2020), "Black Runners on Ahmaud Arbery and the Unique Treachery of a Simple Job," *Mic*.

30. Joshua Bote (2020), "George Floyd Told Officers He 'Can't Breathe' Nearly 30 Times, Newly Released Body Cam Transcripts Show," *USA Today*.

31. BBC News (2020), "George Floyd: What Happened in the Final Moments of His Life," *BBC News*.

32. Fox 9 News (2020), "911 Transcript of Call that Brought Police to George Floyd Released," *Fox 9 KMSP News*.

33. Jorge Fitz-Gibbon (2020), "Here's Everything We Know about the Death of George Floyd," *New York Post*.

34. BBC News, "George Floyd: What Happened."

35. BBC News, "George Floyd: What Happened."

36. Chao Xiong (2020), "A Timeline of Events Leading to George Floyd's Death as Outlined in Charging Documents," *Star Tribune*.

37. Fitz-Gibbon, "Here's Everything We Know."

38. BBC News, "George Floyd: What Happened."

39. Lewis Dodley (2020), "Timeline: How George Floyd's Death Sparked a Movement," *Spectrum News NY1*.

40. BBC News, "George Floyd: What Happened."

41. Chao, "A Timeline of Events."

42. BBC News, "George Floyd: What Happened."

43. Bote "George Floyd Told Officers."

44. BBC News, "George Floyd: What Happened."

45. Fitz-Gibbon (2020), "Here's Everything We Know."

46. Chao, "Timeline of Events."

47. BBC News, "George Floyd: What Happened."

48. Dodley, "Timeline: How George Floyd's Death."

49. Meredith Deliso (2020), "Timeline: The Impact of George Floyd's Death in Minneapolis and Beyond," *ABC News*.

50. Cheung (2020), "George Floyd Death."

51. Cheung, "George Floyd Death."

52. BBC News, "George Floyd: What Happened in the Final Moments."

53. Meredith Kornfield, Mark Guarino, Kayla Ruble, and Lenny Bernstein (2020), "Huge, Peaceful Protests Mark Anti-racism Demonstrations around the Globe," *Washington Post*.

54. Cheung, "George Floyd Death: Why US Protests."

55. BBC News, "George Floyd: What Happened in the Final Moments."

56. Kornfield, Guarino, Ruble, and Bernstein, "Huge, Peaceful Protests Mark Anti-racism."

57. BBC News, "George Floyd: What Happened in the Final Moments."

58. Al Jazeera (author unknown) (2020), "International Reaction to George Floyd Killing," *Al Jazeera*.

59. *Al Jazeera*, "International Reaction to George Floyd Killing."

60. Eugene Robinson (2020), "Black Lives Remain Expendable," *Washington Post*.

61. Sara M. Moniuszko (2020), "Billie Eilish, Taylor Swift, Oprah, More Celebrities React to the Death of George Floyd: 'We Must Act,'" *USA Today*.

62. Moniuszko (2020), "Billie Eilish, Taylor Swift, Oprah, More Celebrities React."

63. Moniuszko (2020), "Billie Eilish, Taylor Swift, Oprah, More Celebrities React."

64. Moniuszko (2020), "Billie Eilish, Taylor Swift, Oprah, More Celebrities React."

65. BBC News (2020), "Breonna Taylor: Protestors Call on People to 'Say Her Name.'" *BBC*.

66. Emma Bowman (2022), "4 Current and Former Officers Federally Charged in Raid that Killed Breonna Taylor," *NPR*; BBC News (author unknown) (2022), "Breonna Taylor: Protestors Call on People"; Richard A. Oppel Jr., Derrick Bryson Taylor, and Nicholas Bogel-Burroughs (2022), "What to Know about Breonna Taylor's Death," *New York Times*; Mark Morales, Eric Levenson, Elizabeth Joseph, and Christina Carrega (2020), "Louisville Agrees to Pay Breonna Taylor's Family $12 Million and Enact Police Reforms in Historic Settlement," *CNN*.

67. Bowman, "4 Current and Former Officers," 1.

68. Bowman, "4 Current and Former Officers"; *BBC News*, "Breonna Taylor: Protestors Call on People."

69. *BBC News*, "Breonna Taylor: Protestors Call on People"; Oppel Jr. et al., "What to Know about Breonna Taylor's Death."

70. Oppel Jr. et al., "What to Know about Breonna Taylor's Death."

71. Bowman, "4 Current and Former Officers."

72. Morales et al., "Louisville Agrees to Pay."

73. Morales et al., "Louisville Agrees to Pay."

74. *BBC News* (Author Unknown). "Breonna Taylor: Protestors Call on People."

Chapter 1

1. Richard S. Lazarus and Susan Folkman (1984), *Stress, Appraisal, and Coping*, New York: Springer; Susan Folkman Richard S. Lazarus (1988), "The Relationship between Coping and Emotion: Implications for Theory and Research," *Social Science & Medicine* 26 (3): 309–17.

2. Folkman and Lazarus, "The Relationship between Coping and Emotion"; Lazarus and Folkman (1984), *Stress, Appraisal, and Coping*; Neal E. Miller (1980), "A Perspective on the Effects of Stress and Coping on Disease and Health," in S. Levine and H. Ursin (eds.), *Coping and Health*, New York: Plenum, 323–53; Cynthia L. Radnitz and Lana Tiersky (2007); "Psychodynamic and Cognitive Theories of Coping," in E. Martz and H. Livneh (eds.), *Coping with Chronic Illness and Disability: Theoretical, Empirical, and Clinical Aspects*, New York: Springer Science + Business Media, 29–48; Holger Ursin (1980), "Personality, Activation and Somatic Health: A New Psychosomatic Theory," in S. Levine and H. Ursin (eds.), *Coping and Health*, New York: Plenum, 259–79.

3. Folkman and Lazarus, "The Relationship between Coping and Emotion"; Lazarus and Folkman, *Stress, Appraisal, and Coping*.

4. Lazarus and Folkman, *Stress, Appraisal, and Coping*, 118; Katharine H. Greenaway et al. (2014), "Successful Coping for Psychological Well-Being," in G. Boyle, D. H. Saklofske, and G. Matthews (eds.), *Measures of Personality and Social Psychological Constructs*, Oxford, UK: Elsevier, 322–51; Miller "A Perspective on the Effects of Stress": Holger "Personality, Activation and Somatic Health."

5. Lazarus and Folkman, *Stress, Appraisal, and Coping*; Radnitz and Tiersky, "Psychodynamic and Cognitive Theories of Coping."

6. Folkman and Lazarus, "Relationship between Coping and Emotion"; Lazarus and Folkman, *Stress, Appraisal, and Coping*.

7. Lazarus and Folkman, *Stress, Appraisal, and Coping*, 118.

8. Lazarus and Folkman, *Stress, Appraisal, and Coping*; Karl Menninger (1954), "Regulatory Devices of the Ego under Major Stress" *International Journal of Psychoanalysis* 35: 412–20; Karl Menninger (1963), *The Vital Balance: The Life Process in Mental Health and Illness*, New York: Viking; Radnitz and Tiersky "Psychodynamic and Cognitive Theories of Coping"; George Vaillant (1977), *Adaptation to Life*, Cambridge, MA: Harvard University Press.

9. Menninger, *Vital Balance*.

10. Lazarus and Folkman (1984), *Stress, Appraisal, and Coping*.

11. Lazarus and Folkman, *Stress, Appraisal, and Coping*.

12. Folkman and Lazarus, "Relationship between Coping and Emotion"; Lazarus and Folkman, *Stress, Appraisal, and Coping*.

13. Folkman and Lazarus, "Relationship between Coping and Emotion"; Lazarus and Folkman, *Stress, Appraisal, and Coping*.

14. Lazarus and Folkman, *Stress, Appraisal, and Coping*.

15. Lazarus and Folkman, *Stress, Appraisal, and Coping*, 120–21.

16. Lazarus and Folkman, *Stress, Appraisal, and Coping*.

17. Heinz W. Krohne and Josef Rogner (1982), "Repression-Sensitization as a Central Construct in Coping Research," in H.W. Krohne and L. Laux (eds.), *Series in Clinical & Community Psychology: Achievement, Stress, and Anxiety*, Washington, DC: Hemisphere, 167–93; Robert H. Shipley, James H. Butt, Bruce Horwitz, and John E. Farbry (1978), "Preparation for a Stressful Medical Procedure: Effect of Amount of Stimulus Preexposure and Coping Style," *Journal of Consulting and Clinical Psychology* 46 (3): 499–507; Robert H. Shipley, James H. Butt, and Ellen A. Horwitz (1979), "Preparation to Reexperience a Stressful Medical Examination: Effect of Repetitious Videotape Exposure and Coping Style," *Journal of Consulting and Clinical Psychology* 47 (3): 485–92.

18. Michael J. Goldstein (1959), "The Relationship between Coping and Avoiding Behavior and Response to Fear-Arousing Propaganda," *Journal of Abnormal and Social Psychology* 58 (2): 247–52; Michael J. Goldstein (1973), "Individual Differences in Response to Stress," *American Journal of Community Psychology* 1 (2): 113–37.

19. Julie A. Penley, Joe Tomaka, and John S. Wiebe (2002), "The Association of Coping to Physical and Psychological Health Outcomes: A Meta-Analytic Review," *Journal of Behavioral Medicine* 25 (6): 553; Vaillant, *Adaptation to Life*.

20. Susan Folkman (1982), "An Approach to the Measurement of Coping," *Journal of Occupational Behavior* 3: 95–107; Goldstein, "Individual Differences in Response to Stress"; Stavroula Mitrousi et al. (2013), "Theoretical Approaches to Coping," *International Journal of Caring Sciences* 6 (2): 131–7; Penley, Tomaka, and Wiebe, "The Association of Coping."

21. Goldstein (1973), "Individual Differences in Response to Stress," 114.

22. For example, see Goldstein, "The Relationship between Coping"; Goldstein, "Individual Differences in Response to Stress"; Willard A. Mainord, "Experimental Repression Related to Coping and Avoidance Behavior in the Recall and Relearning of Nonsense Syllables," doctoral diss., University of Washington.

23. For example, see Donn Byrne (1964), "Repression-Sensitization as a Dimension of Personality," in Brendan A. Maher (ed.), *Progress in Experimental Personality Research*, vol. 1, New York: Academic Press, 170–220.

24. For example, see Goldine C. and David Ihilevich (1969), "An Objective Instrument for Measuring Defense Mechanisms," *Journal of Consulting and Clinical Psychology* 33 (1): 51–60.

25. Folkman, "An Approach to the Measurement of Coping"; Susan Folkman and Richard S. Lazarus (1980). "An Analysis of Coping in a Middle-Aged Community Sample" *Journal of Health and Social Behavior* 21 (3): 219–39; Mitrousi et al., "Theoretical Approaches to Coping." For a more thorough review of trait measures, see Rudolf H. Moos (1974), "Psychological Techniques in the Assessment of Adaptive Behavior," in G. V. Coelho, D. A. Hamburg, and J. E. Adams (eds.), *Coping and Adaptation*, New York: Basic Books, 334–99.

26. Folkman, "An Approach to the Measurement of Coping"; Lazarus and Folkman, *Stress, Appraisal, and Coping*; Mitrousi et al., "Theoretical Approaches to Coping."

27. Frances Cohen and Richard S. Lazarus (1973), "Active Coping Processes, Coping Dispositions, and Recovery from Surgery," *Psychosomatic Medicine* 35 (5): 375–89.

28. Folkman, "An Approach to the Measurement of Coping"; Lazarus and Folkman, *Stress, Appraisal, and Coping*.

29. Cohen and Lazarus, "Active Coping Processes"; Folkman, "An Approach to the Measurement of Coping"; Lazarus and Folkman, *Stress, Appraisal, and Coping*.

30. Lazarus and Folkman, *Stress, Appraisal, and Coping*.

31. Cohen and Lazarus, "Active Coping Processes"; Folkman, "An Approach to the Measurement of Coping"; Lazarus and Folkman, *Stress, Appraisal, and Coping*.

32. Cohen and Lazarus, "Active Coping Processes."

33. Cohen and Lazarus, "Active Coping Processes."

34. Cohen and Lazarus, "Active Coping Processes."

35. Cohen and Lazarus, "Active Coping Processes."

36. Lazarus and Folkman, *Stress, Appraisal, and Coping*, 129.

37. Rudolf H. Moos and Vivien Davis Tsu (1977), "The Crisis of Physical Illness: An Overview," in R. H. Moos (ed.), *Coping with Physical Illness*, New York: Plenum, 3–21.

38. Folkman and Lazarus, "An Analysis of Coping"; Lazarus and Folkman, *Stress, Appraisal, and Coping.*

39. Folkman and Lazarus, "An Analysis of Coping"; Lazarus and Folkman, *Stress, Appraisal, and Coping*; Moos and Tsu, "The Crisis of Physical Illness: An Overview."

40. Folkman and Lazarus, "An Analysis of Coping" Lazarus and Folkman, *Stress, Appraisal, and Coping.*

41. Lazarus and Folkman, *Stress, Appraisal, and Coping.*

42. Lazarus and Folkman, *Stress, Appraisal, and Coping.*

43. Sherman A. James, Sue A. Hartnett, and William D. Kalsbeek (1983), "John Henryism and Blood Pressure Differences among Black Men," *Journal of Behavioral Medicine* 6 (3): 263.

44. Lazarus and Folkman, *Stress, Appraisal, and Coping.*

45. Greenaway et al., "Successful Coping for Psychological Well-Being"; Lazarus and Folkman, *Stress, Appraisal, and Coping.*

46. Lazarus and Folkman, *Stress, Appraisal, and Coping.*

47. Lazarus and Folkman, *Stress, Appraisal, and Coping*, 141.

48. Susan Folkman and Richard S. Lazarus (1985), "If It Changes It Must Be a Process: Study of Emotion and Coping during Three Stages of a College Examination," *Journal of Personality and Social Psychology* 48 (1): 150–70; Folkman and Lazarus, "The Relationship between Coping and Emotion"; Susan Folkman, Richard S. Lazarus, Christine Dunkel-Schetter, Anita DeLongis, and Rand J. Gruen (1986), "Dynamics of a Stressful Encounter: Cognitive Appraisal, Coping, and Encounter Outcomes," *Journal of Personality and Social Psychology* 50 (5): 992–1003; Greenaway et al., "Successful Coping for Psychological Well-Being"; Richard S. Lazarus (1991), *Emotion and Adaptation*, New York: Oxford University Press.

49. Bruce E. Compas et al. (2014), "Coping and Emotion Regulation from Childhood to Early Adulthood: Points of Convergence and Divergence," *Australian Journal of Psychology* 66: 71–81; Mitrousi et al., "Theoretical Approaches to Coping."

50. Lazarus and Folkman, *Stress, Appraisal, and Coping.*

51. Penley, Tomaka, and Wiebe, "The Association of Coping," 552.

52. Penley, Tomaka, and Wiebe, "The Association of Coping."

53. Penley, Tomaka, and Wiebe, "The Association of Coping"; Christine J. Yeh, Agnes Kwong Arora, and Katherine A. Wu (2006), "A New Theoretical Model of Collectivistic Coping," in Paul T. P. Wong and Lilian C. J. Wong (eds.), *Handbook of Multicultural Perspectives on Stress and Coping*, New York: Springer.

54. Folkman and Lazarus, "An Analysis of Coping"; Folkman and Lazarus. "If It Changes It Must Be a Process"; Penley, Tomaka, and Wiebe, "The Association of Coping."

55. Lazarus and Folkman, *Stress, Appraisal, and Coping*; Greenaway et al., "Successful Coping for Psychological Well-Being."

56. Lazarus and Folkman, *Stress, Appraisal, and Coping*; Penley, Tomaka, and Wiebe, "The Association of Coping."

57. Amy M. Bippus and Stacy L. Young (2012), "Using Appraisal Theory to Predict Emotional and Coping Responses to Hurtful Messages," *Interpersona* 6 (2): 176–90; Folkman, "An Approach to the Measurement of Coping"; Folkman and Lazarus, "An Analysis of Coping"; Folkman and Lazarus, "If It Changes It Must Be a Process"; Folkman and Lazarus, "The Relationship between Coping and Emotion; Folkman et al., "Dynamics of a Stressful Encounter; Greenaway et al., "Successful Coping for Psychological Well-Being"; Lazarus, *Emotion and Adaptation*; Richard S. Lazarus (1999), *Stress and Emotion: A New Synthesis*, New York: Springer; Lazarus and Folkman, *Stress, Appraisal, and Coping*.

58. Bippus and Young (2012), "Using Appraisal Theory," 176; Lazarus, *Emotion and Adaptation*.

59. Bippus and Young, "Using Appraisal Theory"; Folkman and Lazarus, "If It Changes It Must Be a Process"; Folkman et al., "Dynamics of a Stressful Encounter"; Lazarus and Folkman, *Stress, Appraisal, and Coping*.

60. Lazarus and Folkman, *Stress, Appraisal, and Coping*.

61. Bippus and Young, "Using Appraisal Theory"; Folkman and Lazarus, "If It Changes It Must Be a Process"; Lazarus, *Stress and Emotion*; Lazarus and Folkman, *Stress, Appraisal, and Coping*.

62. Folkman and Lazarus. (1984). *Stress, Appraisal, and Coping*.

63. Folkman and Lazarus, "If It Changes It Must Be a Process."

64. R. S. Bhagat, P. K. Steverson, and Ben C. H. Kuo (2009), "Cultural Variations in Work Stress and Coping in an Era of Globalization," in R. S. Bhagat and R. M. Steers (eds.), *Handbook of Culture, Organizations, and Work*, Cambridge, UK: Cambridge University Press, 418–41; Ben C. H. Kuo (2011), "Culture's Consequences on Coping: Theories, Evidence, and Dimensionalities," *Journal of Cross-Cultural Psychology* 42 (6): 1084–1100; Lazarus and Folkman, *Stress, Appraisal, and Coping*; Paul T. P. Wong and Lilian C. J. Wong (2006), *Handbook of Multicultural Perspectives on Stress and Coping*, New York: Springer.

65. Kuo, "Collectivism and Coping: Current Theories, Evidence, and Measurements of Collective Coping," *International Journal of Psychology* 48 (3): 375.

66. Yeh et al., "A New Theoretical Model of Collectivistic Coping."

67. Ben C. H., Gargi Roysircar, and Ian R. Newby-Clark (2006), "Development of the Cross-Cultural Coping Scale: Collective, Avoidance, and Engagement Strategies." *Measurement and Evaluation in Counseling and Development* 39 (3): 161–81; Kuo, "Culture's Consequences on Coping"; Kuo, "Collectivism and Coping"; Yeh et al., "A New Theoretical Model."

68. Kuo, "Collectivism and Coping," 383; Kuo et al., "Development of the Cross-Cultural Coping Scale."

69. Kuo, "Collectivism and Coping, 383; Kuo, "Culture's Consequences on Coping."

70. Kuo, "Collectivism and Coping."

71. Christine J. Yeh, T. Chang, A. B. Kim, Agnes Kwong Arora, and T. Xin (2003), "Reliability, Validity, and Factor Analysis of the Collectivistic Coping Scale," poster presented at the annual meeting of the American Psychological Association, Toronto, Canada; Yeh et al., "A New Theoretical Model of Collectivistic Coping."

72. P. Paul Heppner et al. (2006), "Development and Validation for a Collectivist Coping Styles Inventory," *Journal of Counseling Psychology* 53 (1): 107–25.

73. Kuo et al., "Development of the Cross-Cultural Coping Scale."

74. James L. Moore and Madonna G. Constantine (2005), "Development and Initial Validation of the Collectivistic Coping Styles Measure with African, Asian, and Latin American International Students," *Journal of Mental Health Counseling* 27 (4): 329–47.

75. For a more thorough review of these—and other—cultural-based measures of coping, please see the original studies. For a review of theories on collectivism and collective coping, including evidence and measurements, see Ben H. C. Kuo (2013), "Collectivism and Coping: Current Theories, Evidence, and Measurements of Collective Coping," *International Journal of Psychology* 48 (3): 374–88.

76. Heinz W. Krohne et al. (2000). "The Assessment of Dispositional Vigilance and Cognitive Avoidance: Factorial Structure, Psychometric Properties, and Validity of the Mainz Coping Inventory," *Cognitive Therapy and Research* 24 (3): 297–311.

77. Byrne, "Repression-Sensitization as a Dimension of Personality."

78. Krohne et al., "The Assessment of Dispositional Vigilance."

79. Heinz W. Krohne (1986), "Coping with Stress: Dispositions, Strategies, and the Problem of Measurement," in M. H. Appley and R. Trumbull (eds.), *Dynamics of Stress: Physiological, Psychological, and Social Perspectives*, New York: Plenum, 207–32; Heinz W. Krohne (1993), "Vigilance and Cognitive Avoidance as Concepts in Coping Research," in H. W. Krohne (ed.), *Attention and Avoidance: Strategies in Coping with Aversiveness*, Seattle, WA: Hogrefe and Huber, 19–50.

80. Krohne et al., "The Assessment of Dispositional Vigilance," 298.

81. Suzanne M. Miller (1987), "Monitoring and Blunting: Validation of a Questionnaire to Assess Styles of Information Seeking under Threat," *Journal of Personality and Social Psychology* 52 (2): 345–53.

82. Miller, "Monitoring and Blunting," 345.

83. Charles S. Carver, Michael F. Scheier, and Jagdish Kumari Weintraub (1989), "Assessing Coping Strategies: A Theoretically Based Approach," *Journal of Personality and Social Psychology* 56 (2): 267–83.

84. Charles S. Carver (1997), "You Want to Measure Coping but Your Protocol's Too Long: Consider the Brief COPE," *International Journal of Behavioral Medicine* 4 (1): 92–100.

85. Carver, Scheier, and Weintraub, "Assessing Coping Strategies"; Carver "You Want to Measure Coping."

86. For a complete breakdown of the COPE inventory, see Charles S. Carver, Michael F. Scheier, and Jagdish Kumari Weintraub (1989), "Assessing Coping Strategies: A Theoretically Based Approach," *Journal of Personality and Social Psychology* 56 (2): 267–83.

For a complete breakdown of the Brief COPE, see Carver, "You Want to Measure Coping."

87. David L. Tobin ([1984] 2001), "User Manual for the Coping Strategies Inventory."

88. Folkman and Lazarus, "An Analysis of Coping."

89. James H. Amirkhan (1990), "A Factor Analytically Derived Measure of Coping: The Coping Strategy Indicator," *Journal of Personality and Social Psychology* 59 (5): 1066–74.

90. Margaret A. Chesney et al. (2006), "A Validity and Reliability Study of the Coping Self-Efficacy Scale," *British Journal of Health Psychology* 11 (3): 421–37.

91. Vaughn G. Sinclair and Kenneth A. Wallston (2004), "The Development and Psychometric Evaluation of the Brief Resilient Coping Scale," *Assessment* 11 (1): 94–101.

92. Esther Greenglass, Ralf Schwarzer, Dagmara Jakubiec, Lisa Fiksenbaum, and Steffen Taubert (1999), "The Proactive Coping Inventory (PCI): A Multidimensional Research Instrument," paper presented at the 20th International Conference of the Stress and Anxiety Research Society (STAR), Cracow, Poland, July 12–14.

93. Alexander Rice, Yunkyoung Loh Garrison, and William Ming Liu (2020), "Spending as Social and Affective Coping (SSAC): Measure Development and Initial Validation," *Counseling Psychologist* 48 (1): 78–105.

94. Bruce Arnow, Justin Kenardy, and W. Stewart Agras (1995), "The Emotional Eating Scale: The Development of a Measure to Assess Coping with Negative Affect by Eating," *International Journal of Eating Disorders* 18 (1): 79–90.

95. Rice et al., "Spending as Social and Affective Coping."

96. James, Sherman A. (1994), "John Henryism and the Health of African-Americans," *Culture, Medicine and Psychiatry* 18: 163–82.

97. James, Hartnett, and Kalsbeek, "John Henryism and Blood Pressure Differences."

98. James, "John Henryism and the Health of African-Americans," 165.

99. S. Leonard Syme (1979), "Psychosocial Determinants of Hypertension," in E. Onesti and C. Klint (eds.), *Hypertension Determinants, Complications and Intervention*, New York: Grune and Stratton, 95–98.

100. Gary G. Bennett et al. (2004), "Stress, Coping, and Health Outcomes among African-Americans: A Review of the John Henryism Hypothesis," *Psychology and Health* 19 (3): 369–83; Ellen C. Bronder et al. (2014), "John Henryism, Depression, and Perceived Social Support in Black Women," *Journal of Black Psychology* 40

(2): 115–37; James, Hartnett, and Kalsbeek, "John Henryism and Blood Pressure Differences"; James, "John Henryism and the Health of African-Americans"; D. R. Williams (1992), "Black-White Differences in Blood Pressure: The Role of Social Factors," *Ethnicity and Disease* 2 (2): 126–41.

101. Syme, "Psychosocial Determinants of Hypertension."

102. James, "John Henryism and the Health of African-Americans," 166.

103. James, "John Henryism and the Health of African-Americans," 166–7; James, Hartnett, and Kalsbeek (1983), "John Henryism and Blood Pressure Differences"; Bennett et al., "Stress, Coping, and Health Outcomes"; Bronder et al., "John Henryism, Depression, and Perceived Social Support"; Shaan Gupta, Emmanuelle Belanger, and Susan P. Phillips (2019), "Low Socioeconomic Status but Resilient: Panacea or Double Trouble? John Henryism in the International IMIAS Study of Older Adults," *Journal of Cross-Cultural Gerontology* 34: 15–24; E. C. McKetney and David R. Ragland (1996), "John Henryism, Education, and Blood Pressure in Young Adults: The CARDIA Study," *American Journal of Epidemiology* 143 (8): 787–91.

104. James, "John Henryism and the Health."

105. Bennett et al., "Stress, Coping, and Health Outcomes"; Bronder et al., "John Henryism, Depression, and Perceived Social Support"; Gupta, Belanger, and Phillips, "Low Socioeconomic Status but Resilient"; James, Hartnett, and Kalsbeek, "John Henryism and Blood Pressure Differences"; James, "John Henryism and the Health"; Syme, "Psychosocial Determinants of Hypertension"; Williams, "Black-White Differences in Blood Pressure."

106. James, "John Henryism and the Health," 167–68.

107. Bennett et al., "Stress, Coping, and Health Outcomes"; James, Hartnett, and Kalsbeek, "John Henryism and Blood Pressure Differences""; James, "John Henryism and the Health."

108. James, Hartnett, and Kalsbeek, "John Henryism and Blood Pressure Differences"; Sherman A. James et al. (1984), "John Henryism and Blood Pressure Differences among Black Men, II: The Role of Occupational Stressors," *Journal of Behavioral Medicine* 7 (3): 259–75.

109. James, "John Henryism and the Health," 169.

110. Scholarly works on the legend of John Henry, which inspired James (1994), include but are not limited to: (1) Lawrence Levine (1977), *Black Culture and Black Consciousness: Afro-American Folk Thought from Slavery to Freedom*, Oxford, UK: Oxford University Press; and (2) Brett Williams (1983), *John Henry: A Bio-bibliography*. Westport, CT: Greenwood Press.

111. Bennett et al., "Stress, Coping, and Health Outcomes"; James, Hartnett, and Kalsbeek, "John Henryism and Blood Pressure Differences"; James et al., "John Henryism and Blood Pressure Differences, II"; James, "John Henryism and the Health."

112. James, "John Henryism and the Health, 169; Bennett et al. (2004), "Stress, Coping, and Health Outcomes."

113. James, "John Henryism and the Health."

114. Vence L. Bonham, Sherrill L. Sellers, and Harold W. Neighbors (2004), "John Henryism and Self-Reported Physical Health among High-Socioeconomic Status African American Men," *American Journal of Public Health* 94 (5): 737–38; James, "John Henryism and the Health."

115. James, "John Henryism and the Health."

116. James, "John Henryism and the Health," 169.

117. Bonham, Sellers, and Neighbors, "John Henryism and Self-Reported Physical Health," 737; Bronder et al., "John Henryism, Depression, and Perceived Social Support"; James et al., "John Henryism and Blood Pressure Differences, II."

118. Julie Doron et al. (2015), "Coping Profiles, Perceived Stress and Health-Related Behaviors: A Cluster Analysis Approach," *Health Promotion International* 30 (1): 88–100; Folkman and Lazarus. "An Analysis of Coping"; Lazarus, *Emotion and Adaptation*; Lazarus and Folkman, *Stress, Appraisal, and Coping*; Penley, Tomaka, and Wiebe, "The Association of Coping."

119. Ellen A. Skinner et al. (2003), "Searching for the Structure of Coping: A Review and Critique of Category Systems for Classifying Ways of Coping," *Psychological Bulletin* 129 (2): 216.

120. Penley, Tomaka, and Wiebe, "The Association of Coping."

121. Folkman and Lazarus, "If It Changes It Must Be a Process."

122. Penley, Tomaka, and Wiebe, "The Association of Coping."

123. James, Hartnett, and Kalsbeek, "John Henryism and Blood Pressure Differences,"; James et al., "John Henryism and Blood Pressure Differences, II";Sherman A. James, and P. E. Thomas (2000), "John Henryism and Blood Pressure in Black Populations: A Review of the Evidence," *African American Research Perspectives* 6 (3): 1–10; Lynda B. Wright et al. (1996), "Relationship of John Henryism to Cardiovascular Functioning at Rest and during Stress in Youth," *Annals of Behavioral Medicine* 18 (3): 146–50.

124. Marcellus M. Merritt et al. (2004), "Low Educational Attainment, John Henryism, and Cardiovascular Reactivity to and Recovery from Personally Relevant Stress," *Psychosomatic Medicine* 66 (1): 49–55; Wright et al. (1996), "Relationship of John Henryism to Cardiovascular."

125. Anita F. Fernander et al. (2005), "Exploring the Association of John Henry Active Coping and Education on Smoking Behavior and Nicotine Dependence among Blacks in the USA," *Social Science and Medicine* 60: 491–500.

126. Bonham et al., "John Henryism and Self-Reported Physical Health"; Bronder et al., "John Henryism, Depression, and Perceived Social Support"; James, Hartnett, and Kalsbeek, "John Henryism and Blood Pressure Differences"; James et al., "John Henryism and Blood Pressure Differences, II";Sherman A. James et al. (1992); "Socioeconomic Status, John Henryism, and Blood Pressure in Black Adults: The Pitt County Study," *American Journal of Epidemiology* 135 (1): 59–67; James and Thomas, "John Henryism and Blood Pressure"; McKetney and Ragland,

"John Henryism, Education, and Blood Pressure"; Merritt et al., "Low Educational Attainment, John Henryism"; Wright et al., "Relationship of John Henryism to Cardiovascular."

127. Bennett et al., "Stress, Coping, and Health Outcomes"; Thomas Duijkers et al. (1988), "'John Henryism' and Blood Pressure in a Dutch Population," *Psychosomatic Medicine* 50 (4): 353–59; James, Hartnett, and Kalsbeek. "John Henryism and Blood Pressure Differences"; James et al., "John Henryism and Blood Pressure Differences, II"; Sherman A. James et al. (1987), "Socioeconomic Status, John Henryism, and Hypertension in Blacks and Whites," *American Journal of Epidemiology* 126 (4): 664–73; James et al., "Socioeconomic Status, John Henryism, and Blood Pressure"; James and Thomas, "John Henryism and Blood Pressure"; Merritt et al., "Low Educational Attainment, John Henryism"; Wright et al., "Relationship of John Henryism to Cardiovascular."

128. Bennett et al., "Stress, Coping, and Health Outcomes"; Bronder et al., "John Henryism, Depression, and Perceived Social Support."

129. Duijkers et al., "'John Henryism' and Blood Pressure"; James, Hartnett, and Kalsbeek, "John Henryism and Blood Pressure Differences"; James et al., "Socioeconomic Status, John Henryism, and Hypertension"; James et al., "Socioeconomic Status, John Henryism, and Blood Pressure"; Nina Markovic et al. (1998), "John Henryism and Blood Pressure among Nigerian Civil Servants," *Journal of Epidemiology and Community Health* 52 (3): 186–90; Merritt et al., "Low Educational Attainment, John Henryism"; Wright et al., "Relationship of John Henryism to Cardiovascular."

130. J. H. Adams, R. E. Aubert, and V. R. Clark (1999), "The Relationship among John Henryism, Hostility, Perceived Stress, Social Support, and Blood Pressure in African-American College Students," *Ethnicity and Disease* 9 (3): 359–68; Rupert A. Francis et al. (1991), "The Relationship of Blood Pressure to a Brief Measure of Anger during Routine Health Screening," *Journal of the National Medical Association* 83 (7): 601–4; McKetney and Ragland, "John Henryism, Education, and Blood Pressure"; G. Nordby et al. (1995), "A Double-Blind Study of Psychosocial Factors in 40-Year-Old Women with Essential Hypertension," *Psychotherapy and Psychosomatics* 63 (3–4): 142–50. For a review of the literature on the John Henryism hypothesis and an overview of the empirical studies testing it, see Bennett et al., "Stress, Coping, and Health Outcomes."

131. Bennett et al., "Stress, Coping, and Health Outcomes."

132. James, "John Henryism and the Health of African-Americans"; Dressler et al. (1998). "John Henryism, Gender, and Arterial Blood Pressure in an African American Community," *Psychosomatic Medicine* 60 (5): 620–24.

133. Bennett et al., "Stress, Coping, and Health Outcomes," 373.

134. Bennett et al., "Stress, Coping, and Health Outcomes"; Duijkers et al., "John Henryism and Blood Pressure"; Gupta et al., "Low Socioeconomic Status but Resilient."

135. Duijkers et al., "John Henryism and Blood Pressure."

136. Gupta et al., "Low Socioeconomic Status but Resilient."

137. Bennett et al., "Stress, Coping, and Health Outcomes"; Bonham et al., "John Henryism and Self-Reported Physical Health"; Bronder et al., "John Henryism, Depression, and Perceived Social Support"; Jelena Čvorović and Sherman A. James (2018), "John Henryism, Gender and Self-Reported Health among Roma/Gypsies in Serbia," *Culture, Medicine and Psychiatry* 42 (2): 295–314; Fernander et al., "Exploring the Association of John Henry Active Coping"; A. Jeanne Van Loon et al. (2001), "Personality and Coping: Their Relationship with Lifestyle Risk Factors for Cancer," *Personality and Individual Differences* 31 (4): 541–53.

138. Bonham et al., "John Henryism and Self-Reported Physical Health."

139. Bonham et al., "John Henryism and Self-Reported Physical Health."

140. Van Loon et al., "Personality and Coping."

141. Fernander et al., "Exploring the Association of John Henry Active Coping."

142. Fernander et al., "Exploring the Association of John Henry Active Coping."

143. Čvorović and James, "John Henryism, Gender and Self-Reported Health . . ."

144. Bronder et al., "John Henryism, Depression, and Perceived Social Support."

145. Lazarus, *Emotion and Adaptation*; Penley, Tomaka, and Wiebe, "The Association of Coping."

146. Lazarus, *Emotion and Adaptation*; Penley, Tomaka, and Wiebe, "The Association of Coping."

147. Carver et al., "Assessing Coping Strategies"; Folkman et al., "Dynamics of a Stressful Encounter"; Penley, Tomaka, and Wiebe, "The Association of Coping."

148. Charles Holahan et al. (2005), "Stress Generation, Avoidance Coping, and Depressive Symptoms: A 10-Year Model," *Journal of Consulting and Clinical Psychology* 73 (4): 658–66.

149. Bronder et al., "John Henryism, Depression, and Perceived Social Support."

150. Holahan et al., "Stress Generation, Avoidance Coping, and Depressive Symptoms."

151. Holahan et al., "Stress Generation, Avoidance Coping, and Depressive Symptoms."

152. Doron et al., "Coping Profiles, Perceived Stress and Health-Related Behaviors."

153. Doron et al., "Coping Profiles, Perceived Stress and Health-Related Behaviors."

154. Holahan et al., "Stress Generation, Avoidance Coping, and Depressive Symptoms"; Penley, Tomaka, and Wiebe, "The Association of Coping."

155. Lazarus, *Emotion and Adaptation*; Penley, Tomaka, and Wiebe, "The Association of Coping."

156. Bronder et al., "John Henryism, Depression, and Perceived Social Support."

157. Peter Muris, Florence J. van Zuuren, and Simon de Vries (1994), "Monitoring, Blunting and Situational Anxiety: A Laboratory Study on Coping with a Quasi-Medical Stressor," *Personality and Individual Differences* 16 (3): 365–72.

158. S. Shiloh et al. (2008), "Monitoring Coping Style Moderates Emotional Reactions to Genetic Testing for Hereditary Nonpolyposis Colorectal Cancer: A Longitudinal Study," *Psycho-Oncology* 17: 746–55; Greenaway et al., "Successful Coping for Psychological Well-Being."

159. F. Jane Wardle et al. (1993), "Psychological Impact of Screening for Familial Ovarian Cancer," *Journal of the National Cancer Institute* 85 (8): 653–57.

160. Suzanne M. Miller et al. (1994), "Effects of Coping Style on Psychological Reactions of Low-Income, Minority Women to Colposcopy," *Journal of Reproductive Medicine* 39 (9): 711–18; Greenaway et al., "Successful Coping for Psychological Well-Being."

161. Penley, Tomaka, and Wiebe (2002), "The Association of Coping."

162. Lazarus and Folkman, *Stress, Appraisal, and Coping*; Penley, Tomaka, and Wiebe, "The Association of Coping."

163. Penley, Tomaka, and Wiebe, "The Association of Coping."

164. Leonard I. Pearlin (1989), "The Sociological Study of Stress," *Journal of Health and Social Behavior* 30 (3): 242.

165. Bronder et al., "John Henryism, Depression, and Perceived Social Support"; James, "John Henryism and the Health of African-Americans."

166. Bronder et al., "John Henryism, Depression, and Perceived Social Support"; James, Hartnett, and Kalsbeek, "John Henryism and Blood Pressure Differences"; James, "John Henryism and the Health of African-Americans."

167. Bennett et al., "Stress, Coping, and Health Outcomes"; Bronder et al., "John Henryism, Depression, and Perceived Social Support."

168. Bonham et al., "John Henryism and Self-Reported Physical Health."

169. Bronder et al., "John Henryism, Depression, and Perceived Social Support."

170. Yeh et al., "A New Theoretical Model of Collectivistic Coping."

171. Sharon Manne et al. (2014), "Unsupportive Partner Behaviors, Social-Cognitive Processing, and Psychological Outcomes in Couples Coping with Early Stage Breast Cancer," *Journal of Family Psychology* 28 (2): 214–24.

172. Manne et al., "Unsupportive Partner Behaviors."

Chapter 2

1. S. A. James, S. A. Hartnett, and W. D. Alsek (1983), "John Henryism and Blood Pressure Differences among Black Men," *Journal of Behavioral Medicine* 6: 259–78.

2. Sherman A. James (1994), "John Henryism and the Health of African-Americans," *Culture, Medicine and Psychiatry* 18: 163–82.

3. James, Hartnett, and Kalsbeek (1983), "John Henryism and Blood Pressure Differences among Black Men," *Journal of Behavioral Medicine* 6 (3): 263.

4. James, "John Henryism and the Health of African-Americans."

5. James, "John Henryism and the Health of African-Americans."

6. Vence L. Bonham, Sherrill L. Sellers, and Harold W. Neighbors (2004), "John Henryism and Self-Reported Physical Health among High-Socioeconomic Status African American Men," *American Journal of Public Health* 94 (5): 737–38.

7. James, Hartnett, and Alsek, "John Henryism and Blood Pressure Differences among Black Men," *Journal of Behavioral Medicine* 6: 259–78; Malavika A. Subramanyam et al. (2013), "Socioeconomic Status, John Henryism and Blood Pressure among African-Americans in the Jackson Heart Study," *Social Science & Medicine* 93: 139–46.

8. W.W. Dressler, J. R. Bandon, and Y. H. Naggers (1998), "John Henryism, Gender, and Arterial Blood Pressure in an African American Community," *Psychosomatic Medicine* 60: 620–24; G. Nordby, Ø. Ekeberg, S. Knardahl, and I. Os (1995), "A Double-Blind Study of Psychosocial Factors in 40-Year-Old Women with Essential Hypertension," *Psychotherapy and Psychosomatics* 63: 142–50; L. I. Somova, K. Diarra and T. Q. Jacobs (1995), "Psychophysiological Study of Hypertension in Black, Indian and White African Students," *Stress and Health* 11: 105–11.

9. L. B. Wright et al. (1996), "Relationship of John Henryism to Cardiovascular Functioning at Rest and during Stress in Youth," *Annals of Behavioral Medicine* 18: 146–50; K. C. Light et al. (1995), "Job Status and High-Effort Coping Influence Work Blood Pressure in Women and Blacks," *Hypertension* 25: 554–59.

10. D. E. Bild et al. (1993), "Physical Activity in Young Black and White Women the CARDIA Study," *Annals of Epidemiology* 3: 636–44; V. L. Bonham, S. L. Sellers, H. W. and Neighbors (2004), "John Henryism and Self-Reported Physical Health among High–Socioeconomic Status African American Men." *American Journal of Public Health* 94: 737–38.

11. W. H. Wiist and J. M. Flack (1992), "A Test of the John Henryism Hypothesis: Cholesterol and Blood Pressure," *Journal of Behavioral Medicine* 15: 15–29.

12. Neighbors, Njai, and Jackson (2007), "Race, Ethnicity, John Henryism, and Depressive Symptoms: The National Survey of American Life Adult Re-Interview," *Research in Human Development* 4: 71–87; D. D. Matthews et al. (2013), "Racial Discrimination and Depressive Symptoms among African-American Men: The Mediating and Moderating Roles of Masculine Self-Reliance and John Henryism," *Psychology of Men & Masculinity* 14: 35; E. C. Bronder et al. (2014), "John Henryism, Depression, and Perceived Social Support in Black Women," *Journal of Black Psychology* 40: 115–37; D. L. Hudson et al. (2016), "Racial Discrimination, John Henryism, and Depression among African Americans," *Journal of Black Psychology* 42: 221–43.

13. A. F. Fernander et al. (2005), "Exploring the Association of John Henry Active Coping and Education on Smoking Behavior and Nicotine Dependence among Blacks in the USA," *Social Science & Medicine* 60: 491–500.

14. S. A. James et al. (1987), "Socioeconomic Status, John Henryism, and Hypertension in Blacks and Whites," *American Journal of Epidemiology* 126 (4): 664–73.

15. M. M. Merritt, T. J. McCallum, and T. Fritsch (2011), "How Much Striving Is Too Much? John Henryism Active Coping Predicts Worse Daily Cortisol Responses for African American but Not White Female Dementia Family Caregivers," *American Journal of Geriatric Psychiatry* 19(5): 451–60.

16. S. A. James (1994), "John Henryism and the Health of African Americans," *Culture, Medicine, and Psychiatry* 18: 163–82.

17. S. A. James (1994), "John Henryism and the Health of African Americans," *Culture, Medicine, and Psychiatry* 18: 163–82; K. Vedhara et al. (2007), "Erratum to 'Psychosocial Factors Associated with Indices of Cortisol Production in Women with Breast Cancer and Controls,'" *Psychoneuroendocrinology* 31: 299–311; W. W. Dressler, J. R. Bindon, and Y. H. Neggers (1998), "John Henryism, Gender, and Arterial Blood Pressure in an African American Community," *Psychosomatic Medicine* 60 (5): 620–24; M. Ford et al. (2000), "Assessing the Reliability of Four Standard Health Measures in a Sample of Older, Urban Adults," *Research on Aging* 22: 774–96.

18. A. F. Fernander et al. (2003), "Assessing the Reliability and Validity of the John Henry Active Coping Scale in an Urban Sample of African Americans and White Americans," *Ethnicity and Health* 8 (2): 147–61.

19. An overview of previous research using JHAC is provided in chapter 2.

20. We are using the restricted data set from ICPSR.

21. D. Hudson et al. (2012), "The Relationship between Socioeconomic Position and Depression among a US Nationally Representative Sample of African Americans," *Social Psychiatry and Psychiatric Epidemiology* 47: 373–81.

22. J. Jackson et al. (2004), "The National Survey of American Life: A Study of Racial, Ethnic and Cultural Influences on Mental Disorders and Mental Health," *International Journal of Methods in Psychiatric Research* 13: 199.

23. R. Njai (2008), "Examining the Measurement of Race and Ethnicity to Inform a Model of Sociocultural Stress and Adaptive Coping," diss., University of Michigan, 117.

24. Jackson et al., "National Survey of American Life," 196.

25. For a detailed discussion regarding NSAL sampling methodology and procedures, see S. Heeringa et al. (2006), "Sample Designs and Sampling Methods for the Collaborative Psychiatric Epidemiology Studies (CPES)," *International Journal of Methods in Psychiatric Research* 13: 221–40. For a similar usage, see Candis Watts-Smith (2014), *Black Mosaic: The Politics of Black Pan-Ethnic Diversity*, New York: NYU Press.

26. S. A. James (1994), "John Henryism and the Health of African Americans," *Culture, Medicine, and Psychiatry* 18: 163–82.

27. Michael Dawson (2001), *Black Vision: The Roots of Contemporary African-American Political Ideologies*, Chicago: University of Chicago Press.

28. R. M. Sellers et al. (1997), "The Multidimensional Inventory of Black Identity: Construct Validity and Reliability," *Journal of Social and Personality Psychology* 73: 805–15.

29. Sellers et al. (1997), "The Multidimensional Inventory of Black Identity," 23.

30. H. E. Hunte and A. E. Barry (2012), "Perceived Discrimination and DSM-IV–Based Alcohol and Illicit Drug Use Disorders," *American Journal of Public Health* 102 (12): e111–e117.

31. D. W. Sue et al. (2007), "Racial Microaggressions in Everyday Life: Implications for Clinical Practice," *American Psychologist* 62 (4): 271.

32. R. C. Kessler, K. D. Mickelson, and D. R. Williams (1999), "The Prevalence, Distribution, and Mental Health Correlates of Perceived Discrimination in the United States," *Journal of Health and Social Behavior*, 208–30.

33. R. C. Kessler, K. D. Mickelson, and D. R. Williams (1999), "The Prevalence, Distribution, and Mental Health Correlates of Perceived Discrimination in the United States," *Journal of Health and Social Behavior*, 208–30.

34. Jim Sidanius and Felicia Pratto (1999), *Social Dominance: An Intergroup Theory of Social Hierarchy and Oppression*, Cambridge, UK: Cambridge University Press, 48.

35. See J. Long and J. Freese (2014), *Regression Models for Categorical and Dependent Variables Using Stata*, 3rd ed., College Station, TX: Stata Press.

Chapter 3

1. Jan Ransom (2020), "Amy Cooper Faces Charges after Calling Police on Black Bird-Watcher," *New York Times*.

2. Brian Price, Checkey Beckford, and Kiki Intarasuwan (2020), "Woman in Racial Central Park Confrontation Is Fired from Job, Gives up Dog," *NBC New York*.

3. Allie Yang (2020), "Christian Cooper Accepts Apology from Woman at Center of Central Park Confrontation," *ABC News*.

4. Price, Beckford, and Intarasuwan, "Woman in Racial Central Park Confrontation."

5. Tom Hays (2020), "White Woman Charged after Racist Central Park Confrontation," *Associated Press*.

6. Ransom, "Amy Cooper Faces Charges."

7. Price, Beckford, and Intarasuwan, "Woman in Racial Central Park Confrontation."

8. Hays, "White Woman Charged."

9. Ransom, "Amy Cooper Faces Charges."

10. Sarah Maslin Nir (2020), "The Bird Watcher, that Incident and His Feelings on the Woman's Fate," *New York Times*.

11. Bill de Blasio (2020), Twitter, https://twitter.com/nycmayor/status/1265 265665755230209?lang=en.

12. Janelle Griffith (2020), "NYC Officials Call for Police Probe of White Woman's 911 Call on Black Man in Central Park," *NBC News*.

13. Ray Sanchez and Elizabeth Joseph (2020), "Black Birdwatcher Christian Cooper Says Prosecuting Amy Cooper 'Lets White People Off the Hook,'" *CNN*.

14. Price, Beckford, and Intarasuwan, "Woman in Racial Central Park Confrontation."

15. Allie Yang (2020), "Christian Cooper Accepts Apology from Woman at Center of Central Park Confrontation," *ABC News*.

16. Helier Cheung (2020), "George Floyd Death: Why US Protests Are so Powerful This Time," *BBC News*.

17. Chauncey Alcorn (2020), "#BlackOutDay2020 Is Today: Here's What You Need to Know," *CNN*.

18. Joel Anderson (2020), "No Justice, No Football: The Only Way College Players Can Force Change Is to Boycott Games," *Slate*; Barrett Sallee (2020), "Kansas State Players Announce Boycott of Program in Wake of Offensive Social Media Post by Student," *CBS*.

19. Alex Hern (2020), "Facebook to Be Hit by Its Largest Ever Advertiser Boycott over Racism," *Guardian*; Rachel Hosie (2020), "The World's Top Crossfit Athletes Are Boycotting the Sport Following the CEO's Insensitive Comments on George Floyd," *Insider*.

20. Richard Y. Bourhis (2020), "A Journey Researching Prejudice and Discrimination," *Canadian Psychology/Psychologie Canadienne*, CPA Awards and Convention Keynotes/Prix de la SCP et allocutions au Congrés 61 (2): 95–100; Yin Paradies et al. (2015), "Racism as a Determinant of Health: A Systematic Review and Meta-Analysis," *PLoS ONE* 10 (9): e0138511.

21. Jas M. Sullivan (2020), "Does Region Matter on African Americans' Reaction to Discrimination? An Exploratory Study," in L. Martin (ed.), *Introduction to Africana Demography*, Boston, MA: Brill, 3; Philomena Essed (1991), *Understanding Everyday Racism: An Interdisciplinary Theory*, Newbury Park, CA: Sage; Philomena Essed (2002), "Everyday Racism," in D. T. Goldberg and J. Solomos (eds.), *A Companion to Racial and Ethnic Studies*, Malden, MA: Blackwell, 202–17; Ryan C. T. Delapp and Monnica T. Williams (2015), "Professional Challenges Facing African American Psychologists: The Presence and Impact of Racial Microaggressions," *Behavior Therapist* 38 (4): 101–5; Jason A. Nier and Samuel L. Gaertner (2012), "The Challenge of Detecting Contemporary Forms of Discrimination," *Journal of Social Issues* 68 (2): 207–20; Derald Wing Sue (2010), *Microaggressions in Everyday Life: Race, Gender, and Sexual Orientation*, New Jersey: John Wiley.

22. Bourhis, "A Journey Researching Prejudice."

23. Robert T. Carter et al. (2017), "Racial Discrimination and Health Outcomes among Racial/Ethnic Minorities: A Meta-Analytic Review," *Journal of Multicultural Counseling and Development* 45 (4): 232–59.

24. Carter et al., "Racial Discrimination and Health Outcomes," 233; Rodney Clark et al. (1999), "Racism as a Stressor for African Americans: A Biopsychosocial Model," *American Psychologist* 54 (10): 805–16.

25. Nier and Gaertner, "The Challenges of Detecting Contemporary Forms"; Heather R. Farmer, Linda A. Wray, and Jason R. Thomas (2019), "Do Race and Everyday Discrimination Predict Mortality Risk? Evidence from the Health and Retirement Study," *Gerontology and Geriatric Medicine* 5 (June); Paradies et al., "Racism as a Determinant of Health"; Sullivan, "Does Region Matter"; Natalie N. Watson-Singleton et al. (2020), "Racism's Effect on Depressive Symptoms: Examining Perseverative Cognition and Black Lives Matter Activism as Moderators," *Journal of Counseling Psychology* (April).

26. Carter et al., "Racial Discrimination and Health Outcomes"; Farmer et al., "Do Race and Everyday Discrimination Predict?"; Frederick X. Gibbons et al. (2010), "Exploring the Link between Racial Discrimination and Substance Use: What Mediates? What Buffers?" *Journal of Personality & Social Psychology* 99 (5): 785; Nancy Krieger et al. (1993), "Racism, Sexism, and Social Class: Implications for Studies of Health, Disease, and Well-Being," *American Journal of Preventive Medicine* 9 (6, Suppl): 82–122; Nancy Krieger and Stephen Sidney (1996), "Racial Discrimination and Blood Pressure: The CARDIA Study of Young Black and White Adults," *American Journal of Public Health* 96 (10): 1370–78; Nier and Gaertner, "The Challenges of Detecting Contemporary Forms"; Paradies et al., "Racism as a Determinant of Health"; David R. Williams, Risa Lavizzo-Mourey, and Rueben C. Warren (1994), "The Concept of Race and Health Status in America," *Public Health Reports* 109 (1): 26–41; Watson-Singleton et al. (2020), "Racism's Effect on Depressive Symptoms."

27. Robert T. Carter (2007), "Racism and Psychological and Emotional Injury: Recognizing and Assessing Race-Based Traumatic Stress," *Counseling Psychologist* 35 (1): 13–105; Alexander R. Green et al. (2007), "Implicit Bias among Physicians and Its Prediction of Thrombolysis Decisions for Black and White Patients," *Journal of General Internal Medicine* 22 (9): 1231–38; Sullivan, "Does Region Matter?"

28. Jeroan Allison et al. (1996). "Racial Differences in the Medical Treatment of Elderly Medicare Patients with Acute Myocardial Infarction," *Journal of General Internal Medicine* 11 (12): 736–43; Luisa Borrell et al. (2007), "Self-Reported Racial Discrimination and Substance Use in the Coronary Artery Risk Development in Adults Study," *American Journal of Epidemiology* 166 (9): 1068–79; David H. Chae et al. (2010), "Do Experiences of Racial Discrimination Predict Cardiovascular Disease among African American Men? The Moderating Role of Internalized Negative Racial Group Attitudes." *Social Science & Medicine* 71 (6): 1182–88; Ann Ashley Dondanville and Patrick Pössel (2019), "The Impact of Cognitive Styles and Depressive Symptoms on the Relation between Perceived Everyday Discrimination and Blood Pressure in Adolescents," Psychological Science to Reduce and Prevent Health Disparities, *Translational Issues in Psychological Science* 5 (4): 335–45; Bridget Goosby et al. (2015), "Perceived Discrimination and Markers of Cardiovascular Risk among Low-Income African American Youth," *American Journal of Human Biology* 27 (4): 546–52; Green et al., "Implicit Bias among Physicians"; Nancy R. Kressin and

Laura A. Petersen (2001), "Racial Differences in the Use of Invasive Cardiovascular Procedures: Review of the Literature and Prescription for Future Research," *Annals of Internal Medicine* 135 (5): 352–66; Nancy Krieger et al. (2013), "Racial Discrimination & Cardiovascular Disease Risk: My Body My Story Study of 1005 US-Born Black and White Community Health Center Participants (US)," *PLoS ONE* 8 (10): 1–15; Sullivan, "Does Region Matter?"; Tomoko Udo and Carlos M. Grilo (2017), "Cardiovascular Disease and Perceived Weight, Racial, and Gender Discrimination in U.S. Adults," *Journal of Psychosomatic Research* 100 (September): 83–88.

29. Chae et al., "Do Experiences of Racial Discrimination Predict?"

30. Samaah Sullivan et al. (2019), "An Investigation of Racial/Ethnic and Sex Differences in the Association between Experiences of Everyday Discrimination and Leukocyte Telomere Length among Patients with Coronary Artery Disease," *Psychoneuroendocrinology* 106 (August): 122–28.

31. Krieger et al., "Racism, Sexism, and Social Class."

32. Krieger et al., "Racism, Sexism, and Social Class."

33. Borrell et al., "Self-Reported Racial Discrimination and Substance Use"; Dondanville and Pössel, "The Impact of Cognitive Styles"; Goosby et al., "Perceived Discrimination and Markers"; Saffron Karlsen and James Y. Nazroo (2002), "Relation between Racial Discrimination, Social Class, and Health among Ethnic Minority Groups," *American Journal of Public Health* 92 (4): 624–31; Krieger and Sidney, "Racial Discrimination and Blood Pressure."

34. Dondanville and Pössel, "The Impact of Cognitive Styles"; Devon English, Sharon F. Lambert, and Nicholas S. Ialongo (2014), "Longitudinal Associations between Experienced Racial Discrimination and Depressive Symptoms in African American Adolescents," *Developmental Psychology* 50 (4): 1190–96; Lauren Hayes, Patrick Pössel, and Sarah J. Roane (2019), "Perceived Everyday Discrimination and Depressive Symptoms: Does Cognitive Style Mediate?" *Journal of Counseling & Development* 97 (4): 427–36; Akiko S. Hosler, Jamie R. Kammer, and Xiao Cong (2019), "Everyday Discrimination Experience and Depressive Symptoms in Urban Black, Guyanese, Hispanic, and White Adults," *Journal of the American Psychiatric Nurses Association* 25 (6): 445–52; Karlsen and Nazroo (2002), "Relation between Racial Discrimination"; Watson-Singleton et al., "Racism's Effect on Depressive Symptoms"; Larrell L. Wilkinson et al. (2020), "The Association of Emotional and Physical Reactions to Perceived Discrimination with Depressive Symptoms among African American Men in the Southeast," *International Journal of Environmental Research and Public Health* 17 (1): 322.

35. Anton Hart (2019), "The Discriminatory Gesture: A Psychoanalytic Consideration of Posttraumatic Reactions to Incidents of Racial Discrimination," *Psychoanalytic Social Work* 26 (1): 5–24; James M. Henson et al. (2013), "African American Students' Responses to Racial Discrimination: How Race-Based Rejection Sensitivity and Social Constraints Are Related to Psychological Reactions," *Journal of Social & Clinical Psychology* 32 (5): 504–29; Paradies et al., "Racism as a Determinant

of Health"; Watson-Singleton et al., "Racism's Effect on Depressive Symptoms."

36. Borrell et al., "Self-Reported Racial Discrimination and Substance Use"; Karlsen and Nazroo, "Relation between Racial Discrimination"; Watson-Singleton et al., "Racism's Effect on Depressive Symptoms."

37. Borrell et al., "Self-Reported Racial Discrimination"; Carter et al., "Racial Discrimination and Health Outcomes"; Meg Gerrard et al. (2012), "Coping with Racial Discrimination: The Role of Substance Use," *Psychology of Addictive Behaviors* 26 (3): 550; Gibbons et al., "Exploring the Link"; Haslyn E. R. Hunte and Adam E. Barry (2012), "Perceived Discrimination and DSM-IV–Based Alcohol and Illicit Drug Use Disorders," *American Journal of Public Health* 102 (12): e111–e17; Sullivan, "Does Region Matter?"

38. Bourhis, "A Journey Researching Prejudice"; Karlsen and Nazroo, "Relation between Racial Discrimination"; Nier and Gaertner, "The Challenge of Detecting"; Sullivan, "Does Region Matter?"

39. Krieger and Sidney, "Racial Discrimination and Blood Pressure."

40. Krieger and Sidney, "Racial Discrimination and Blood Pressure."

41. Marc Benedick Jr., Charles W. Jackson, and Victor A. Reinoso (1994), "Measuring Employment Discrimination through Controlled Experiments," *Review of Black Political Economy* 23 (1): 25–48; Devah Pager and Bruce Western (2012), "Identifying Discrimination at Work: The Use of Field Experiments," *Journal of Social Issues* 68 (2): 221–37; Sullivan, "Does Region Matter?"

42. Lincoln Quillian, John J. Lee, and Brandon Honore (2020), "Racial Discrimination in the U.S. Housing and Mortgage Lending Markets: A Quantitative Review of Trends, 1976–2016," *Race and Social Problems* 12: 13–28.

43. Tabbye M. Chavous et al. (2008), "Gender Matters, Too: The Influences of School Racial Discrimination and Racial Identity on Academic Engagement Outcomes among African American Adolescents," *Developmental Psychology* 44 (3): 637–54; Krieger and Sidney (1996), "Racial Discrimination and Blood Pressure"; Sullivan, "Does Region Matter?"

44. Chavous et al., "Gender Matters, Too."

45. Nier and Gaertner, "The Challenge of Detecting"; Melody S. Sadler et al. (2012), "The World Is Not Black and White: Racial Bias in the Decision to Shoot in a Multiethnic Context," *Journal of Social Issues* 68 (2): 286–313; Sullivan, "Does Region Matter?"

46. Joshua Correll et al. (2002), "The Police Officer's Dilemma: Using Ethnicity to Disambiguate Potentially Threatening Individuals," *Journal of Personality and Social Psychology* 83 (6): 1314–29.

47. Sadler et al., "The World Is Not Black and White," 290; Correll et al., "The Police Officer's Dilemma."

48. E. Ashby Plant and B. Michelle Peruche (2005), "The Consequences of Race for Police Officers' Responses to Criminal Suspects," *Psychological Science* 16 (3): 180–83.

49. Sadler et al., "The World Is Not Black and White"; Plant and Peruche, "The Consequences of Race for Police."

50. Sadler et al., "The World Is Not Black and White."

51. Sadler et al., "The World Is Not Black and White," 306.

52. Sadler et al., "The World Is Not Black and White."

53. For example, Krieger and Sidney, "Racial Discrimination and Blood Pressure."

54. For example, Robert T. Carter and Jessica Forsyth (2010), "Reactions to Racial Discrimination: Emotional Stress and Help-Seeking Behaviors," *Psychological Trauma: Theory, Research, Practice, and Policy* 2 (3): 183–91; Henson et al. (2013), "African American Students' Responses."

55. For example, Sullivan "Does Region Matter?"

56. For example, Hart (2019), "The Discriminatory Gesture."

57. Krieger and Sidney (1996), "Racial Discrimination and Blood Pressure," 1374.

58. Krieger and Sidney (1996), "Racial Discrimination and Blood Pressure."

59. Meg Gerrard et al. (2018), "Moderation of the Effects of Discrimination-Induced Affective Responses on Health Outcomes," *Psychology & Health* 33 (2): 193–212.

60. Gerrard et al. (2018), "Moderation of the Effects," 207.

61. Gerrard et al., "Moderation of the Effects."

62. Gerrard et al., "Moderation of the Effects."

63. Carter and Forsyth, "Reactions to Racial Discrimination."

64. Carter and Forsyth, "Reactions to Racial Discrimination."

65. Carter and Forsyth, "Reactions to Racial Discrimination."

66. Carter and Forsyth, "Reactions to Racial Discrimination," 189.

67. Carter and Forsyth, "Reactions to Racial Discrimination."

68. Henson et al., "African American Students' Responses."

69. Henson et al., "African American Students' Responses," 520.

70. Henson et al. (2013). "African American Students' Responses to Racial Discrimination."

71. Henson et al., "African American Students' Responses."

72. Sullivan, "Does Region Matter?"

73. Sullivan, "Does Region Matter?"

74. Sullivan, "Does Region Matter?"

75. Carter and Forsyth, "Reactions to Racial Discrimination."

76. Krieger and Sidney, "Racial Discrimination and Blood Pressure."

77. Sullivan, "Does Region Matter?"

78. Krieger and Sidney, "Racial Discrimination and Blood Pressure."

79. Krieger and Sidney, "Racial Discrimination and Blood Pressure."

80. Chae et al., "Do Experiences of Racial Discrimination Predict?"

81. Carter and Forsyth, "Reactions to Racial Discrimination."

82. Clark et al., "Racism as a Stressor."

83. Carter and Forsyth, "Reactions to Racial Discrimination"; Hart, "The Discriminatory Gesture."

Chapter 4

1. Darryl Dickson-Carr (2005), "Black Nationalism," *The Columbia Guide to Contemporary African American Fiction*, New York: Columbia University Press, 54.

2. David H. Demo and Michael Hughes (1990), "Socialization and Racial Identity among Black Americans," *Social Psychology Quarterly* 53 (4): 367.

3. Darryl Dickson-Carr "Black Nationalism," 54.

4. Duchess Harris (2018), *Black Lives Matter*, Minneapolis, MN: Abdo.

5. Harris, *Black Lives Matter*.

6. Kay Lim (2020), "Alicia Garza on the Origin of Black Lives Matter," *CBS News*.

7. Larry Buchanan, Quoctrung Bui, and Jugal K. Patel (2020), "Black Lives Matter May Be the Largest Movement in U.S. History," *New York Times*.

8. Fabiola Cineas (2020), "Black Lives Matter Activists Plan to Organize Even Harder after the Election—No Matter Who Wins," *Vox*.

9. Anthonia Akitunde (2019), "Buying Black, Rebooted," *New York Times*.

10. Felicia Craddock (2020), "Black-Owned Watch Brands Rising," *New York Times*.

11. Simon Hall (2011), *American Patriotism, American Protest: Social Movements since the Sixties*, Philadelphia: University of Pennsylvania Press.

12. ACLED (2020), "US Crisis Monitor Releases Full Data for Summer 2020," Accessed online at https://acleddata.com/acleddatanew/wp-content/uploads/2020/08/ACLED_US-Crisis-Monitor-Summer-2020_Overview.pdf; Sanya Mansoor (2020), "93% of Black Lives Matter Protests Have Been Peaceful, New Report Finds," *Time*.

13. Hall *American Patriotism, American Protest*, 9.

14. Jennifer Wolak and David A. M. Peterson (2020), "The Dynamic American Dream," *American Journal of Political Science* 64 (4): 968.

15. Joslyn Armstrong et al. (2019), "'A Dream Deferred': How Discrimination Impacts the American Dream Achievement for African Americans," *Journal of Black Studies* 50 (3): 228; S. L. Hanson and J. Zogby (2010), "The Polls-Trends: Attitudes about the American Dream," *Public Opinion Quarterly* 74: 570–84; S. Hanson and J. White (2011), *The American Dream in the 21st Century*, Philadelphia, PA: Temple University Press; R. C. Hauhart (2015), "American Sociology's Investigations of the American Dream: Retrospect and Prospect," *American Sociology* 46: 65–98; N. O. A. Kwate and I. H. Meyer (2010), "The Myth of Meritocracy and African American Health," *American Journal of Public Health* 100: 1831–34.

16. Vence L. Bonham, Sherrill L. Sellers, and Harold W. Neighbors (2004), "John Henryism and Self-Reported Physical Health among High-Socioeconomic Status African American Men," *American Journal of Public Health* 94 (5): 737; Ellen C. Bronder et al. (2014), "John Henryism, Depression, and Perceived Social Support in Black Women," *Journal of Black Psychology* 40 (2): 115–37; Sherman A. James et al. (1984), "John Henryism and Blood Pressure Differences among Black Men, II: The Role of Occupational Stressors," *Journal of Behavioral Medicine* 7 (3): 259–75.

17. Wolak and Peterson, "The Dynamic American Dream."

18. Wolak and Peterson, "The Dynamic American Dream," 970; Sandra L. Hanson (2011), "Whose Dream? Gender and the American Dream," in *The American Dream in the 21st Century*, ed. Sandra L. Hanson and John Kenneth White, Philadelphia, PA: Temple University Press, 77–104; Jennifer L. Hochschild (1995), *Facing Up to the American Dream: Race, Class, and the Soul of the Nation*, Princeton, NJ: Princeton University Press; Matt Vasilogambros (2016), "The Ethnic Groups that Still Believe in the American Dream," *The Atlantic.*

19. Armstrong et al., " 'A Dream Deferred': How Discrimination Impacts"; Hanson and Zogby, "The Polls-Trends: Attitudes about the American Dream"; Wolak and Peterson, "The Dynamic American Dream."

20. Armstrong et al., " 'A Dream Deferred': How Discrimination Impacts."

21. Armstrong et al., " 'A Dream Deferred': How Discrimination Impacts."

22. Armstrong et al., " 'A Dream Deferred': How Discrimination Impacts"; Wolak and Peterson, "The Dynamic American Dream."

23. Armstrong et al., " 'A Dream Deferred.' "

24. Wolak and Peterson, "The Dynamic American Dream."

25. Lazarus and Folkman, *Stress, Appraisal, and Coping*; Penley, Tomaka, and Wiebe, "The Association of Coping."

26. Bonham, Sellers, and Neighbors, "John Henryism and Self-Reported Physical Health," 737; Bronder et al., "John Henryism, Depression, and Perceived Social Support"; James et al., "John Henryism and Blood Pressure Differences, II."

27. Sherman A. James (1994), "John Henryism and the Health of African-Americans," *Culture, Medicine and Psychiatry* 18: 169; Gary G. Bennett et al. (2004), "Stress, Coping, and Health Outcomes among African-Americans: A Review of the John Henryism Hypothesis," *Psychology and Health* 19 (3): 369–83.

28. John Mirowsky and Catherine E. Ross (2003), *Social Causes of Psychological Distress*, 2nd ed., Hawthorne, NY: Aldine De Gruyter.

29. For example, see James, "John Henryism and the Health."

30. Demo and Hughes, "Socialization and Racial Identity," 367.

31. This scale was similar to that used in other studies, including Richard L. Allen and Shirley Hatchett (1986), "The Media and Social Reality Effects: Self and System Orientations of Blacks," *Communication Research* 13: 97–123; and Richard L. Allen, Michael C. Dawson, and Ronald E. Brown (1989), "A Schema-Based

Approach to Modeling an African-American Racial Belief System," *American Political Science Review* 83: 421–41. However, we have left out the two questions regarding dating, because they correlated strongly, as found in Demo and Hughes's 1990 study.

32. W. E. B. Du Bois [1934] (1996), "The Board of Directors on Segregation," in Cary D. Wintz, ed. *African American Political Thought, 1890–1930*, New York: M. E. Sharpe.

33. Elijah Muhammad (1965), *Message to the Black Man in America*, Chicago, IL: Muhammad's Temple of Islam No. 2.

34. M. Garvey [1923] (1996), "The Negro's Greatest Enemy," in Cary D. Wintz, ed., *African-American Political Thought, 1890–1930*, New York: M. E. Sharpe.

35. Hanes Walton (1972), *Black Political Parties: An Historical and Political Analysis*, New York: The Free Press, 199.

36. Hanes Walton (1972), *Black Political Parties: An Historical and Political Analysis*, New York: The Free Press, 200.

37. Willie Legette (2000), "The South Carolina Legislative Black Caucus, 1970 to 1988," *Journal of Black Studies* 30: 839–58.

38. R. Brown R. and Todd Shaw (2002), "Separate Nations: Two Attitudinal Dimensions of Black Nationalism," *Journal of Politics* 64: 22–44; Michael Dawson (2001), *Black Vision: The Roots of Contemporary African American Political Ideologies*, Chicago, IL: University of Chicago Press; D. W. Davis and R. E. Brown (2002), "The Antipathy of Black Nationalism: Behavioral and Attitudinal Implications of an African American Ideology," *American Journal of Political Science*, 46 (2): 239–52.

39. Brown and Shaw (2002), "Separate Nations: Two Attitudinal Dimensions"; Davis and Brown, "The Antipathy of Black Nationalism.

40. Brown and Shaw (2002), "Separate Nations: Two Attitudinal Dimensions."

41. Hochschild, *Facing Up to the American Dream*.

42. M. Dawson (1994). *Behind the Mule: Race and Class in African American Politics*. Princeton, NJ: Princeton University Press.

43. Brown and Shaw (2002), "Separate Nations: Two Attitudinal Dimensions."

44. Allen, Dawson, and Brown (1989), "A Schema-Based Approach to Modeling."

45. L. A. Reese, R. E. Brown, and J. D. Ivers (2007), "Some Children See Him . . . : Political Participation and the Black Christ," *Political Behavior* 29 (4): 517–37.

46. C. G. Ellison (1991), "Identification and Separatism: Religious Involvement and Racial Orientations among Black Americans," *Sociological Quarterly* 32 (3): 477–94.

47. R. Allen, M. Dawson, and R. Brown (1989), "A Schema-Based Approach to Modeling an African American Racial Belief System," *American Political Science Review* 83: 421–41; M. Dawson (2001), *Black Vision: The Roots of Contemporary African American Political Ideologies*, Chicago, IL: University of Chicago Press.

48. R. Block Jr. (2011), "What about Disillusionment? Exploring the Pathways to Black Nationalism," *Political Behavior* 33: 27–51.

49. Brown and Shaw (2002), "Separate Nations: Two Attitudinal Dimensions"; Dawson (2001), *Black Vision: The Roots* R. C. Smith (1996), *We Have No Leaders: African Americans in the Post-Civil Rights Era*, Albany: State University of New York Press.

50. J. M. Sullivan, J. Winburn, and W. E. Cross Jr. (2018), *Dimensions of Blackness: Racial Identity and Political Beliefs*, State University of New York Press.

51. Bart Bonikowski and Paul DiMaggio (2016), "Varieties of American Popular Nationalism," *American Sociological Review* 81 (5): 949–80; Kristin Hanson and Emma O'Dwyer (2019), "Patriotism and Nationalism, Left and Right: A Q-Methodology Study of American National Identity," *Political Ideology* 40 (4): 777–96; Deborah J. Schildkraut (2014), "Boundaries of American Identity: Evolving Understandings of 'Us,'" *Annual Review of Political Science* 17: 441–60; Elizabeth Theiss-Morse (2009), *Who Counts as an American? The Boundaries of National Identity*, Cambridge, UK: Cambridge University Press.

52. Hanson and O'Dwyer, "Patriotism and Nationalism, Left and Right," 779.

53. Rui J. P. De Figueiredo and Zachary Elkins (2003), "Are Patriots Bigots? An Inquiry into the Vices of Ingroup Pride," *American Journal of Political Science* 47 (1): 171–88.

54. Hanson and O'Dwyer, "Patriotism and Nationalism, Left and Right."

55. Hanson and O'Dwyer, "Patriotism and Nationalism, Left and Right," 779.

56. De Figueiredo and Elkins, "Are Patriots Bigots?," 175.

57. Gayle Porter (2010), "Work Ethic and Ethical Work: Distortions in the American Dream," *Journal of Business Ethics* 96: 535–50; Wolak and Peterson, "The Dynamic American Dream."

58. Wolak and Peterson. "The Dynamic American Dream"; Sandra L. Hanson (2011), "Whose Dream? Gender and the American Dream," in *The American Dream in the 21st Century*, ed. Sandra L. Hanson and John Kenneth White, Philadelphia, PA: Temple University Press, 77–104; Hochschild, *Facing Up to the American Dream*; Matt Vasilogambros, "Ethnic Groups that Still Believe."

59. Hanson and Zogby, "The Polls-Trends: Attitudes about the American Dream," 572–73.

60. Wolak and Peterson, "The Dynamic American Dream."

61. Hanson and Zogby, "The Polls-Trends: Attitudes about the American Dream," 581.

62. Bonham, Sellers, and Neighbors, "John Henryism and Self-Reported Physical Health," 737–38; Bronder, Speight, Witherspoon, and Thomas, "John Henryism, Depression, and Perceived Social Support"; James et al. "John Henryism and Blood Pressure Differences, II."

63. Pamela J. Conover and Stanley Feldman (1987), "Memo to NES Board of Overseers Regarding 'Measuring Patriotism and Nationalism.'"

64. Bonikowski and DiMaggio, "Varieties of American Popular Nationalism."

65. Bonikowski and DiMaggio, "Varieties of American Popular Nationalism," 959.

66. Hanson and O'Dwyer, "Patriotism and Nationalism, Left and Right," 778; Michael Billig (1995), *Banal Nationalism*, Thousand Oaks, CA: Sage; Huddy, Leonie, and Nadia Khatib (2007). "American Patriotism, National Identity, and Political Involvement," *American Journal of Political Science* 51 (1): 63–77; Rick Kosterman and Seymour Feshbach (1989), "Toward a Measure of Patriotic and Nationalistic Attitudes," *Political Psychology* 29 (6): 859–79.

67. Hanson and O'Dwyer (2019), "Patriotism and Nationalism, Left and Right," 778; Huddy and Khatib (2007).

68. Huddy and Khatib, "American Patriotism, National Identity," 71.

69. James, "John Henryism and the Health."

70. Huddy and Khatib, "American Patriotism, National Identity," 64.

71. Elizabeth A. LeCuyer and Dena Phillips Swanson (2017), "A Within-Group Analysis of African American Mothers' Authoritarian Attitudes, Limit-Setting and Children's Self-Regulation," *Journal of Child and Family Studies* 26: 833–42; Veronica Smith (2020), "African American Authoritarianism, Child Rearing Beliefs and Academic Outcomes: A Qualitative Ethnography," Northcentral University ProQuest Dissertations Publishing (27735916), https://www-proquest-com.libezp.lib.lsu.edu/docview/2354894825?accountid=12154.

72. LeCuyer and Swanson, "A Within-Group Analysis."

73. H.-J. Cha and H.-S. Cho (2016), "An Exploratory Study on the Factors of Parental Rearing Behavior Based on Vygotsky's Theory of Social Constructivism for Developing Convergence Digital Contents," *Journal of Digital Convergence* 14 (3): 453–64.

74. L. S. Vygotsky (1978), *Mind in Society*, in M. Cole et al. (Eds.), *The Development of Higher Psychological Processes*. Cambridge, MA: MIT Press.

75. Smith, *African American Authoritarianism*, 23.

Chapter 5

1. Justin Worland (2020), "America's Long Overdue Awakening to Systemic Racism," *Time*.

2. Meryl Kornfield et al. (2020), "Huge, Peaceful Protests Mark Anti-Racism Demonstrations around the Globe," *Washington Post*.

3. Worland, "America's Long Overdue Awakening."

4. Worland, "America's Long Overdue Awakening."

5. Stephen Eide (2020), "Why New York's New 'Anti-Karen' Law Will Backfire," *New York Post*.

6. Jan Ransom (2020), "Amy Cooper Faces Charges after Calling Police on Black Bird-Watcher," *New York Times*.

7. Brian Price, Checkey Beckford and Kiki Intarasuwan (2020), "Woman in Racial Central Park Confrontation Is Fired from Job, Gives Up Dog," *NBC New York*.

8. Rebecca Rosenberg (2020), "Central Park 'Karen' Case: Details Of Previously Unheard Second 911 Call Revealed," *New York Post.*

9. Eide, "Why New York's New 'Anti-Karen' Law Will Backfire."

10. Worland, "America's Long Overdue Awakening."

11. Kim Hjelmgaard (2020), "Reparations Bill Gets New Attention Amid BLM: Could Other Nations Provide a Blueprint?," *USA Today.*

12. Jason E. Shelton and George Wilson (2009), "Race, Class, and the Basis of Group Alignment: An Analysis of Support for Redistributive Policy among Privileged Blacks," *Sociological Perspectives* 52: 385–408; Michael Dawson (1994), *Behind the Mule: Race and Class in African-American Politics*, Princeton, NJ: Princeton University Press; Franklin D. Gilliam and Kenny J. Whitby (1989), "Race, Class, and Attitudes toward Social Welfare Spending: An Ethclass Interpretation," *Social Science Quarterly* 70 (1): 89–99; Dennis Chong and Reuel Rogers (2005), "Racial Solidarity and Political Participation," *Political Behavior* 27: 347–74; Lee Sigelman and Susan Welch (1991), *Black Americans' Views of Racial Inequality: The Dream Deferred*, New York: Cambridge University Press; Lawrence Bobo and James R. Kluegel (1993), "Opposition to Race-Targeting: Self-Interest, Stratification Ideology, or Racial Attitudes?," *American Sociological Review* 58 (4): 443–64.

13. William Julius Wilson (1978), *The Declining Significance of Race*, Chicago, IL: University of Chicago Press.

14. E. Franklin Frazier (1957), *Black Bourgeoisie*, New York: The Free Press.

15. Frazier, *Black Bourgeoisie*, 126.

16. Dawson, *Behind the Mule.*

17. Dawson, *Behind the Mule*, 76.

18. Dawson, *Behind the Mule.*

19. Charles Jaret and Donald C. Reitzes (1999), "The Importance of Racial-Ethnic Identity and Social Setting for Blacks, Whites, and Multiracials," *Sociological Perspectives* 42 (4): 711–37; Dawson, *Behind the Mule*; Patricia Gurin, Shirley Hatchett, and James S. Jackson (1989), *Hope and Independence: Blacks' Response to Electoral Party Politics*, New York: Russell Sage; Katherine Tate (1993), *From Protest to Politics: The New Black Voters in American Elections*, Cambridge, MA: Harvard University Press; Mary Herring, Thomas B. Jankowski, and Ronald E. Brown (1999), "Pro-Black Doesn't Mean Anti-White: The Structure of African-American Group Identity," *Journal of Politics* 61 (2): 363–86; Clifford L. Broman, Harold W. Neighbors, and James S. Jackson (1988), "Racial Group Identification among Black Adults," *Social Forces* 67 (1): 146–58; Pamela J. Conover (1984), "The Influence of Group Identifications on Political Perception and Evaluation," *Journal of Politics* 46 (3): 760–85; Richard L. Allen and Shirley Hatchett (1986), "The Media and Social Reality Effects: Self and System Orientations of Blacks," *Communication Research* 13: 97–123; Richard L. Allen, Michael C. Dawson, and Ronald E. Brown (1989), "A Schema-Based Approach to Modeling an African-American Racial Belief System," *American Political Science Review* 83: 421–41; Judith R. Porter and Robert

E. Washington (1979), "Black Identity and Self-Esteem," *Annual Review of Sociology* 5: 53–74; Cheryl Grills and Douglas Longshore (1996), "Africentrism: Psychometric Analyses of a Self-Report Measure," *Journal of Black Psychology* 22: 86–106; Chong and Rogers, "Racial Solidarity and Political Participation"; Patricia Gurin, Arthur H. Miller, and Gerald Gurin (1980), "Stratum Identification and Consciousness," *Social Psychology Quarterly* 43: 30–47; Arthur H. Miller et al. (1981), "Group Consciousness and Political Participation," *American Journal of Political Science* 25: 494–511.

20. Tate, *From Protest to Politics*; Dawson, *Behind the Mule*; Michael Dawson (2001), *Black Vision: The Roots of Contemporary African-American Political Ideologies*, Chicago, IL: University of Chicago Press; Evelyn M. Simeon and Rosalee A. Clawson (2004), "The Intersection of Race and Gender: An Examination of Black Feminist Consciousness, Race Consciousness, and Policy Attitudes," *Social Science Quarterly* 85 (3): 793–810.

Byron D'Andra Orey et al. (2013), "Black Opposition to Welfare in the Age of Obama," *Race, Gender & Class* 20 (3/4): 114–29;Cardell K. Jacobson (1983), "Black Support for Affirmative Action," *Journal of Conflict Resolution* 29: 306–29; Ellis Cose (1993), *The Rage of a Privileged Class*, New York: HarperCollins; Jennifer Hochschild (1995), *Facing Up to the American Dream*, Princeton, NJ: Princeton University Press; Linda Lopez and Adrian D. Pantoja (2004), "Beyond Black and White: General Support for Race-Conscious Policies among African Americans, Latinos, Asian Americans, and Whites," *Political Research Quarterly* 57: 633–42.

21. Orey et al., "Black Opposition to Welfare."

22. Tate, *From Protest to Politics*; Dawson, *Behind the Mule*; Donald R. Kinder and Nicholas Winter (2001), "Exploring the Racial Divide: Blacks, Whites, and Opinion on National Policy," *American Journal of Political Science* 45: 439–56; Anke Schmermund et al. (2001), "Attitudes toward Affirmative Action as a Function of Racial Identity among African American College Students," *Political Psychology* 22: 759–74.

23. Tate, *From Protest to Politics*.

24. Michael C. Dawson and Rovana Popoff (2004), "Reparations: Justice and Greed in Black and White," *Du Bois Review* 1: 47–91.

25. Cardell K. Jacobson (1985), "Resistance to Affirmative Action," *Journal of Conflict Resolution* 29: 306–29; James R. Kluegel and Eliot R. Smith (1983), "Affirmative Action Attitudes: Effects of Self-Interest, Racial Affect, and Stratification Beliefs on Whites' Views," *Social Forces* 61: 797–824; David Kravitz and Stephen Klineberg (2000), "Reactions to Two Versions of Affirmative Action among Whites, Blacks, and Hispanics," *Journal of Applied Psychology* 85: 597–611; David Kravitz et al. (2006), "Attitudes toward Affirmative Action: Correlations with Demographic Variables and with Beliefs about Targets, Actions, and Economic Effects," *Journal of Applied Social Psychology* 30: 1109–36; David A. Harrison et al. (2006), "Understanding Attitudes toward Affirmative Action Programs in Employment: Summary and Meta-Analysis of 35 Years of Research." *Journal of Applied Psychology* 91 (5): 1013–36.

26. Harold W. Neighbors, Rashid Njai, and James S. Jackson (2007), "Race, Ethnicity, John Henryism, and Depressive Symptoms: The National Survey of American Life Adult Reinterview," *Research in Human Development* 4: 71–87.

27. Sherman A. James (1994), "John Henryism and the Health of African Americans," *Culture, Medicine, and Psychiatry* 18: 163–82; Michael V. Stanton et al. (2010), "Socioeconomic Status Moderates the Association between John Henryism and NEO PI-R Personality Domains," *Psychosomatic Medicine* 72 (2): 141; Gene H. Brody et al. (2013), "Is Resilience Only Skin Deep? Rural African Americans' Socioeconomic Status-Related Risk and Competence in Preadolescence and Psychological Adjustment and Allostatic Load at Age 19," *Psychological Science* 24 (7): 1285–93.

28. *Thornburg v. Gingles*, 478 U.S. 30. (1986).

29. David Butler and Bruce E. Cain (1992), *Congressional Redistricting: Comparative and Theoretical Perspectives*, New York: Macmillan, 36.

Chapter 6

1. BBC News (2020), "George Floyd: What Happened in the Final Moments of His Life," *BBC News*; Meryl Kornfield et al. (2020), "Huge, Peaceful Protests Mark Anti-racism Demonstrations around the Globe," *Washington Post*; Helier Cheung (2020), "George Floyd Death: Why US Protests Are so Powerful This Time," *BBC News*.

2. Cheung, "George Floyd Death."

3. Cheung, "George Floyd Death."

4. Pam Ramsden (2020), "How the Pandemic Changed Social Media and George Floyd's Death Created a Collective Conscience," *The Conversation*.

5. Cheung "George Floyd Death."

6. Anthonia Akitunde (2019), "Buying Black, Rebooted," *New York Times*.

7. Nielsen Company (2019), "Diverse Intelligence Series 2019. It's in the Bag: Black Consumers' Path to Purchase," accessed online at https://www.nielsen.com/wp-content/uploads/sites/3/2019/09/2019-african-american-DIS-report.pdf.

8. Quoted in Akitunde, "Buying Black, Rebooted."

9. Akitunde "Buying Black, Rebooted."

10. R. Thomas Umstead (2019), "African-Americans Are Leaders in Media Consumption," *Multichannel News*.

11. Felecia G. Jones (1990), "The Black Audience and the BET Channel," *Journal of Broadcasting & Electronic Media* 34 (4): 477.

12. iHeartMedia (2020). "BIN: Black Information Network Launches Today as the First-of-Its-Kind 24/7 National and Local All News Audio Service for the Black Community," *iHeartMedia*.

13. Jones, "Black Audience and the BET Channel"; Maria E. Len-Rios, Elisia Cohen, and Charlene Caburnay (2010), "Readers Use Black Newspapers for Health/Cancer Information," *Newspaper Research Journal* 31 (1): 20–35; Jas M. Sullivan

and Gheni N. Platenburg (2017), "From Black-ish to Blackness: An Analysis of Black Information Sources' Influence on Black Identity Development," *Journal of Black Studies* 48 (3): 215–34.

14. Sullivan and Platenburg, "From Black-ish to Blackness."

15. Michele Lamont and Virag Molnar (2001), "How Blacks Use Consumption to Shape Their Collective Identity: Evidence from Marketing Specialists," *Journal of Consumer Culture* 1 (1): 31–32.

16. Lamont and Molnar, "How Blacks Use Consumption," 32.

17. Jones, "Black Audience and the BET Channel," 478.

18. David H. Demo and Michael Hughes (1990), "Socialization and Racial Identity among Black Americans," *Social Psychology Quarterly* 53 (4): 367.

19. Oscar H. Gandy Jr. (2001), "Racial Identity, Media Use, and the Social Construction of Risk among African Americans," *Journal of Black Studies* 31 (5): 601.

20. Carolyn A. Stroman (1984), "The Socialization Influence of Television on Black Children," *Journal of Black Studies* 15 (1): 79; Peter L. Berger and Thomas Luckmann (1967), *The Social Construction of Reality*, Garden City, NY: Doubleday; Aimee Dorr (1982), "Television and the Socialization of the Minority Child," in G. L. Berry and C. Mitchell-Kernan (eds.), *Television and the Socialization of the Minority Child*, New York: Academic.

21. Gordon L. Berry (1980), "Children, Television, and Social Class Roles: The Medium as an Unplanned Educational Curriculum," in E. L. Palmer and A. Dorr (eds.), *Children and the Faces of Television*, New York: Academic; George A. Comstock et al. (1978), *Television and Human Behavior*, New York: Columbia University Press; Stroman, "The Socialization Influence of Television."

22. Berry, "Children, Television, and Social Class"; Comstock et al. (1978), *Television and Human Behavior*; Stroman, "The Socialization Influence of Television."

23. TV One (n.d.), *About TV One*, retrieved from http://tvone.tv/about-tvone/.

24. ABC Television Network (2014), *Black-ish: The Nod*, YouTube video, 1:33, https://www.youtube.com/watch?v=k0Zn4NCsP9Q; Sullivan and Platenburg, "From Black-ish to Blackness," 216.

25. Karsten Renckstorf (1996), "Media Use as Social Action: A Theoretical Perspective," in K. Renckstorf (ed.). *Media Use as Social Action: European Approach to Audience Studies*, London: John Libby, 18–31.

26. Gandy, "Racial Identity, Media Use," 600.

27. Gandy, "Racial Identity, Media Use," 601.

28. Jannette L. Dates (1979), "The Relationship of Demographic Variables and Racial Attitudes to Adolescent Perceptions of Black Television Characters," *Dissertation Abstracts International Section A: Humanities and Social Sciences* 40 (5-A): 2333; Bradley Greenberg and Brenda Dervin (1970), *Use of the Mass Media by the Urban Poor*, New York: Praeger; Bradley S. Greenberg and Gerhard J. Hanneman (1970), "Racial Attitudes and the Impact of TV Blacks," *Educational Broadcasting Review* 4 (2): 27–34; Shosteck, Herschel. (1969). "Some Influences of Television

on Civil Unrest," *Journal of Broadcasting* 13: 371–85; Robert L. Stevenson (1979), "Use of Public Television by Blacks," *Journalism Quarterly* 56: 141–47.

29. Jones, "Black Audience and the BET Channel," 478.

30. Kerry Ann Rockquemore, David L. Brunsma, and Daniel J. Delgago (2009), "Racing to Theory or Retheorizing Race? Understanding the Struggle to Build a Multiracial Identity Theory," *Journal of Social Issues* 65 (1): 14.

31. Sullivan and Platenburg, "From Black-ish to Blackness," 218.

32. Ruthann Weaver Lariscy, Bryan H. Reber, and Hye-Jin Paek (2010), "Examination of Media Channels and Types as Health Information Sources for Adolescents: Comparisons for Black/White, Male/Female, Urban/Rural," *Journal of Broadcasting & Electronic Media* 54 (1): 104; K. Kline (2003), "Popular Media and Health: Images, Effects, and Institutions," in T. L. Thompson, A. M. Dorsey, K. I. Miller, and R. Parrott (eds.), *Handbook of Health Communication*, Mahwah, NJ: Lawrence Erlbaum, 557–81.

33. Lariscy et al., "Examination of Media Channels," 104;Aletha C. Huston, Ellen Wartella, and Edward Donnerstein (1998), "Measuring the Effects of Sexual Content in the Media," A Report to the Kaiser Foundation, available at: https:// www.kff.org/hivaids/report/measuring-the-effects-of-sexual-content-in/; L. M. Ward and R. Rivadeneyra (1999), "Contributions of Entertainment Television to Adolescents' Sexual Attitudes and Expectations: The Role of Viewing Amount versus Viewer Involvement," *Journal of Sex Research* 36 (3): 223–42.

34. Lariscy et al., "Examination of Media Channels," 104–5.

35. Maria E. Len-Rios et al. (2008), "Study Asks If Reporter's Gender or Audience Predict Paper's Cancer Coverage," *Newspaper Research Journal* 29 (2): 91–9; Len-Rios et al. (2010), "Readers Use Black Newspapers," 22.

36. Len-Rios et al., "Readers Use Black Newspapers," 21.

37. Lamont and Molnar, "How Blacks Use Consumption," 36.

38. Christy Fisher (1996), "Black, Hip, and Primed (to Shop)," *American Demographics* 18 (9): 52; Lamont and Molnar, "How Blacks Use Consumption," 36.

39. Sullivan and Platenburg, "From Black-ish to Blackness," 227.

40. E. Shohat and R. Stamm (1994), *Unthinking Eurocentrism: Multiculturalism and the Media*, New York: Routledge; Gandy, "Racial Identity, Media Use," 602.

41. Lariscy et al., "Examination of Media Channels," 104.

42. Sherman A. James (1994), "John Henryism and the Health of African-Americans," *Culture, Medicine and Psychiatry* 18: 169; Gary G. Bennett et al. (2004), "Stress, Coping, and Health Outcomes among African-Americans: A Review of the John Henryism Hypothesis," *Psychology and Health* 19 (3): 369–83.

43. Darryl Dickson-Carr (2005),"Black Nationalism," *The Columbia Guide to Contemporary African American Fiction*, New York: Columbia University Press, 54.

44. David H. Demo and Michael Hughes (1990), "Socialization and Racial Identity among Black Americans," *Social Psychology Quarterly* 53 (4): 367.

45. Lamont and Molnar, "How Blacks Use Consumption."

46. Gandy, "Racial Identity, Media Use."

47. Bradley and Hanneman (1970), "Racial Attitudes and the Impact"; Dates, "Relationship of Demographic Variables"; Greenberg and Dervin, *Use of the Mass Media*; Jones, "Black Audience and the BET Channel"; Stevenson, "Use of Public Television."

48. Akitunde, "Buying Black, Rebooted"; Nielsen Company, "Diverse Intelligence Series 2019."

Chapter 7

1. Holly Ellyatt (2020), " 'The Fight for America': The World Is Watching the U.S. Election. Here's What It Thinks," *CNBC*; Mike Hills, Evisa Terziu, and Prina Shah (2020), "US Election 2020: A Really Simple Guide," *BBC News*.

2. Clive Myrie (2020), "US Election 2020: Why Racism Is Still a Problem for the World's Most Powerful Country," *BBC News*; Donna Owens (2020), "From Covid-19 to Racial Justice, How 2020's Biggest Issues Influenced the Black Vote," *NBC News*.

3. Owens, "From Covid-19 to Racial Justice."

4. Lynne Peeples (2020), "What the Data Say about Police Brutality and Racial Bias—and which Reforms Might Work," *Nature*.

5. Myrie (2020), "US Election 2020"; Owens, "From Covid-19 to Racial Justice."

6. Myrie (2020), "US Election 2020."

7. Scott Desposato and Barbara Norrander (2008), "The Gender Gap in Latin America: Contextual and Individual Influences on Gender and Political Participation," *British Journal of Political Science* 39: 141–62; Allyson L. Holbrook et al. (2016), "Racial Disparities in Political Participation across Issues: The Role of Issue-Specific Motivators," *Political Behavior* 38: 1–32.

8. Andrew S. Fullerton and Michael J. Stern (2013), "Racial Differences in the Gender Gap in Political Participation in the American South, 1952–2004," *Social Science History* 37 (2): 145–76; Sidney Verba, Kay Lehman Schlozman, and Henry E. Brady (1995), *Voice and Equality: Civic Voluntarism in American Politics*, Cambridge, MA: Harvard University Press.

9. Hilde Coffé (2013), "Gender and Political Participation in Western and Eastern Europe" in K. N. Demetriou (ed.), *Democracy in Transition*, Berlin: Springer, 95–107; Desposato and Norrander, "Gender Gap in Latin America."

10. Desposato and Norrander, "Gender Gap in Latin America."

11. Hilde Coffé and Catherine Bolzendahl (2010), "Same Game, Different Rules? Gender Differences in Political Participation," *Sex Roles* 62 (5–6): 318–33.

12. Desposato and Norrander (2008), "Gender Gap in Latin America"; Coffé, "Gender and Political Participation."

13. Coffé and Bolzendahl, "Same Game, Different Rules?," 319.

14. Coffé, "Gender and Political Participation"; Coffé and Bolzendahl, "Same Game, Different Rules?"; Desposato and Norrander, "Gender Gap in Latin America"; Heather L. Ondercin and Daniel Jones-White (2011), "Gender Jeopardy: What Is the Impact of Gender Differences in Political Knowledge on Political Participation?," *Social Science Quarterly* 92 (3): 675–94.

15. Holbrook et al., "Racial Disparities in Political Participation"; Arend Lijphart (1997), "Unequal Participation: Democracy's Unresolved Dilemma—Presidential Address," American Political Science Association, 1996, *American Political Science Review* 91 (1): 1–14.

16. Coffé, "Gender and Political Participation."

17. Desposato and Norrander, "The Gender Gap in Latin America"; Aina Gallego (2007), "Unequal Political Participation in Europe," *International Journal of Sociology* 37 (4): 10–25.

18. Desposato and Norrander, "The Gender Gap in Latin America."

19. Coffé and Bolzendahl, "Same Game, Different Rules?"; Desposato and Norrander, "The Gender Gap in Latin America."

20. Coffé and Bolzendahl, "Same Game, Different Rules?"; Kay Lehman Schlozman, Nancy Burns, and Sidney Verba (1999), "'What Happened at Work Today?': A Multistage Model of Gender, Employment, and Political Participation," *Journal of Politics* 61: 29–53.

21. Jeanne A. Batalova and Philip N. Cohen (2002), "Premarital Cohabitation and Housework: Couples in Cross-National Perspective," *Journal of Marriage and the Family* 64: 743–55; Coffé and Bolzendahl (2010), "Same Game, Different Rules?"; Knud Knudsen and Kari Waerness (2008), "National Context and Spouses' Housework in 34 Countries." *European Sociological Review* 24 (1): 97–113; Schlozman, Burns, and Verba, "'What Happened at Work Today?'"

22. Coffé, "Gender and Political Participation"; Coffé and Bolzendahl, "Same Game, Different Rules?"; Sidney Verba, Nancy Burns, and Kay Lehman Schlozman (1997), "Knowing and Caring about Politics: Gender and Political Engagement," *Journal of Politics* 59 (4): 1051–72.

23. Coffé and Bolzendahl, "Same Game, Different Rules?"; Ondercin and Jones-White, "Gender Jeopardy"; Verba, Burns, and Schlozman, "Knowing and Caring about Politics."

24. Coffé and Bolzendahl, "Same Game, Different Rules?"; Verba, Burns, and Schlozman, "Knowing and Caring about Politics."

25. Ondercin and Jones-White, "Gender Jeopardy."

26. Belinda Robnett and James A. Bany (2011), "Gender, Church Involvement, and African American Political Participation," *Sociological Perspectives* 54 (4): 689–712.

27. Frederick Harris, Valeria Sinclair-Chapman, and Brian D. McKenzie (2005), "Macrodynamics of Black Political Participation in the Post-Civil Rights Era," *Journal of Politics* 67 (4): 1143–63; John C. Pierce, William P. Avery, and

Addison Carey Jr. (1973), "Sex Differences in Black Political Beliefs and Behavior," *American Journal of Political Science* 17 (2): 422–30.

28. Verba and Nie, *Participation in America*; Linda F. Williams (1987), "Black Political Progress in the 1980s: The Electoral Arena," in M. B. Preston, L. J. Henderson Jr., and P. Puryear (eds.), *The New Black Politics*, New York: Longman, 97–136.

29. Nancy Burns, Kay Lehman Schlozman, and Sidney Verba (2001), *The Private Roots of Public Action: Gender, Equality, and Political Participation*, Cambridge, MA: Harvard University Press; Kay Lehman Schlozman, Nancy Burns, and Sidney Verba (1994), "Gender and the Pathways to Participation: The Role of Resources," *Journal of Politics* 56 (4): 963–90.

30. Robnett and Bany, "Gender, Church Involvement," 702.

31. Holbrooke et al., "Racial Disparities in Political Participation"; Steven J. Rosenstone and John Mark Hansen (1993), *Mobilization, Participation, and Democracy in America*, New York: Macmillan.

32. Holbrooke et al., "Racial Disparities in Political Participation";Marvin E. Olsen (1970), "Social and Political Participation of Blacks," *American Sociological Review* 35 (4): 682–97; Richard D. Shingles (1981), "Black Consciousness and Political Participation: The Missing Link," *American Political Science Review* 75 (1): 76–91.

33. Holbrooke et al., "Racial Disparities in Political Participation"; Shingles, "Black Consciousness and Political Participation"; Sidney Verba and Norman H. Nie (1972), *Participation in America*, New York: Harper & Row.

34. William A. Gamson (1968), *Power and Discontent*, Homewood, IL: Dorsey Press; William A. Gamson (1971), "Political Trust and Its Ramifications," in Gilbert Abcarian and John W. Soule, eds., *Social Psychology and Political Behavior*, New York: Charles E. Merrill, 40–55; Patricia Gurin, Gerald Gurin, and Leo M. Beattie (1969), "Internal-External Control in the Motivational Dynamics of Negroes," *Journal of Social Issues* 25: 29–53; Patricia Gurin and Edgar Epps (1975), *Black Consciousness, Identity and Achievement*, New York: John Wiley; Shingles, "Black Consciousness and Political Participation"; Verba and Nie (1972), *Participation in America*.

35. Shingles (1981), "Black Consciousness and Political Participation"; Verba and Nie, *Participation in America*

36. Shingles, "Black Consciousness and Political Participation"; Verba and Nie, *Participation in America*.

37. Gamson. (1968). *Power and Discontent*; Shingles (1981). "Black Consciousness and Political Participation."

38. Shingles, "Black Consciousness and Political Participation," 77; Gamson, *Power and Discontent*.

39. Gamson, *Power and Discontent*; Shingles, "Black Consciousness and Political Participation."

40. Gamson, *Power and Discontent*; Gurin et al., "Internal-External Control"; Gurin and Epps, *Black Consciousness, Identity, and Achievement*; Shingles, "Black Consciousness and Political Participation."

41. Gurin et al., "Internal-External Control"; Gurin and Epps, *Black Consciousness, Identity, and Achievement*; Shingles, "Black Consciousness and Political Participation."

42. Gamson, *Power and Discontent*; Gamson, "Political Trust and Its Ramifications"; Gurin, Gurin, and Beattie, "Internal-External Control"; Gurin and Epps, *Black Consciousness, Identity and Achievement*; Shingles. "Black Consciousness and Political Participation."

43. Shingles (1981), "Black Consciousness and Political Participation," 76.

44. John R. Arvizu and F. Chris Garcia (1996), "Latino Voting Participation: Explaining and Differentiating Latino Voting Turnout," *Hispanic Journal of Behavioral Sciences* 18 (2): 104–28; Holbrooke et al., "Racial Disparities in Political Participation"; Katherine Tate (1991), "Black Political Participation in the 1984 and 1988 Presidential Elections," *American Political Science Review* 85 (4): 1159–76; Sidney Verba, Kay Lehman Schlozman, and Henry E. Brady (1995), *Voice and Equality: Civic Voluntarism in American Politics*, Cambridge, MA: Harvard University Press.

45. Yvette Alex-Assensoh and A. B. Assensoh (2001), "Inner-City Contexts, Church Attendance, and African-American Political Participation," *Journal of Politics* 63 (3): 886–901; Holbrooke et al. (2016), "Racial Disparities in Political Participation."

46. Holbrooke et al. (2016), "Racial Disparities in Political Participation"; Richard J. Timpone (1998), "Structure, Behavior, and Voter Turnout in the United States," *American Political Science Review* 92 (1): 145–58.

47. Lawrence Bobo and Franklin D. Gilliam Jr. (1990), "Race, Sociopolitical Participation, and Black Empowerment," *American Political Science Review* 84 (2): 377–93.

48. Bobo and Gilliam Jr., "Race, Sociopolitical Participation, and Black Empowerment"; Holbrooke et al., "Racial Disparities in Political Participation."

49. Holbrooke et al., "Racial Disparities in Political Participation."

50. Holbrooke et al., "Racial Disparities in Political Participation," 23.

51. Alex-Assensoh and Assensoh, "Inner-City Contexts, Church Attendance"; Coffé and Bolzendahl, "Same Game, Different Rules?"; Brian D. McKenzie (2004), "Religious Social Networks, Indirect Mobilization, and African-American Political Participation," *Political Research Quarterly* 57 (4): 621–32; Belinda Robnett and James A. Bany (2011), "Gender, Church Involvement, and African-American Political Participation," *Sociological Perspectives* 54 (4): 689–712.

52. Coffé and Bolzendahl (2010), "Same Game, Different Rules?"; Frederick Harris (1994), "Something within: Religion as a Mobilizer of African-American Political Activism," *Journal of Politics* 56 (1): 42–68; Mary Patillo-McCoy (1998), "Church Culture as a Strategy of Action in the Black Community," *American Sociological Review* 63 (6): 767–84; Putnam, Robert D. (2000), *Bowling Alone: The Collapse and Revival of American Community*, New York: Simon & Schuster; Robnett and Bany, "Gender, Church Involvement"; Schlozman, Burns, and Verba, "Gender and the Pathways."

53. Coffé and Bolzendahl (2010), "Same Game, Different Rules?"; Robnett and Bany, "Gender, Church Involvement."

54. Robnett and Bany, "Gender, Church Involvement," 707.

55. O'Neil, Aaron (2020), "Voter Turnout among Black Voters in U.S. Presidential Elections 1964–2016," *Statista.*

56. O'Neil (2020), "Voter Turnout among Black Voters."

57. Holbrooke et al. (2016), "Racial Disparities in Political Participation."

58. Jas M. Sullivan (2020), "Does Region Matter on African Americans' Reaction to Discrimination?: An Exploratory Study," in L. Martin (ed.), *Introduction to Africana Demography*, Boston, MA: Brill.

Conclusion

1. Benjamin Siefel (2021), "House Democrats Pass Election Reforms as GOP Moves to Change Voting Laws," *ABC News*; Zachary B. Wolf (2021), "Watch These States as GOP Tries to Make It Harder to Vote," *CNN.*

2. Wolf (2021), "Watch These States"; Brennan Center for Justice (2021), "State Voting Bills Tracker 2021," Brennan Center for Justice.

3. Brennan Center for Justice, "State Voting Bills Tracker 2021."

4. Nick Corasaniti and Jim Rutenberg (2021), "In Georgia, Republicans Take Aim at Role of Black Churches in Elections," *New York Times.*

5. Nolan D. McCaskill (2021), "After Trump's Loss and False Fraud Claims, GOP Eyes Voter Restrictions across Nation," *Politico.*

6. Corasaniti and Rutenberg, "In Georgia, Republicans Take Aim."

7. Derrick Bryson Taylor (2020), "A Timeline of the Coronavirus Pandemic," *New York Times.*

8. Sui-Lee Wee, Donald G. McNeil Jr., and Javier C. Hernandez (2020), "WHO Declares Global Emergency as Wuhan Coronavirus Spreads." Last updated April 16, 2020, *New York Times.*

9. American Journal of Managed Care Staff (2021), "A Timeline of COVID-19 Developments in 2020," *American Journal of Managed Care.*

10. Madeline Holcombe and Dakin Andone (2020), "A Variety of Responses by US States Hurt the Country's Ability to Contain the Coronavirus Pandemic, Fauci says," *CNN.*

11. CDC (2020), "Health Equity Considerations and Racial and Ethnic Minority Groups," *Centers for Disease Control and Prevention*; Eboni G. Price-Haywood, Jeffrey Burton, Daniel Fort, and Leonardo Seoane (2020), "Hospitalization and Mortality among Black Patients and White Patients with COVID-19," *New England Journal of Medicine* 382: 2534–43.

12. CDC (2020), "Health Equity Considerations and Racial and Ethnic Minority Groups," *Centers for Disease Control and Prevention*; Jack Cordes and Marcia

C. Castro (2020), "Spatial Analysis of COVID-19 Clusters and Contextual Factors in New York City," *Spatial and Spatio-Temporal Epidemiology* 34 (100355): 1–8; Yin Paradies (2006), "A Systematic Review of Empirical Research on Self-Reported Racism and Health." *International Journal of Epidemiology* 35 (4): 888–901; Price-Haywood et al. (2020), "Hospitalization and Mortality among Black Patients and White Patients with Covid-19"; Ronald L. Simons et al. (2018), "Discrimination, Segregation, and Chronic Inflammation: Testing the Weathering Explanation for the Poor Health of Black Americans," *Developmental Psychology* 54 (10): 1993–2006.

13. E. J. Mundell (2020), "Mental Health Issues Soaring during COVID Pandemic," *WebMD* and *HealthDay News*; Nirmita Panchal et al. (2020), "The Implications of COVID-19 for Mental Health and Substance Use," *KFF.*

14. Mundell (2020), "Mental Health Issues Soaring."

15. Assistant Secretary for Public Affairs (ASPA) (2020), "Mental Health and Coping during the Coronavirus (COVID-19) Pandemic," *U.S. Department of Health & Human Services.*

16. CDC (2020), "Coping with Stress," *Centers for Disease Control and Prevention.*

17. WHO (2020), "Mental Health and Psychosocial Considerations during the COVID-19 Outbreak," *World Health Organization.*

18. Karmel Choi and Jordan W. Smoller (2020), "General Mental Health & Coping," *Massachusetts General Hospital—Psychiatry.*

19. K. J. Korte et al. (2020), "Managing Stress: Tips for Coping with the Stress of COVID-19," *Harvard T. H. Chan School of Public Health.*

20. Joshua Morganstein (2020), "Coronavirus and Mental Health: Taking Care of Ourselves during Infectious Disease Outbreaks," *American Psychiatric Association.*

21. Long Huang, et al. (2020), "Emotional Responses and Coping Strategies in Nurses and Nursing Students during COVID-19 Outbreak: A Comparative Study," *PLoS ONE* 15 (8): e0237303; Ghada Shahrour and Latefa Ali Dardas (2020), "Acute Stress Disorder, Coping Self-Efficacy and Subsequent Psychological Distress among Nurses amid COVID-19," *Journal of Nursing Management* 28 (7): 1686–95; Zhi Ye, Xueying Yang, et al. (2020), "Resilience, Social Support, and Coping as Mediators between COVID-19-Related Stressful Experiences and Acute Stress Disorder among College Students in China," *Applied Psychology: Health and Well-Being* 12 (4): 1074–94.

22. Bethany Albertson and Shana Kushner Gadarian (2015), *Anxious Politics: Democratic Citizenship in a Threatening World*, New York: Cambridge University Press.

23. Albertson and Gadarian (2015), *Anxious Politics.*

24. BBC News (2020), "George Floyd: What Happened in the Final Moments of His Life," *BBC News*; Helier Cheung (2020), "George Floyd Death: Why US Protests Are so Powerful this Time," *BBC News*; Lewis Dodley (2020), "Timeline: How George Floyd's Death Sparked a Movement," *Spectrum News NY1*; Richard Faussett (2020), "What We Know about the Shooting Death of Ahmaud Arbery,"

New York Times; Jan Ransom (2020), "Amy Cooper Faces Charges after Calling Police on Black Bird-Watcher," *New York Times*; Chao Xiong (2020), "A Timeline of Events Leading to George Floyd's Death as Outlined in Charging Documents," *Star Tribune.*

25. Dakin Andone (2020), "A Black Doctor Died Of Covid-19 Weeks after Accusing Hospital Staff of Racist Treatment," *CNN.*

26. Andone, "Black Doctor Died of Covid-19"; John Eligon (2020), "Black Doctor Dies of Covid-19 after Complaining of Racist Treatment," *New York Times.*

27. Marianne Bertrand et al. (2020), "How COVID-19 Is Changing Americans' Behaviors, Expectations, and Political Views," *University of Chicago—Rustandy Center for Social Sector Innovation and the Poverty Lab*, 1.

28. Bertrand et al. (2020), "How COVID-19 Is Changing Americans' Behaviors," 1.

29. Aaron O'Neil (2020), "Voter Turnout among Black Voters in U.S. Presidential Elections 1964–2016," *Statista.*

Bibliography

ABC News. (2020). "Three Men Indicted with Murder of Black Jogger Ahmaud Arbery in Georgia." *ABC News.* https://www.abc.net.au/news/2020-06-25/black-lives-matter-protest-updates-murder-charges-ahmaud-arbery/12390598.

ABC Television Network. (2014). Black-ish: The Nod. Youtube video, 1:33. https://www.youtube.com/watch?v=k0Zn4NCsP9Q.

Armed Conflict Location and Event Data (ACLED). (2020). "US Crisis Monitor Releases Full Data for Summer 2020." *ACLED.*

Adams, J. H., R. E. Aubert, and V. R. Clark. (1999). "The Relationship among John Henryism, Hostility, Perceived Stress, Social Support, and Blood Pressure in African-American College Students." *Ethnicity and Disease* 9 (3): 359–68.

American Journal of Managed Care (AJMC) Staff. (2021). "A Timeline of COVID-19 Developments in 2020." *American Journal of Managed Care.* https://www.ajmc.com/view/a-timeline-of-covid19-developments-in-2020.

Akitunde, Anthonia. (2019). "Buying Black, Rebooted." *New York Times.*

Albertson, Bethany, and Shana Kushner Gadarian. (2015). *Anxious Politics: Democratic Citizenship in a Threatening World.* New York: Cambridge University Press.

Al Jazeera. (2020). "International Reaction to George Floyd Killing." *Al Jazeera.*

Alcorn, Chauncey. (2020). "#BlackOutDay2020 is today. Here's what you need to know." *CNN.* https://www.cnn.com/2020/07/06/business/blackout-day-2020/index.html.

Alex-Assensoh, Yvette, and A. B. Assensoh. (2001). "Inner-City Contexts, Church Attendance, and African-American Political Participation." *Journal of Politics* 63 (3): 886–901.

Allen, Richard L., Michael C. Dawson, and Ronald E. Brown. (1989). "A Schema-Based Approach to Modeling an African American Racial Belief System." *American Political Science Review* 83 (2): 421–41.

Allen, Richard L., and Shirley Hatchett. (1986). "The Media and Social Reality Effects: Self and System Orientations of Blacks." *Communication Research* 13: 97–123.

Allison, Jeroan, Catarina Kiefe, Robert Centor, J. Box, and Robert Farmer. (1996). "Racial Differences in the Medical Treatment of Elderly Medicare Patients with Acute Myocardial Infarction." *Journal of General Internal Medicine* 11 (12): 736–43.

Amirkhan, James H. (1990). "A Factor Analytically Derived Measure of Coping: The Coping Strategy Indicator." *Journal of Personality and Social Psychology* 59 (5): 1066–74.

Anderson, Joel. (2020). "No Justice, No Football: The Only Way College Players Can Force Change Is to Boycott Games." *Slate.* https://slate.com/culture/2020/06/mike-gundy-chuba-hubbard-oklahoma-state-college-football-protests.html.

Anderson, Norman B. (1998). "Levels of Analysis in Health Science: A Framework for Integrating Sociobehavioral and Biomedical Research." In S. M. McCann and J. M. Lipton (Eds.), *Annals of the New York Academy of Sciences, Neuroimmunomodulation: Molecular Aspects, Integrative Systems, and Clinical Advances,* vol. 840, 563–76. New York: New York Academy of Sciences.

Andone, Dakin. (2020). "A Black Doctor Died of Covid-19 Weeks after Accusing Hospital Staff of Racist Treatment." *CNN.* https://www.cnn.com/2020/12/24/us/black-doctor-susan-moore-covid-19/index.html.

Armstrong, Joslyn, Fiorella L. Carlos Chavez, Julia H. Jones, Shar'Dane Harris, and Gregory J. Harris. (2019). "'A Dream Deferred': How Discrimination Impacts the American Dream Achievement for African Americans." *Journal of Black Studies* 50 (3): 227–50.

Arnow, Bruce, Justin Kenardy, W. Stewart Agras. (1995). "The Emotional Eating Scale: The Development of a Measure to Assess Coping with Negative Affect by Eating." *International Journal of Eating Disorders* 18 (1): 79–90.

Arvizu, John R., and F. Chris Garcia. (1996). "Latino Voting Participation: Explaining and Differentiating Latino Voting Turnout." *Hispanic Journal of Behavioral Sciences* 18 (2): 104–28.

Assistant Secretary for Public Affairs (ASPA). (2020). "Mental Health and Coping during the Coronavirus (COVID-19) Pandemic." U.S. Department of Health & Human Services. https://www.hhs.gov/coronavirus/mental-health-and-coping/index.html.

New York Times. (2020). "Ahmaud Arbery Shooting: A Timeline of the Case." *New York Times.* https://www.nytimes.com/article/ahmaud-arbery-timeline.html.

iHeartMedia. (2020). "BIN: Black Information Network Launches Today as the First-of-Its-Kind 24/7 National and Local All News Audio Service for the Black Community." iHeartMedia.

Banks, Kira Hudson, Laura P. Kohn-Wood, and Michael Spencer. (2006). "An Examination of the African American Experience of Everyday Discrimination and Symptoms of Psychological Distress." *Community Mental Health Journal* 42 (6): 555–70.

Barajas, Angela. (2020). "Man who Recorded Ahmaud Arbery's Killing tried to 'Confine and Detain' Him with his Vehicle, Warrant Says." *CNN.*

Barnhill, George E. (2020). "Glynn County: The Shooting Death of Ahmaud Arbery, Feb 23rd, 2020." Office of the District Attorney: Waycross Judicial District.

Batalova, Jeanne A., and Philip N. Cohen. (2002). "Premarital Cohabitation and Housework: Couples in Cross-National Perspective." *Journal of Marriage and the Family* 64: 743–55.

Baxter, Sandra, and Marjorie Lansing. (1983). *Women and Politics: The Visible Majority*. Ann Arbor: University of Michigan Press.

BBC News. (2020). "George Floyd: What Happened in the Final Moments of His Life." *BBC News*.

BBC News. (2020). "Breonna Taylor: Protestors Call on People to 'Say Her Name.'" *BBC News*.

Benedick, Marc, Jr., Charles W. Jackson, and Victor A. Reinoso. (1994). "Measuring Employment Discrimination through Controlled Experiments." *Review of Black Political Economy* 23 (1): 25–48.

Bennett, Gary G., Marcellus M. Merritt, John J. Sollers III, Christopher L. Edwards, Keith E. Whitfield, Dwayne T. Brandon, and Reginald D. Tucker. (2004). "Stress, Coping, and Health Outcomes among African-Americans: A Review of the John Henryism Hypothesis." *Psychology and Health* 19 (3): 369–83.

Berger, Peter L., and Thomas Luckmann. (1967). *The Social Construction of Reality*. Garden City, NY: Doubleday.

Berry, Gordon L. (1980). "Children, Television, and Social Class Roles: The Medium as an Unplanned Educational Curriculum." In E. L. Palmer and A. Dorr (Eds.), *Children and the Faces of Television*. New York: Academic.

Bertrand, Marianne, Guglielmo Briscese, Maddalena Grignani, and Salma Nassar. (2020). "How COVID-19 is Changing Americans' Behaviors, Expectations, and Political Views." University of Chicago—Rustandy Center for Social Sector Innovation and the Poverty Lab. https://www.chicagobooth.edu/research/rustandy/blog/2020/wave-3-how-covid19-is-changing-americans-behaviors-expectations-and-political-views.

Bhagat, Rabi S., Pamela K. Steverson, and Ben C. H. Kuo. (2009). "Cultural Variations in Work Stress and Coping in an Era of Globalization." In R. S. Bhagat, and R. M. Steers (Eds.), *Handbook of Culture, Organizations, and Work*, 418–41. Cambridge, UK: Cambridge University Press.

Bild, Diane E., David R. Jacobs Jr., Stephen Sidney, William L. Haskell, Norman Anderssen, N., and Albert Oberman. (1993). "Physical Activity in Young Black and White Women the CARDIA Study." *Annals of Epidemiology* 3 (6): 636–44.

Billig, Michael. (1995). *Banal Nationalism*. Thousand Oaks, CA: Sage.

Bippus, Amy M., and Stacy L. Young. (2012). "Using Appraisal Theory to Predict Emotional and Coping Responses to Hurtful Messages." *Interpersona* 6 (2): 176–90.

Block, Ray, Jr. (2011). "What about Disillusionment? Exploring the Pathways to Black Nationalism." *Political Behavior* 33: 27–51.

Bobo, Lawrence, and Franklin D. Gilliam Jr. (1990). "Race, Sociopolitical Participation, and Black Empowerment." *American Political Science Review* 84 (2): 377–93.

Bobo, Lawrence, and James R. Kluegel. (1993). "Opposition to Race-Targeting: Self-Interest, Stratification Ideology, or Racial Attitudes?" *American Sociological Review* 58 (4): 443–64.

Bonham, Vence L., Sherrill L. Sellers, and Harold W. Neighbors. (2004). "John Henryism and Self-Reported Physical Health among High-Socioeconomic Status African American Men." *American Journal of Public Health* 94 (5): 737–38.

Bonikowski, Bart, and Paul DiMaggio. (2016). "Varieties of American Popular Nationalism." *American Sociological Review* 81 (5): 949–80.

Borrell, Luisa N., David R. Jacobs Jr., David R. Williams, Mark J. Pletcher, Thomas K. Houston, and Catarina I. Kiefe. (2007). "Self-Reported Racial Discrimination and Substance Use in the Coronary Artery Risk Development in Adults Study." *American Journal of Epidemiology* 166 (9): 1068–79.

Bote, Joshua. (2020). "George Floyd Told Officers He 'Can't Breathe' Nearly 30 Times, Newly Released Body Cam Transcripts Show." *USA Today.*

Bourhis, Richard Y. (2020). "A Journey Researching Prejudice and Discrimination." *Canadian Psychology/Psychologie Canadienne, CPA Awards and Convention Keynotes/Prix de la SCP et allocutions au Congrès* 61 (2): 95–100.

Bowman, Emma. (2022). "4 Current and Former Officers Federally Charged in Raid that Killed Breonna Taylor." *NPR.* https://www.npr.org/2022/08/04/1115659537/breonna-taylor-police-charges-ky.

Brandeberry, J. (2020). "Glynn County Police Department Public Release Incident Report for G20-11303." *New York Times.* https://int.nyt.com/data/documenthelper/6915-arbery-shooting/b52fa09cdc974b970b79/optimized/full.pdf.

Brennan Center for Justice. (2021). "State Voting Bills Tracker 2021." Brennan Center for Justice. https://www.brennancenter.org/our-work/research-reports/state-voting-bills-tracker-2021.

Brody, Gene H., Tianyi Yu, Edith Chen, Gregory E. Miller, Steven M. Kogan, and Steven R. H. Beach. (2013). "Is Resilience Only Skin Deep? Rural African Americans' Socioeconomic Status–Related Risk and Competence in Preadolescence and Psychological Adjustment and Allostatic Load at Age 19." *Psychological Science* 24 (7): 1285–93.

Broman, Clifford L., Harold W. Neighbors, and James S. Jackson. (1988). "Racial Group Identification among Black Adults." *Social Forces* 67 (1): 146–58.

Bronder, Ellen C., Suzette L. Speight, Karen M. Witherspoon, and Anita J. Thomas. (2014). "John Henryism, Depression, and Perceived Social Support in Black Women." *Journal of Black Psychology* 40 (2): 115–37.

Brown, Robert A., and Todd C. Shaw. (2002). "Separate Nations: Two Attitudinal Dimensions of Black Nationalism." *Journal of Politics* 64 (1): 22–44.

Buchanan, Larry, Quoctrung Bui, and Jugal K. Patel. (2020). "Black Lives Matter May Be the Largest Movement in U.S. History." *New York Times.*

Burke, Minyvonne. (2020). "White Man Accused of Killing Ahmaud Arbery Allegedly Used Racial Slur after Shooting, Investigator Says." *NBC News.*

Burns, Nancy, Kay Lehman Schlozman, and Sidney Verba. (2001). *The Private Roots of Public Action: Gender, Equality, and Political Participation.* Cambridge, MA: Harvard University Press.

Butler, David, and Bruce E. Cain. (1992). *Congressional Redistricting: Comparative and Theoretical Perspectives.* New York: Macmillan.

Byrne, Donn. (1961). "The Repression-Sensitization Scale: Rationale, Reliability, and Validity." *Journal of Personality* 29 (3): 334–49.

———. (1964). "Repression-Sensitization as a Dimension of Personality." In Brendan A. Maher (Ed.), *Progress in Experimental Personality Research*, vol. 1, 170–220. New York: Academic Press.

Campbell, Angus, Gerald Gurin, and Warren E. Miller. (1954). *The Voter Decides.* Evanston, IL: Row, Peterson.

Carter, Robert T. (2007). "Racism and Psychological and Emotional Injury: Recognizing and Assessing Race-Based Traumatic Stress." *Counseling Psychologist* 35 (1): 13–105.

Carter, Robert T., and Jessica Forsyth. (2010). "Reactions to Racial Discrimination: Emotional Stress and Help-Seeking Behaviors." *Psychological Trauma: Theory, Research, Practice, and Policy* 2 (3): 183–91.

Carter, Robert T., Michael Y. Lau, Veronica Johnson, and Katherine Kirkinis. (2017). "Racial Discrimination and Health Outcomes among Racial/Ethnic Minorities: A Meta-analytic Review." *Journal of Multicultural Counseling and Development* 45 (4): 232–59.

Carver, Charles S. (1997). "You Want to Measure Coping but Your Protocol's Too Long: Consider the Brief COPE." *International Journal of Behavioral Medicine* 4 (1): 92–100.

Carver, Charles S., Michael F. Scheier, and Jagdish Kumari Weintraub. (1989). "Assessing Coping Strategies: A Theoretically Based Approach." *Journal of Personality and Social Psychology* 56 (2): 267–83.

CBS News. (2020). "The World Reacts as American Cities Erupt in Anger over George Floyd's Death." *CBS News.* Updated June 1, 2020. Accessed online at https://www.cbsnews.com/news/protests-around-the-world-george-floyd-death-international-sympathy-and-scorn-today-2020-06-01/.

CDC. (2020). "Coping with Stress." Centers for Disease Control and Prevention. https://www.cdc.gov/coronavirus/2019-ncov/daily-life-coping/managing-stress-anxiety.html?CDC_AA_refVal=https%3A%2F%2Fwww.cdc.gov%2Fcoronavirus%2F2019-ncov%2Fprepare%2Fmanaging-stress-anxiety.html.

———. (2020). "Health Equity Considerations and Racial and Ethnic Minority Groups." Centers for Disease Control and Prevention. https://www.cdc.gov/coronavirus/2019-ncov/community/health-equity/race-ethnicity.html.

Cha, Hyeon-Ju, and Hee-Sun Cho. (2016). "An Exploratory Study on the Factors of Parental Rearing Behavior based on Vygotsky's Theory of Social Constructivism for Developing Convergence Digital Contents." *Journal of Digital Convergence* 14 (3): 453–64.

Chae, David H., Karen D. Lincoln, Nancy E. Adler, and S. Leonard Syme. (2010). "Do Experiences of Racial Discrimination Predict Cardiovascular Disease among African American Men? The Moderating Role of Internalized Negative Racial Group Attitudes." *Social Science & Medicine* 71 (6): 1182–88.

Chavous, Tabbye M., Deborah Rivas-Drake, Ciara Smalls, Tiffany Griffin, and Courtney Cogburn. (2008). "Gender Matters, Too: The Influences of School Racial Discrimination and Racial Identity on Academic Engagement Outcomes among African American Adolescents." *Developmental Psychology* 44 (3): 637–54.

Chesney, Margaret A., Torsten B. Neilands, Donald B. Chambers, Jonelle M. Taylor, and Susan Folkman. (2006). "A Validity and Reliability Study of the Coping Self-Efficacy Scale." *British Journal of Health Psychology* 11 (3): 421–37.

Cheung, Helier. (2020). "George Floyd Death: Why US Protests Are so Powerful This Time." *BBC News*. https://www.bbc.com/news/world-us-canada-52969905.

Choi, Karmel, and Jordan W. Smoller. (2020). "General Mental Health & Coping." *Massachusetts General Hospital—Psychiatry*. https://www.massgeneral.org/psychiatry/guide-to-mental-health-resources/general-mental-health-and-coping

Chong, Dennis, and Reuel Rogers. (2005). "Racial Solidarity and Political Participation." *Political Behavior* 27: 347–74.

Cineas, Fabiola. (2020). "Black Lives Matter Activists Plan to Organize Even Harder after the Election—No Matter Who Wins." *Vox*.

Clark, Rodney, Norman B. Anderson, Vernessa R. Clark, and David R. Williams. (1999). "Racism as a Stressor for African Americans: A Biopsychosocial Model." *American Psychologist* 54 (10): 805–16.

Coffé, Hilde. (2013). "Gender and Political Participation in Western and Eastern Europe." In K. N. Demetriou (Ed.), *Democracy in Transition*. Berlin: Springer, 95–107.

Coffé, Hilde, and Catherine Bolzendahl. (2010). "Same Game, Different Rules? Gender Differences in Political Participation." *Sex Roles* 62 (5–6): 318–33.

Cohen, Frances, and Richard S. Lazarus. (1973). "Active Coping Processes, Coping Dispositions, and Recovery from Surgery." *Psychosomatic Medicine* 35 (5): 375–89.

Compas, Bruce E., Sarah S. Jaser, Jennifer P. Dunbar, Kelly H. Watson, Alexandra H. Bettis, Meredith A. Gruhn, and Ellen K. Williams. (2014). "Coping and Emotion Regulation from Childhood to Early Adulthood: Points of Convergence and Divergence." *Australian Journal of Psychology* 66: 71–81.

Comstock, George A., Steven H. Chaffee, Thomas Bowers, and Natan Katzman. (1978). *Television and Human Behavior*. New York: Columbia University Press.

Conover, Pamela J. (1984). "The Influence of Group Identification on Political Perception and Evaluation." *Journal of Politics* 46 (3): 760–85.

Corasaniti, Nick, and Jim Rutenberg. (2021). "In Georgia, Republicans Take Aim at Role of Black Churches in Elections." *New York Times*. https://www.nytimes.com/2021/03/06/us/politics/churches-black-voters-georgia.html

Cordes, Jack, and Marcia C. Castro. (2020). "Spatial Analysis of COVID-19 Clusters and Contextual Factors in New York City." *Spatial and Spatio-Temporal Epidemiology* 34 (100355): 1–8.

Correll, Joshua, Bernadette Park, Charles M. Judd, and Bernd Wittenbrink. (2002). "The Police Officer's Dilemma: Using Ethnicity to Disambiguate Potentially Threatening Individuals." *Journal of Personality and Social Psychology* 83 (6): 1314–29.

Cose, Ellis. (1993). The Rage of a Privileged Class. New York: HarperCollins.

Craddock, Felicia. (2020). "Black-Owned Watch Brands Rising." *New York Times*.

Cvorovic, Jelena, and Sherman A. James. (2018). "John Henryism, Gender and Self-Reported Health among Roma/Gypsies in Serbia." *Culture, Medicine and Psychiatry* 42 (2): 295–314.

Dates, Jannette L. (1979). "The Relationship of Demographic Variables and Racial Attitudes to Adolescent Perceptions of Black Television Characters." *Dissertation Abstracts International Section A: Humanities and Social Sciences* 40 (5-A): 2333.

Davis, Darren W., and Ronald E. Brown. (2002). "The Antipathy of Black Nationalism: Behavioral and Attitudinal Implications of an African American Ideology." *American Journal of Political Science* 46 (2): 239–52.

Dawson, Michael. (1994). *Behind the Mule: Race and Class in African American Politics*. Princeton, NJ: Princeton University Press.

———. (2001). *Black Vision: The Roots of Contemporary African American Political Ideologies*. Chicago, IL: University of Chicago Press.

Dawson, Michael C., and Rovana Popoff. (2004). "Reparations: Justice and Greed in Black and White." *Du Bois Review* 1: 47–91.

De Blasio, Bill. (2020). Twitter. https://twitter.com/nycmayor/status/1265265665755230209?lang=en.

De Figueiredo, Rui J. P., and Zachary Elkins. (2003). "Are Patriots Bigots? An Inquiry into the Vices of Ingroup Pride." *American Journal of Political Science* 47 (1): 171–88.

Deegan-McCree, Michael. (2020). "An Anti-Lynching Law Would Not Get Rid of Bad Cops, But It Would Go a Long Way toward Acknowledging America's Troubled History on Race, Abuse." *USA Today*.

Delapp, Ryan C. T., and Monnica T. Williams. (2015). "Professional Challenges Facing African American Psychologists: The Presence and Impact of Racial Microaggressions." *Behavior Therapist* 38 (4): 101–105.

Deliso, Meredith. (2020). "Timeline: The Impact of George Floyd's Death in Minneapolis and Beyond." *ABC News*.

Demo, David H., and Michael Hughes. (1990). "Socialization and Racial Identity among Black Americans." *Social Psychology Quarterly* 53 (4): 364–74.

Desposato, Scott, and Barbara Norrander. (2008). "The Gender Gap in Latin America: Contextual and Individual Influences on Gender and Political Participation." *British Journal of Political Science* 39: 141–62.

Dickson-Carr, Darryl. (2005). *The Columbia Guide to Contemporary African American Fiction*, 54–56. Columbia University Press.

Dodley, Lewis. (2020). "Timeline: How George Floyd's Death Sparked a Movement." *Spectrum News NY1*.

Dondanville, Ashley Ann, and Patrick Pössel. (2019). "The Impact of Cognitive Styles and Depressive Symptoms on the Relation between Perceived Everyday Discrimination and Blood Pressure in Adolescents." *Translational Issues in Psychological Science, Psychological Science to Reduce and Prevent Health Disparities* 5 (4): 335–45.

Doron, Julie, Raphael Trouillet, Anais Maneveau, Dorine Nevue, and Gregory Ninot. (2015). "Coping Profiles, Perceived Stress and Health-Related Behaviors: A Cluster Analysis Approach." *Health Promotion International* 30 (1): 88–100.

Dorr, Aimee. (1982). "Television and the Socialization of the Minority Child." In G. L. Berry and C. Mitchell-Kernan (Eds.), *Television and the Socialization of the Minority Child*. New York: Academic.

Dressler, William W., James R. Bindon, and Yasmin H. Neggers. (1998). "John Henryism, Gender, and Arterial Blood Pressure in an African American Community." *Psychosomatic Medicine* 60 (5): 620–24.

Du Bois, W. E. B. [1903] (1993). *The Souls of Black Folk*. New York: Alfred A. Knopf.

———. [1934] (1996). "The Board of Directors on Segregation." In Cary D. Wintz (Ed.), *African American Political Thought, 1890–1930*. New York: M. E. Sharpe.

Duijkers, Thomas J., Marjon Drjver, Daan Kromhout, and Sherman A. James. (1988). "'John Henryism' and Blood Pressure in a Dutch Population." *Psychosomatic Medicine* 50 (4): 353–59.

Eide, Stephen. (2020). "Why New York's New 'Anti-Karen' Law will Backfire." *New York Post*.

Eligon, John. (2020). "Black Doctor Dies of Covid-19 after Complaining of Racist Treatment." *New York Times*. https://www.nytimes.com/2020/12/23/us/susan-moore-black-doctor-indiana.html.

Elliot, Josh K. (2020). "Outrage Erupts over 'Karen' who Called Cops on Black Birdwatcher in Central Park." *Global News*. May 26, 2020; updated May 27, 2020. Accessed at https://globalnews.ca/news/6986111/central-park-karen-amy-cooper-dog/.

Ellison, Christopher G. (1991). "Identification and Separatism: Religious Involvement and Racial Orientations among Black Americans." *Sociological Quarterly* 32 (3): 477–94.

Ellyatt, Holly. (2020). "'The Fight for America': The World Is Watching the U.S. Election. Here's What It Thinks." *CNBC*. https://www.cnbc.com/2020/11/03/the-whole-world-is-wthe-us-election-the-worlds-media-is-watching-on-.html.

English, Devin, Sharon F. Lambert, and Nicholas S. Ialongo. (2014). "Longitudinal Associations between Experienced Racial Discrimination and Depressive Symptoms in African American Adolescents." *Developmental Psychology* 50 (4): 1190–96.

Epstein, Seymour, and Walter D. Fenz. (1967). "The Detection of Areas of Emotional Stress through Variations in Perceptual Threshold and Physiological Arousal." *Journal of Experimental Research in Personality* 2 (3): 191–99.

Essed, Philomena. (2002). "Everyday Racism." In D. T. Goldberg and J. Solomos (Eds.), *A Companion to Racial and Ethnic Studies*, 202–17. Malden, MA: Blackwell.

———. (1991). Understanding Everyday Racism: An Interdisciplinary Theory. Newbury Park, CA: Sage.

Eversley, Melanie. (2020). "Running while Black: Ahmaud Arbery's Killing Reveals Runners' Shared Fears of Profiling." *The Undefeated*. https://theundefeated.com/features/running-while-black-ahmaud-arberys-killing-reveals-runners-shared-fears-of-profiling/.

Farmer, Heather R., Linda A. Wray, and Jason R. Thomas. (2019). "Do Race and Everyday Discrimination Predict Mortality Risk? Evidence From the Health and Retirement Study." *Gerontology and Geriatric Medicine* 5 (June).

Faussett, Richard. (2020). "What We Know about the Shooting Death of Ahmaud Arbery." *New York Times*.

Fernander, Anita F., Ron E. F. Duran, Patrice G. Saab, Maria M. Llabre, and Neil Schneiderman. (2003). "Assessing the Reliability and Validity of the John Henry Active Coping Scale in an Urban Sample of African Americans and White Americans." *Ethnicity & Health* 8 (2): 147–61.

Fernander, Anita F., Christi A. Patten, Darrell R. Schroeder, Susanna R. Stevens, Kay M. Ebermnan, and Richard D. Hurt. (2005). "Exploring the Association of John Henry Active Coping and Education on Smoking Behavior and Nicotine Dependence among Blacks in the USA." *Social Science and Medicine* 60: 491–500.

Fisher, Christy. (1996). "Black, Hip, and Primed (to Shop)." *American Demographics* 18 (9): 52–58.

Fitz-Gibbon, Jorge. (2020). "Here's Everything We Know about the Death of George Floyd." *New York Post*.

Folkman, Susan. (1982). "An Approach to the Measurement of Coping." *Journal of Occupational Behavior* 3: 95–107.

Folkman, Susan, and Richard S. Lazarus. (1980). "An Analysis of Coping in a Middle-Aged Community Sample." *Journal of Health and Social Behavior* 21 (3): 219–39.

———. (1985). "If It Changes It Must Be a Process: Study of Emotion and Coping During Three Stages of a College Examination." *Journal of Personality and Social Psychology* 48 (1): 150–70.

———. (1988). "The Relationship between Coping and Emotion: Implications for Theory and Research." *Social Science & Medicine* 26 (3): 309–17.

Folkman, Susan, Richard S. Lazarus, Christine Dunkel-Schetter, Anita DeLongis, and Rand J. Gruen. (1986). "Dynamics of a Stressful Encounter: Cognitive Appraisal, Coping, and Encounter Outcomes." *Journal of Personality and Social Psychology* 50 (5): 992–1003.

Ford, Marvella E., Suzanne L. Havstad, Deanna D. Hill, and Cary S. Kart. (2000). "Assessing the Reliability of Four Standard Health Measures in a Sample of Older, Urban Adults." *Research on Aging* 22 (6): 774–96.

Fox 9 News. (2020). "911 Transcript of Call that Brought Police to George Floyd Released." *Fox 9 KMSP News.*

Francis, Rupert A., Frederick A. Ernst, Harold Nevels, and Carol A. Lemeh. (1991). "The Relationship of Blood Pressure to a Brief Measure of Anger during Routine Health Screening." *Journal of the National Medical Association* 83 (7): 601–4.

Frazier, E. Franklin. (1957). *Black Bourgeoisie.* New York: Free Press Paperbacks.

Fullerton, Andrew S., and Michael J. Stern. (2013). "Racial Differences in the Gender Gap in Political Participation in the American South, 1952–2004." *Social Science History* 37 (2): 145–76.

Gallego, Aina. (2007). "Unequal Political Participation in Europe." *International Journal of Sociology* 37 (4): 10–25.

Gamson, William A. (1971). "Political Trust and Its Ramification." In Gilbert Abcarian and John W. Soule (Eds.), *Social Psychology and Political Behavior.* New York: Charles E. Merrill, 40–55.

———. (1968). *Power and Discontent.* Homewood, IL: Dorsey Press.

Gandy, Oscar H., Jr. (2001). "Racial Identity, Media Use, and the Social Construction of Risk among African Americans." *Journal of Black Studies* 31 (5): 600–18.

Garvey, Marcus. [1923] (1996). "The Negro's Greatest Enemy." In Cary D. Wintz (Ed.), *African-American Political Thought, 1890–1930.* New York: M. E. Sharpe.

Gerrard, Meg, Frederick X. Gibbons, Mary E. Fleischli, Carolyn E. Cutrona, and Michelle L. Stock. (2018). "Moderation of the Effects of Discrimination-Induced Affective Responses on Health Outcomes." *Psychology & Health* 33 (2): 193–212.

Gerrard, Meg, Michelle L. Stock, Megan E. Roberts, Frederick X. Gibbons, Ross E. O'Hara, Chih-Yuan Weng, and Thomas A. Wills. (2012). "Coping with Racial Discrimination: The Role of Substance Use." *Psychology of Addictive Behaviors* 26 (3): 550–60.

Gibbons, Frederick X., Paul E. Etcheverry, Michelle L. Stock, Meg Gerrard, Chih-Yuan Weng, Marc Kiviniemi, and Ross E. O'Hara. (2010). "Exploring the Link Between Racial Discrimination and Substance Use: What Mediates? What Buffers?" *Journal of Personality & Social Psychology* 99 (5): 785–801.

Gilliam, Franklin D., and Kenny J. Whitby. (1989). "Race, Class, and Attitudes toward Social Welfare Spending: An Ethclass Interpretation." *Social Science Quarterly* 70 (1): 89–99.

Gleser, Goldine C., and David Ihilevich. (1969). "An Objective Instrument for Measuring Defense Mechanisms." *Journal of Consulting and Clinical Psychology* 33 (1): 51–60.

Goldstein, Michael J. (1973). "Individual Differences in Response to Stress." *American Journal of Community Psychology* 1 (2): 113–37.

———. (1959). "The Relationship between Coping and Avoiding Behavior and Response to Fear-Arousing Propaganda." *Journal of Abnormal and Social Psychology* 58 (2): 247–52.

Goosby, Bridget J., Sarah Malone, Elizabeth A. Richardson, Jacob E. Cheadle, and Deadric T. Williams. (2015). "Perceived Discrimination and Markers of Cardiovascular Risk among Low-Income African American Youth." *American Journal of Human Biology* 27 (4): 546–52.

Green, Alexander R., Dana R. Carney, Daniel J. Pallin, Long H. Ngo, Kristal L. Raymond, Lisa I. Iezzoni, and Mahzarin R. Banaji. (2007). "Implicit Bias among Physicians and Its Prediction of Thrombolysis Decisions for Black and White Patients." *Journal of General Internal Medicine* 22 (9): 1231–38.

Greenaway, Katharine H., Winnifred R. Louis, Stacey L. Parker, Elise K. Kalokerinos, Joanne R. Smith, and Deborah J. Terry. (2014). "Successful Coping for Psychological Well-Being." In G. Boyle, D. H. Saklofske, and G. Matthews (Eds.), *Measures of Personality and Social Psychological Constructs*, 322–51. Oxford, UK: Elsevier.

Greenberg, Bradley, and Brenda Dervin. (1970). *Use of the Mass Media by the Urban Poor*. New York: Praeger.

Greenberg, Bradley S., and Gerhard J. Hanneman. (1970). "Racial Attitudes and the Impact of TV Blacks." *Educational Broadcasting Review* 4 (2): 27–34.

Greene, David. (2020). "During Court Hearing, Details Emerge about Black Jogger's Death." *NPR*.

Greenglass, Esther, Ralf Schwarzer, Dagmara Jakubiec, Lisa Fiksenbaum, and Steffen Taubert. (1999). "The Proactive Coping Inventory (PCI): A Multidimensional Research Instrument." Paper presented at the 20th International Conference of the Stress and Anxiety Research Society (STAR), Cracow, Poland, July 12–14, 1999.

Griffith, Janelle. (2020). "Owner of Empty House Ahmaud Arbery Allegedly Entered before Shooting Might Not Move in because of Threats." *NBC News*.

———. (2020). "NYC Officials Call for Police Probe of White Woman's 911 Call on Black Man in Central Park." *NBC News*.

Grills, Cheryl, and Douglas Longshore. (1996). "Africentrism: Psychometric Analyses of a Self-Report Measure." *Journal of Black Psychology* 22: 86–106.

Gupta, Shaan, Emmanuelle Belanger, and Susan P. Phillips. (2019). "Low Socioeconomic Status but Resilient: Panacea or Double Trouble? John Henryism in the International IMIAS Study of Older Adults." *Journal of Cross-Cultural Gerontology* 34: 15–24.

Gurin, Patricia, and Edgar Epps. (1975). *Black Consciousness, Identity and Achievement*. New York: John Wiley.

Gurin, Patricia, Gerald Gurin, and Leo M. Beattie. (1969). "Internal-External Control in the Motivational Dynamics of Negroes." *Journal of Social Issues* 25: 29–53.

Gurin, Patricia, Shirley Hatchett, and James S. Jackson, J. (1989). *Hope and Independence: Blacks' Response to Electoral Party Politics*. New York: Russell Sage Foundation.

Gurin, Patricia, Arthur H. Miller, and Gerald Gurin. (1980). "Stratum Identification and Consciousness." *Social Psychology Quarterly* 43: 30–47.

Hall, Simon. (2011). *American Patriotism, American Protest: Social Movements since the Sixties*. Philadelphia, PA: University of Pennsylvania Press.

Hanson, Kristin, and Emma O'Dwyer. (2019). "Patriotism and Nationalism, Left and Right: A Q-Methodology Study of American National Identity." *Political Ideology* 40 (4): 777–96.

Hanson, Sandra L. (2011). "Whose Dream? Gender and the American Dream." In *The American Dream in the 21st Century*, ed. Sandra L. Hanson and John Kenneth White. Philadelphia, PA: Temple University Press, 77–104.

Hanson, Sandra, and John White. (2011). *The American Dream in the 21st Century.* Philadelphia, PA: Temple University Press.

Hanson, Sandra L., and John Zogby. (2010). "The Polls-Trends: Attitudes about the American Dream." *Public Opinion Quarterly* 74 (3): 570–84.

Harris, Duchess. (2018). *Black Lives Matter*. Minneapolis, MN: Abdo.

Harris, Frederick. (1994). "Something within: Religion as a Mobilizer of African-American Political Activism." *Journal of Politics* 56 (1): 42–68.

Harris, Frederick, Valeria Sinclair-Chapman, and Brian D. McKenzie. (2005). "Macrodynamics of Black Political Participation in the Post-Civil Rights Era." *Journal of Politics* 67 (4): 1143–63.

Harrison, David A., David A. Kravitz, David M. Mayer, Lisa M. Leslie, and Dalit Lev-Arey. (2006). "Understanding Attitudes toward Affirmative Action Programs in Employment: Summary and Meta-Analysis of 35 Years of Research." *Journal of Applied Psychology* 91 (5): 1013–36.

Hart, Anton. (2019). "The Discriminatory Gesture: A Psychoanalytic Consideration of Posttraumatic Reactions to Incidents of Racial Discrimination." *Psychoanalytic Social Work* 26 (1): 5–24.

Hauhart, Robert C. (2015). "American Sociology's Investigations of the American Dream: Retrospect and Prospect." *American Sociologist* 46: 65–98.

Hayes, Lauren, Patrick Pössel, and Sarah J. Roane. (2019). "Perceived Everyday Discrimination and Depressive Symptoms: Does Cognitive Style Mediate?" *Journal of Counseling & Development* 97 (4): 427–36.

Hays, Tom. (2020). "White Woman Charged after Racist Central Park Confrontation." *Associated Press*. July 6.

Heeringa, Steven G., James Wagner, Myriam Torres, Naihua Duan, Terry Adams, and Patricia Berglund. (2006). "Sample Designs and Sampling Methods for the Collaborative Psychiatric Epidemiology Studies (CPES)." *International Journal of Methods in Psychiatric Research* 13 (4): 221–40.

Henson, James M., Valerian J. Derlega, Matthew R. Pearson, Rebecca Ferrer, and Karen Holmes. (2013). "African American Students' Responses to Racial Discrimination: How Race-Based Rejection Sensitivity and Social Constraints Are Related to Psychological Reactions." *Journal of Social & Clinical Psychology* 32 (5): 504–29.

Heppner, P. Paul, Mary J. Heppner, Dong-gwi Lee, Yu-Wei Wang, Hyun-joo Park, and Li-fei Wang. (2006). "Development and Validation for a Collectivist Coping Styles Inventory." *Journal of Counseling Psychology* 53 (1): 107–25.

Hern, Alex. (2020). "Facebook to Be Hit by Its Largest Ever Advertiser Boycott over Racism." *Guardian.* https://www.theguardian.com/business/2020/jun/24/ben-and-jerrys-joins-facebook-advertising-boycott-racism.

Herring, Mary, Thomas B. Jankowski, and Ronald E. Brown. (1999). "Pro-Black Doesn't Mean Anti-White: The Structure of African-American Group Identity." *Journal of Politics* 61: 363–86.

Hills, Mike, Evisa Terziu, and Prina Shah. (2020). "US Election 2020: A Really Simple Guide." *BBC News.* https://www.bbc.com/news/election-us-2020-53785985.

Hjelmgaard, Kim. (2020). "Reparations Bill Gets New Attention amid BLM. Could Other Nations Provide a Blueprint?" *USA Today.*

Hobbs, Larry. (2020). "Dispatcher: 'What Was He Doing Wrong?' " *Brunswick News.*

Hochschild, Jennifer L. (1995). *Facing Up to the American Dream: Race, Class, and the Soul of the Nation.* Princeton, NJ: Princeton University Press.

Holahan, Charles J., Rudolf H. Moos, Carole K. Holahan, Penny L. Brennan, and Kathleen K. Schutte. (2005). "Stress Generation, Avoidance Coping, and Depressive Symptoms: A 10-Year Model." *Journal of Consulting and Clinical Psychology* 73 (4): 658–66.

Holbrook, Allyson L., David Sterrett, Timothy P. Johnson, and Maria Krysan. (2016). "Racial Disparities in Political Participation across Issues: The Role of Issue-Specific Motivators." *Political Behavior* 38: 1–32.

Holcombe, Madeline, and Dakin Andone. (2020). "A Variety of Responses by US States Hurt the Country's Ability to Contain the Coronavirus Pandemic, Fauci Says." *CNN.* Updated July 31, 2020. https://www.cnn.com/2020/07/31/health/us-coronavirus-friday/index.html.

Hosie, Rachel. (2020). "The World's Top CrossFit Athletes are Boycotting the Sport following the CEO's Insensitive Comments on George Floyd." Insider. https://www.insider.com/crossfit-athletes-boycott-sport-games-after-ceo-george-floyd-comment-2020-6.

Hosler, Akiko S., Jamie R. Kammer, and Xiao Cong. (2019). "Everyday Discrimination Experience and Depressive Symptoms in Urban Black, Guyanese,

Hispanic, and White Adults." *Journal of the American Psychiatric Nurses Association* 25 (6): 445–52.

Huang, Long, Wansheng Lei, Fuming Xu, Hairong Liu, and Liang Yu. (2020). "Emotional Responses and Coping Strategies in Nurses and Nursing Students During COVID-19 Outbreak: A Comparative Study." *PLoS ONE* 15 (8): e0237303.

Huddy, Leonie, and Nadia Khatib. (2007). "American Patriotism, National Identity, and Political Involvement." *American Journal of Political Science* 51 (1): 63–77.

Hudson, Darrell L., Harold W. Neighbors, Arline T. Geronimus, and James S. Jackson. (2016). "Racial Discrimination, John Henryism, and Depression among African Americans." *Journal of Black Psychology* 42 (3): 221–43.

Hudson, Darrell L., Harold W. Neighbors, Arline T. Geronimus, and James S. Jackson. (2012). "The Relationship between Socioeconomic Position and Depression among a US Nationally Representative Sample of African Americans." *Social Psychiatry and Psychiatric Epidemiology* 47 (3): 373–81.

Hunte, Haslyn E. R., and Adam E. Barry. (2012). "Perceived Discrimination and DSM-IV–based Alcohol and Illicit Drug Use Disorders." *American Journal of Public Health* 102 (12): e111–17.

Huston, Aletha C., Ellen Wartella, and Edward Donnerstein. (1998). "Measuring the Effects of Sexual Content in the Media." A Report to the Kaiser Foundation. https://www.kff.org/hivaids/report/measuring-the-effects-of-sexual-content-in/.

Hutchison, Bill, and Rachel Katz. (2020). "Ahmaud Arbery Was Struck by Vehicle before He Was Shot Dead; Suspect Yelled Racial Slur: Investigator." *ABC News.* https://abcnews.go.com/US/suspects-struck-ahmaud-arbery-vehicle-shot-dead-yelled/story?id=71066667.

Italiano, Laura. (2020). "William Roddie Bryan Tried to 'Confine and Detain' Ahmaud Arbery, Warrant Says." *New York Post.*

Jackson, James S., Myriam Torres, Cleopatra H. Caldwell, Harold W. Neighbors, Randolph M. Nesse, Robert Joseph Taylor, Steven J. Trierweiler, and David R. Williams. (2004). "The National Survey of American Life: A Study of Racial, Ethnic and Cultural Influences on Mental Disorders and Mental Health." *International Journal of Methods in Psychiatric Research* 13 (4): 196–207.

Jacobson, Cardell K. (1983). "Black Support for Affirmative Action Programs." *Phylon* 44 (4): 299–311.

———. (1985). "Resistance to Affirmative Action." *Journal of Conflict Resolution* 29: 306–29.

James, Sherman A. (1994). "John Henryism and the Health of African-Americans." *Culture, Medicine and Psychiatry* 18: 163–82.

James, Sherman A., Sue A. Hartnett, and William D. Kalsbeek. (1983). "John Henryism and Blood Pressure Differences among Black Men." *Journal of Behavioral Medicine* 6 (3): 259–78.

James, Sherman A., Nora L. Keenan, David S. Strogatz, Steven R. Browning, and Joanne M. Garrett. (1992). "Socioeconomic Status, John Henryism, and Blood Pressure in Black Adults: The Pitt County Study." *American Journal of Epidemiology* 135 (1): 59–67. James, Sherman A., Andrea Z. LaCroix, David G. Kleinbaum, and David S. Strogatz. (1984). "John Henryism and Blood Pressure Differences among Black Men, II: The Role of Occupational Stressors." *Journal of Behavioral Medicine* 7 (3): 259–75.

James, Sherman A., David S. Strogatz, Steven B. Wing, and Diane L. Ramsey. (1987). "Socioeconomic Status, John Henryism, and Hypertension in Blacks and Whites." *American Journal of Epidemiology* 126 (4): 664–73.

James, Sherman A., and P. E. Thomas. (2000). "John Henryism and Blood Pressure in Black Populations: A Review of the Evidence." *African American Research Perspectives* 6 (3): 1–10.

Jaret, Charles, and Donald C. Reitzes. (1999). "The Importance of Racial-Ethnic Identity and Social Setting for Blacks, Whites, and Multiracials." *Sociological Perspectives* 42 (4): 711–37.

Jones, Felicia G. (1990). "The Black Audience and the BET Channel." *Journal of Broadcasting & Electronic Media* 34 (4): 477–86.

Karlsen, Saffron, and James Y. Nazroo. (2002). "Relation between Racial Discrimination, Social Class, and Health among Ethnic Minority Groups." *American Journal of Public Health* 92 (4): 624–31.

Kessler, Ronald C., Kristin D. Mickelson, and David R. Williams. (1999). "The Prevalence, Distribution, and Mental Health Correlates of Perceived Discrimination in the United States." *Journal of Health and Social Behavior* 40 (3): 208–30.

Kinder, Donald R., and Nicholas Winter. (2001). "Exploring the Racial Divide: Blacks, Whites, and Opinion on National Policy." *American Journal of Political Science* 45: 439–56.

Kline, Kimberly N. (2003). "Popular Media and Health: Images, Effects, and Institutions." In T. L. Thompson, A. M. Dorsey, K. I. Miller, and R Parrott (Eds.), *Handbook of Health Communication*, 557–81. Mahwah, NJ: Lawrence Erlbaum.

Kluegel, James R., and Eliot R. Smith. (1983). "Affirmative Action Attitudes: Effects of Self-Interest, Racial Affect, and Stratification Beliefs on Whites' Views." *Social Forces* 61: 797–824.

Knudsen, Knud, and Kari Waerness. (2008). "National Context and Spouses' Housework in 34 Countries." *European Sociological Review* 24 (1): 97–113.

Kornfield, Meryl, Mark Guarino, Kayla Ruble, and Lenny Bernstein. (2020). "Huge, Peaceful Protests Mark Anti-Racism Demonstrations around the Globe." *Washington Post*.

Korte, K. J., C. A. Denckla, A. A. Ametaj, and K. C. Koenen. (2020). "Managing Stress: Tips for Coping with the Stress of COVID-19." Harvard T. H.

Chan School of Public Health. https://www.massgeneral.org/assets/MGH/pdf/psychiatry/HSPH-COVID-19-mental-health-tips-3-11-20_kk.pdf.

Kosterman, Rick, and Seymour Feshbach. (1989). "Toward a Measure of Patriotic and Nationalistic Attitudes." *Political Psychology* 29 (6): 859–79.

Kravitz, David, and Stephen Klineberg. (2000). "Reactions to Two Versions of Affirmative Action among Whites, Blacks, and Hispanics." *Journal of Applied Psychology* 85: 597–611.

Kravitz, David, Stephen Klineberg, Derek Avery, Ann Kim Nguyen, Christopher Lund, and Emery J. Fu. (2006). "Attitudes toward Affirmative Action: Correlations with Demographic Variables and with Beliefs about Targets, Actions, and Economic Effects." *Journal of Applied Social Psychology* 30: 1109–36.

Kressin, Nancy R., and Laura A. Petersen. (2001). "Racial Differences in the Use of Invasive Cardiovascular Procedures: Review of the Literature and Prescription for Future Research." *Annals of Internal Medicine* 135 (5): 352–66.

Krieger, Nancy, Diane L. Rowley, Allen A. Herman, Byllye Avery, and Mona T. Phillips. (1993). "Racism, Sexism, and Social Class: Implications for Studies of Health, Disease, and Well-Being." *American Journal of Preventive Medicine* 9 (6, Suppl): 82–122.

Krieger, Nancy, and Stephen Sidney. (1996). "Racial Discrimination and Blood Pressure: The CARDIA Study of Young Black and White Adults." *American Journal of Public Health* 96 (10): 1370–78.

Krieger, Nancy, Pamela D. Waterman, Anna Kosheleva, Jarvis T. Chen, Kevin W. Smith, Dana R. Carney, Gary G. Bennett, David R. Williams, Gisele Thornhill, and Elmer R. Freeman. (2013). "Racial Discrimination & Cardiovascular Disease Risk: My Body My Story Study of 1005 US-Born Black and White Community Health Center Participants (US)." *PLoS ONE* 8 (10): 1–15.

Krohne, Heinz W. (1989). "The Concept of Coping Modes: Relating Cognitive Person Variables to Actual Coping Behavior." *Advances in Behavior Research and Therapy* 11: 235–48.

Krohne, Heinz W. (1986). "Coping with Stress: Dispositions, Strategies, and the Problem of Measurement." In M. H. Appley and R. Trumbull (Eds.), *Dyanmics of Stress: Physiological, Psychological, and Social Perspectives*, 207–32. New York: Plenum Press.

Krohne, Heinz W. (1993). "Vigilance and Cognitive Avoidance as Concepts in Coping Research." In H. W. Krohne (Ed.), Attention and Avoidance: Strategies in Coping with Aversiveness, 19–50. Seattle, WA: Hogrefe and Huber.

Krohne, Heinz W., Boris Egloff, Larry J. Varner, Lawrence R. Burns, Gerdi Weidner, and Henry C. Ellis. (2000). "The Assessment of Dispositional Vigilance and Cognitive Avoidance: Factorial Structure, Psychometric Properties, and Validity of the Mainz Coping Inventory." *Cognitive Therapy and Research* 24 (3): 297–311.

Krohne, Heinz W., and Josef Rogner. (1982). "Repression-Sensitization as a Central Construct in Coping Research." *Series in Clinical & Community Psychology: Achievement, Stress, and Anxiety*, 167–93.

Kuo, Ben C. H. (2013). "Collectivism and Coping: Current Theories, Evidence, and Measurements of Collective Coping." *International Journal of Psychology* 48 (3): 374–88.

———. "Culture's Consequences on Coping: Theories, Evidence, and Dimensionalities." *Journal of Cross-Cultural Psychology* 42 (6): 1084–100.

Kuo, Ben C. H., Gargi Roysircar, and Ian R. Newby-Clark. (2006). "Development of the Cross-Cultural Coping Scale: Collective, Avoidance, and Engagement Strategies." *Measurement and Evaluation in Counseling and Development* 39 (3): 161–81.

Kwate, Naa Oyo A., and Ilan H. Meyer. (2010). "The Myth of Meritocracy and African American Health." *American Journal of Public Health* 100 (10): 1831–34.

Lamont, Michele, and Virag Molnar. (2001). "How Blacks Use Consumption to Shape their Collective Identity: Evidence from Marketing Specialists." *Journal of Consumer Culture* 1 (1): 31–45.

Lariscy, Ruthann Weaver, Bryan H. Reber, and Hye-Jin Paek. (2010). "Examination of Media Channels and Types as Health Information Sources for Adolescents: Comparisons for Black/White, Male/Female, Urban/Rural." *Journal of Broadcasting & Electronic Media* 54 (1): 102–20.

Lazarus, Richard S. (1991). *Emotion and Adaptation*. New York: Oxford University Press.

———. (1999). *Stress and Emotion: A New Synthesis*. New York: Springer.

Lazarus, Richard S., and Susan Folkman. (1984). *Stress, Appraisal, and Coping*. New York: Springer.

LeCuyer, Elizabeth A., and Dena Phillips Swanson. (2017). "A Within-Group Analysis of African American Mothers' Authoritarian Attitudes, Limit-Setting and Children's Self-Regulation." *Journal of Child and Family Studies* 26: 833–42.

Legette, Willie. (2000). "The South Carolina Legislative Black Caucus, 1970 to 1988." *Journal of Black Studies* 30: 839–58.

Len-Rios, Maria E., Sun-A Park, Glen T. Cameron, Douglas A. Luke, and Matt Kreuter. (2008). "Study Asks if Reporter's Gender or Audience Predict Paper's Cancer Coverage." *Newspaper Research Journal* 29 (2): 91–99.

Levine, Lawrence. (1977). *Black Culture and Black Consciousness: Afro-American Folk Thought from Slavery to Freedom*. Oxford, UK: Oxford University Press.

Light, Kathleen C., Kimberly A. Brownley, J. Rick Turner, Alan L. Hinderliter, Susan S. Girdler, Andrew Sherwood, and Norman B. Anderson. (1995). "Job Status and High-Effort Coping Influence Work Blood Pressure in Women and Blacks." *Hypertension* 25 (4): 554–59.

Lijphart, Arend. (1997). "Unequal Participation: Democracy's Unresolved Dilemma—Presidential Address." *American Political Science Review* 91 (1): 1–14.

Lim, Kay. (2020). "Alicia Garza on the Origin of Black Lives Matter." *CBS News.*

Long, J. Scott, and Jeremy Freese. (2014). *Regression Models for Categorical Dependent Variables Using Stata.* 3rd ed. College Station, TX: Stata Press.

Lopez, Linda, and Adrian D. Pantoja. (2004). "Beyond Black and White: General Support for

Race-Conscious Policies among African Americans, Latinos, Asian Americans, and Whites." *Political Research Quarterly* 57: 633–42.

Mainord, Willard A. (1956). "Experimental Repression Related to Coping and Avoidance Behavior in the Recall and Relearning of Nonsense Syllables." Doctoral dissertation, University of Washington.

Manne, Sharon, Deborah A. Kashy, Scott Siegel, Shannon Myers Virtue, Carolyn Heckman, and Danielle Ryan. (2014). "Unsupportive Partner Behaviors, Social-Cognitive Processing, and Psychological Outcomes in Couples Coping with Early Stage Breast Cancer." *Journal of Family Psychology* 28 (2): 214–24.

Mansoor, Sanya. (2020). "93% of Black Lives Matter Protests Have Been Peaceful, New Report Finds." *Time.*

Markovic, Nina, Clareann H. Bunker, Flora A. M. Ukoli, and Lewis H. Kuller. (1998). "John Henryism and Blood Pressure among Nigerian Civil Servants." *Journal of Epidemiology and Community Health* 52 (3): 186–90.

Matthews, Derrick D., Wizdom Powell Hammond, Yasmin Cole-Lewis, Amani Nuru-Jeter, and Travis Melvin. (2013). "Racial Discrimination and Depressive Symptoms among African-American Men: The Mediating and Moderating Roles of Masculine Self-Reliance and John Henryism." *Psychology of Men & Masculinity* 14 (1): 35–46.

McCaskill, Nolan D. (2021). "After Trump's Loss and False Fraud Claims, GOP Eyes Voter Restrictions across Nation." *Politico.* https://www.politico.com/news/2021/03/15/voting-restrictions-states-475732.

McKenzie, Brian D. (2004). "Religious Social Networks, Indirect Mobilization, and African-American Political Participation." *Political Research Quarterly* 57 (4): 621–32.

McKetney, E. C., and David R. Ragland. (1996). "John Henryism, Education, and Blood Pressure in Young Adults: The CARDIA Study." *American Journal of Epidemiology* 143 (8): 787–91.

Menninger, Karl. (1954). "Regulatory Devices of the Ego under Major Stress." *International Journal of Psychoanalysis* 35: 412–20.

———. (1963). *The Vital Balance: The Life Process in Mental Health and Illness.* New York: Viking.

Merritt, Marcellus M., Gary G. Bennett, Redford B. Williams, John J. Sollers III, and Julian F. Thayer. (2004). "Low Educational Attainment, John Henryism, and Cardiovascular Reactivity to and Recovery from Personally Relevant Stress." *Psychosomatic Medicine* 66 (1): 49–55.

Merritt, Marcellus M., T. J. McCallum, and Thomas Fritsch. (2011). "How Much Striving Is too Much? John Henryism Active Coping Predicts Worse Daily Cortisol Responses for African American but not White Female Dementia Family Caregivers." *American Journal of Geriatric Psychiatry* 19 (5): 451–60.

Miller, Arthur H., Patricia Gurin, Gerald Gurin, and Oksana Malanchuk. (1981). "Group Consciousness and Political Participation." *American Journal of Political Science* 25: 494–511.

Miller, Neal E. (1980). "A Perspective on the Effects of Stress and Coping on Disease and Health." In S. Levine and H. Ursin (Eds.), *Coping and Health*, 323–53. New York: Plenum.

Miller, Suzanne M. (1987). "Monitoring and Blunting: Validation of a Questionnaire to Assess Styles of Information Seeking Under Threat." *Journal of Personality and Social Psychology* 52 (2): 345–53.

Miller, Suzanne M., Pagona Roussi, D. Altman, W. Helm, and A. Steinberg. (1994). "Effects of Coping Style on Psychological Reactions of Low-Income, Minority Women to Colposcopy." *Journal of Reproductive Medicine* 39 (9): 711–18.

Mirowsky, John, and Catherine E. Ross. (2003). *Social Causes of Psychological Distress*. 2nd ed. Hawthorne, NY: Aldine De Gruyter.

Mitrousi, Stavroula, Antonios Travlos, Evmorfia Koukia, and Sofia Zyga. (2013). "Theoretical Approaches to Coping." *International Journal of Caring Sciences* 6 (2): 131–37.

Moniuszko, Sara M. (2020). "Billie Eilish, Taylor Swift, Oprah, More Celebrities React to the Death of George Floyd: 'We Must Act.'" *USA Today*. https://flipboard.com/@USAToday/cardi-b-justin-bieber-and-more-celebrities-react-to-the-death-of-george-floyd-/a-7KLpqzrtRDKc_WVDoCDGNQ%3Aa%3A3199709-5665958922%2Fusatoday.com?format=amp.

Moore, James L., and Madonna G. Constantine. (2005). "Development and Initial Validation of the Collectivistic Coping Styles Measure with African, Asian, and Latin American International Students." *Journal of Mental Health Counseling* 27 (4): 329–47.

Moos, Rudolf H. (1974). "Psychological Techniques in the Assessment of Adaptive Behavior." In G. V. Coelho, D. A. Hamburg, and J. E. Adams (Eds.), *Coping and Adaptation*, 334–99. New York: Basic Books.

Moos, Rudolf H., and Vivien Davis Tsu. (1977). "The Crisis of Physical Illness: An Overview." In R. H. Moos (Ed.), *Coping with Physical Illness*, 3–21. New York: Plenum.

Morales, Mark, Eric Levenson, Elizabeth Joseph, and Christina Carrega. (2020). "Louisville Agrees to Pay Breonna Taylor's Family $12 Million and Enact Police Reforms in Historic Settlement." *CNN*. https://www.cnn.com/2020/09/15/us/breonna-taylor-louisville-settlement.

Morganstein, Joshua. (2020). "Coronavirus and Mental Health: Taking Care of Ourselves during Infectious Disease Outbreaks." *American Psychiatric Association*. https://www.psychiatry.org/news-room/apa-blogs/apa-blog/2020/02/coronavirus-and-mental-health-taking-care-of-ourselves-during-infectious-disease-outbreaks.

Muhammad, Elijah. (1965). *Message to the Black Man in America.*

Mundell, E. J. (2020). "Mental Health Issues Soaring during COVID Pandemic." *WebMD and HealthDay News.* https://www.webmd.com/lung/news/20200813/levels-of-anxiety-addiction-suicidal-thoughts-are-soaring-in-the-pandemic#1.

Muris, Peter, Florence J. van Zuuren, and Simon de Vries. (1994). "Monitoring, Blunting and Situational Anxiety: A Laboratory Study on Coping with a Quasi-Medical Stressor." *Personality and Individual Differences* 16 (3): 365–72.

Myrie, Clive. (2020). "US Election 2020: Why Racism Is Still a Problem for the World's Most Powerful Country." *BBC News.* https://www.bbc.com/news/election-us-2020-54738922.

Neighbors, Harold W., Rashid Njai, and James S. Jackson. (2007). "Race, Ethnicity, John Henryism, and Depressive Symptoms: The National Survey of American Life Adult Reinterview." *Research in Human Development* 4: 71–87.

Nelson, Scott R. (2006). *Steel-Drivin' Man, The Untold Story of an American Legend.* New York: Oxford University Press.

Nielsen. (2019). "Diverse Intelligence Series 2019. It's In the Bag: Black Consumers' Path to Purchase." Nielsen.

Nier, Jason A., and Samuel L. Gaertner. (2012). "The Challenge of Detecting Contemporary Forms of Discrimination." *Journal of Social Issues* 68 (2): 207–20.

Nir, Sarah Maslin. (2020). "The Bird Watcher, That Incident and His Feeling on the Woman's Fate." *New York Times.* https://www.nytimes.com/2020/05/27/nyregion/amy-cooper-christian-central-park-video.html.

Njai, Rashid S. (2008). "Examining the Measurement of Race and Ethnicity to Inform a Model of Sociocultural Stress and Adaptive Coping." *Dissertation Abstracts International: Section B: The Sciences and Engineering,* 69 (3-B), 1599. University of Michigan.

Nordby, G., Ø. Ekeberg, S. Knardahl, and I. Os. (1995). "A Double-Blind Study of Psychosocial Factors in 40-Year-Old Women with Essential Hypertension." *Psychotherapy and Psychosomatics* 63: 142–50.

Obama, Michelle. (2020). "The Gift of Girlfriends with Denielle, Sharon, and Kelly." *Spotify.* https://open.spotify.com/episode/67ixgWUlHwa1mptT4GkmWh.

Olsen, Marvin E. (1970). "Social and Political Participation of Blacks." *American Sociological Review* 35 (4): 682–97.

Ondercin, Heather L., and Daniel Jones-White. (2011). "Gender Jeopardy: What Is the Impact of Gender Differences in Political Knowledge on Political Participation?" *Social Science Quarterly* 92 (3): 675–94.

O'Neil, Aaron. (2020). "Voter Turnout among Black Voters in U.S. Presidential Elections 1964–2016." Statista. https://www.statista.com/statistics/1096577/voter-turnout-black-voters-presidential-elections-historical/.

Oppel, Richard A., Jr., Derrick Bryson Taylor, and Nicholas Bogel-Burroughs. (2022). "What to Know about Breonna Taylor's Death." *New York Times.* https://www.nytimes.com/article/breonna-taylor-police.html.

Orey, Byron D'Andra, Athena M. King, Shonda K. Lawrence, and Brian E. Anderson. (2013). "Black Opposition to Welfare in the Age of Obama." *Race, Gender & Class* 20 (3/4): 114–29.

Owens, Donna. (2020). "From Covid-19 to Racial Justice, How 2020's Biggest Issues Influenced the Black Vote." *NBC News.* https://www.nbcnews.com/news/nbcblk/covid-19-racial-justice-how-2020-s-biggest-issues-influenced-n1248961.

Pager, Devah, and Bruce Western. (2012). "Identifying Discrimination at Work: The Use of Field Experiments." *Journal of Social Issues* 68 (2): 221–37.

Panchal, Nirmita, Rabah Kamal, Kendal Orgera, Cynthia Cox, Rachel Garfield, Liz Hamel, Cailey Munana, and Priya Chidambaram. (2020). "The Implications of COVID-19 for Mental Health and Substance Use." Kaiser Family Foundation. https://www.kff.org/coronavirus-covid-19/issue-brief/the-implications-of-covid-19-for-mental-health-and-substance-use/.

Paradies, Yin. (2006). "A Systematic Review of Empirical Research on Self-Reported Racism and Health." *International Journal of Epidemiology* 35 (4): 888–901.

Paradies, Yin, Jehonathan Ben, Nida Denson, Amanuel Elias, Naomi Priest, Alex Pieterse, Arpana Gupta, Margaret Kelaher, and Gilbert Gee. (2015). "Racism as a Determinant of Health: A Systematic Review and Meta-Analysis." *PLoS ONE* 10 (9): e0138511. doi:10.1371/journal.pone.0138511.

Patillo-McCoy, Mary. (1998). "Church Culture as a Strategy of Action in the Black Community." *American Sociological Review* 63 (6): 767–84.

Pearlin, Leonard I. (1989). "The Sociological Study of Stress." *Journal of Health and Social Behavior* 30 (3): 241–56.

Peeples, Lynne. (2020). "What the Data Say about Police Brutality and Racial Bias—and which Reforms Might Work." *Nature.* https://www.nature.com/articles/d41586-020-01846-z#ref-CR1.

Penley, Julie A., Joe Tomaka, and John S. Wiebe. (2002). "The Association of Coping to Physical and Psychological Health Outcomes: A Meta-Analytic Review." *Journal of Behavioral Medicine* 25 (6): 551–603.

Pierce, John C., William P. Avery, and Addison Carey Jr. (1973). "Sex Differences in Black Political Beliefs and Behavior." *American Journal of Political Science* 17 (2): 422–30.

Plant, E. Ashby, and B. Michelle Peruche. (2005). "The Consequences of Race for Police Offers' Responses to Criminal Suspects." *Psychological Science* 16 (3): 180–83.

Porter, Gayle. (2010). "Work Ethic and Ethical Work: Distortions in the American Dream." *Journal of Business Ethics* 96: 535–50.

Porter, Judith R., and Robert E. Washington. (1979). "Black Identity and Self-Esteem." *Annual Review of Sociology* 5: 53–74.

Price, Brian, Checkey Beckford, and Kiki Intarasuwan. (2020). "Woman in Racial Central Park Confrontation Is Fired from Job, Gives up Dog." *NBC New York*.

Price-Haywood, Eboni G., Jeffrey Burton, Daniel Fort, and Leonardo Seoane. (2020). "Hospitalization and Mortality among Black Patients and White Patients with COVID-19." *New England Journal of Medicine* 382: 2534–43.

Putnam, Robert D. (2000). *Bowling Alone: The Collapse and Revival of American Community*. New York: Simon & Schuster.

Quillian, Lincoln, John J. Lee, and Brandon Honore. (2020). "Racial Discrimination in the U.S. Housing and Mortgage Lending Markets: A Quantitative Review of Trends, 1976–2016." *Race and Social Problems* 12: 13–28.

Radnitz, Cynthia L., and Lana Tiersky. (2007). "Psychodynamic and Cognitive Theories of Coping." In E. Martz and H. Livneh (Eds.), *Coping with Chronic Illness and Disability: Theoretical, Empirical, and Clinical Aspects*, 29–48. Springer Science + Business Media.

Ransom, Jan. (2020). "Amy Cooper Faces Charges after Calling Police on Black Bird-Watcher." *New York Times*.

Reese, Laura A., Ronald E. Brown, and James David Ivers. (2007). " 'Some Children See Him . . .': Political Participation and the Black Christ." *Political Behavior* 29 (4): 517–37.

Renckstorf, Karsten. (1996). "Media Use as Social Action: A Theoretical Perspective." In K. Renckstorf (Ed.), *Media Use as Social Action: European Approach to Audience Studies*, 18–31), London: John Libby.

Rice, Alexander, Yunkyoung Loh Garrison, and William Ming Liu. (2020). "Spending as Social and Affective Coping (SSAC): Measure Development and Initial Validation." *Counseling Psychologist* 48 (1): 78–105.

Robinson, Eugene. (2020). "Black Lives Remain Expendable." *Washington Post*.

Robnett, Belinda, and James A. Bany. (2011). "Gender, Church Involvement, and African-American Political Participation." *Sociological Perspectives* 54 (4): 689–712.

Rockquemore, Kerry Ann, David L. Brunsma, and Daniel J. Delgago. (2009). "Racing to Theory or Retheorizing Race? Understanding the Struggle to Build a Multiracial Identity Theory." *Journal of Social Issues* 65 (1): 13–34.

Rosenberg, Rebecca. (2020). "Central Park 'Karen' Case: Details of Previously Unheard Second 911 Call Revealed." *New York Post*.

Rosenstone, Steven J., and John Mark Hansen. (1993). *Mobilization, Participation, and Democracy in America*. New York: Macmillan.

Sadler, Melody S., Joshua Correll, Bernadette Park, and Charles M. Judd. (2012). "The World Is Not Black and White: Racial Bias in the Decision to Shoot in a Multiethnic Context." *Journal of Social Issues* 68 (2): 286–313.

Sallee, Barrett. (2020). "Kansas State Players Announce Boycott of Program in Wake of Offensive Social Media Post by Student." *CBS*. https://www.cbssports.com/college-football/news/kansas-state-players-announce-boycott-of-program-in-wake-of-offensive-social-media-post-by-student/.

Sanchez, Ray, and Elizabeth Joseph. (2020). "Black Birdwatcher Christian Cooper Says Prosecuting Amy Cooper 'Lets White People off the Hook.'" *CNN*.

Schildkraut, Deborah J. (2014). "Boundaries of American Identity: Evolving Understandings of 'Us.'" *Annual Review of Political Science* 17: 441–60.

Schlozman, Kay Lehman, Nancy Burns, and Sidney Verba. (1994). "Gender and the Pathways to Participation: The Role of Resources." *Journal of Politics* 56 (4): 963–90.

———. (1999). "What Happened at Work Today?": A Multistage Model of Gender, Employment, and Political Participation." *Journal of Politics* 61: 29–53.

Schmermund, Anke, Robert Sellers, Birgit Mueller, and Faye Crosby. (2001). "Attitudes toward Affirmative Action as a Function of Racial Identity among African American College Students." *Political Psychology* 22: 759–74.

Schrade, Brad, and Bert Roughton. (2020). "'It Just Startled Me.' Travis McMichael Dialed 911 Days before Shooting." *Atlanta Journal Constitution*. https://www.ajc.com/news/crime—law/just-startled-travis-mcmichael-dialed-911-days-before-shooting/cW9EyvfTBkwv6n16B4GT7I/.

Sellers, Robert M., Stephanie A. J. Rowley, Tabbye M. Chavous, J. Nicole Shelton, and Mia A. Smith. (1997). "Multidimensional Inventory of Black Identity: A Preliminary Investigation of Reliability and Construct Validity." *Journal of Personality and Social Psychology* 73 (4): 805–15.

Shahrour, Ghada, and Latefa Ali Dardas. (2020). "Acute Stress Disorder, Coping Self-Efficacy and Subsequent Psychological Distress among Nurses amid COVID-19." *Journal of Nursing Management* 28 (7): 1686–95.

Shelton, Jason E., and George Wilson. (2009). "Race, Class, and the Basis of Group Alignment: An Analysis of Support for Redistributive Policy among Privileged Blacks." *Sociological Perspectives* 52: 385–408.

Shiloh, S., L. Koehly, J. Jenkins, J. Martin, and D. Hadley. (2008). "Monitoring Coping Style Moderates Emotional Reactions to Genetic Testing for Hereditary Nonpolyposis Colorectal Cancer: A Longitudinal Study." *Psycho-Oncology* 17: 746–55.

Shingles, Richard D. (1981). "Black Consciousness and Political Participation: The Missing Link." *American Political Science Review* 75 (1): 76–91.

Shipley, Robert H., James H. Butt, and Ellen A. Horwitz. (1979). "Preparation to Reexperience a Stressful Medical Examination: Effect of Repetitious Videotape Exposure and Coping Style." *Journal of Consulting and Clinical Psychology* 47 (3): 485–92.

Shipley, Robert H., James H. Butt, Bruce Horwitz, and John E. Farbry. (1978). "Preparation for a Stressful Medical Procedure: Effect of Amount of Stimulus Preexposure and Coping Style." *Journal of Consulting and Clinical Psychology* 46 (3): 499–507.

Shohat, Ella, and Robert Stamm. (1994). *Unthinking Eurocentrism: Multiculturalism and the Media*. New York: Routledge.

Shosteck, Herschel. (1969). "Some Influences of Television on Civil Unrest." *Journal of Broadcasting* 13: 371–85.

Sidanius, Jim, and Felicia Pratto. (1999). *Social Dominance: An Intergroup Theory of Social Hierarchy and Oppression.* Cambridge, UK: Cambridge University Press, 48.

Siddiqui, Shamsul. (2015). "Impact of Self-Efficacy on Psychological Well-Being among Undergraduate Students." *International Journal of Indian Psychology* 2: 5–16.

Siegel, Benjamin. (2021). "House Democrats Pass Election Reforms as GOP Moves to Change Voting Laws." *ABC News.* https://abcnews.go.com/Politics/house-democrats-push-pass-election-reforms-gop-moves/story?id=76182685.

Sigelman, Lee, and Susan Welch. (1991). *Black Americans' Views of Racial Inequality: The Dream Deferred.* New York: Cambridge University Press.

Silverman, Hollie. (2020). "Surveillance Videos Show Multiple People Had Trespassed at the Home Ahmaud Arbery Visited. He was the Only One Killed." *CNN.*

Simien, Evelyn M., and Rosalee A. Clawson. (2004). "The Intersection of Race and Gender: An Examination of Black Feminist Consciousness, Race Consciousness, and Policy Attitudes." *Social Science Quarterly* 85 (3): 793–810.

Simons, Ronald L., Man-Kit Lei, Steven R. H. Beach, Ashley B. Barr, Leslie G. Simons, Frederick X. Gibbons, and Robert A. Philibert. (2018). "Discrimination, Segregation, and Chronic Inflammation: Testing the Weathering Explanation for the Poor Health of Black Americans." *Developmental Psychology* 54 (10): 1993–2006.

Sinclair, Vaughn G., and Kenneth A. Wallston. (2004). "The Development and Psychometric Evaluation of the Brief Resilient Coping Scale." *Assessment* 11 (1): 94–101.

Skinner, Ellen A., Kathleen Edge, Jeffrey Altman, and Hayley Sherwood. (2003). "Searching for the Structure of Coping: A Review and Critique of Category Systems for Classifying Ways of Coping." *Psychological Bulletin* 129 (2): 216–69.

Slough, Nancy, Ronald A. Kleinknecht, and Robert M. Thorndike. (1984). "Relationship of the Repression-Sensitization Scales to Anxiety." *Journal of Personality Assessment* 48 (4): 378–79.

Smith, Craig A., and Leslie D. Kirby. (2001). "Toward Delivering on the Promise of Appraisal Theory." In K. R. Scherer, A. Schorr, and T. Johnstone (Eds.), *Appraisal Processes in Emotion: Theory, Methods and Research,* 121–38. New York: Oxford University Press.

Smith, Robert Charles. (1996). *We Have No Leaders: African Americans in the Post-Civil Rights Era.* Albany: State University of New York Press.

Smith, Veronica. (2020). "African American Authoritarianism, Child Rearing Beliefs & Academic Outcomes: A Qualitative Ethnography." Northcentral University ProQuest Dissertations Publishing (27735916). https://www.proquest.com/openview/3dc22ecad89c088fa4a272837fc15faa/1?pq-origsite=gscholar&cbl=18750&diss=y.

Somova, L. I., K. Diarra, and T. Q. Jacobs. (1995). "Psychophysiological Study of Hypertension in Black, Indian and White African Students." *Stress and Health* 11: 105–11.

Stanton, Michael V., Charles R. Jonassaint, Redford B. Williams, and Sherman A. James. (2010). "Socioeconomic Status Moderates the Association between John Henryism and NEO PI-R Personality Domains." *Psychosomatic Medicine* 72 (2): 141–47.

Stevenson, Robert L. (1979). "Use of Public Television by Blacks." *Journalism Quarterly* 56: 141–47.

Stroman, Carolyn A. (1984). "The Socialization Influence of Television on Black Children." *Journal of Black Studies* 15 (1): 79–100.

Subramanyam, Malavika A., Sherman A. James, Ana V. Diez-Roux, DeMarc A. Hickson, Daniel Sarpong, Mario Sims, Herman A. Taylor, and Sharon B. Wyatt. (2013). "Socioeconomic Status, John Henryism and Blood Pressure among African-Americans in the Jackson Heart Study." *Social Science & Medicine* 93: 139–46.

Sue, Derald Wing. (2010). *Microaggressions in Everyday Life: Race, Gender, and Sexual Orientation*. John Wiley.

Sue, Derald Wing, Christina M. Capodilupo, Gina C. Torino, Jennifer M. Bucceri, Aisha M. B. Holder, Kevin L. Nadal, and Marta Esquilin. (2007). "Racial Microaggressions in Everyday Life: Implications for Clinical Practice." *American Psychologist* 62 (4): 271–86.

Sullivan, Jas M. (2020). "Does Region Matter on African Americans' Reaction to Discrimination?: An Exploratory Study." In L. Martin (Ed.), *Introduction to Africana Demography*. Boston, MA: Brill.

Sullivan, Jas M., Jonathan Winburn, and William E. Cross Jr. (2018). *Dimensions of Blackness: Racial Identity and Political Beliefs*. Albany: State University of New York Press.

Sullivan, Samaah, Muhammad Hammadah, Ibhar Al Mheid, Amit Shah, Yan V. Sun, Michael Kutner, Laura Ward, Elizabeth Blackburn, Jinying Zhao, Jue Lin, J. Douglas Bremner, Arshed A. Quyyumi, Viola Vaccarino, and Tene T. Lewis. (2019). "An Investigation of Racial/Ethnic and Sex Differences in the Association between Experiences of Everyday Discrimination and Leukocyte Telomere Length among Patients with Coronary Artery Disease." *Psychoneuroendocrinology* 106 (August): 122–28.

Syme, S. Leonard. (1979). "Psychosocial Determinants of Hypertension." In E. Oresti and C. Klint (Eds.), *Hypertension Determinants, Complications and Intermention*, 95–98. New York: Grune and Stratton.

Tate, Katherine (1991). "Black Political Participation in the 1984 and 1988 Presidential Elections." *American Political Science Review* 85 (4): 1159–76.

———. (1993). *From Protest to Politics: The New Black Voters in American Elections*. Cambridge, MA: Harvard University Press.

Taylor, Derrick Bryson. (2020). "A Timeline of the Coronavirus Pandemic." *New York Times.* https://www.nytimes.com/article/coronavirus-timeline.html.

Taylor, Vanessa. (2020). "Black Runners on Ahmaud Arbery and the Unique Treachery of a Simple Job." Mic. https://www.mic.com/p/black-runners-on-ahmaud-arbery-the-unique-treachery-of-a-simple-jog-22890046.

Theiss-Morse, Elizabeth. (2009). *Who Counts as an American? The Boundaries of National Identity.* Cambridge, UK: Cambridge University Press.

Thomson-DeVeaux, Amelia, and Meredith Conroy. (2020). "Women Won the Right to vote 100 Years Ago. They Didn't Start Voting Differently from Men until 1980." *FiveThirtyEight.* https://fivethirtyeight.com/features/women-won-the-right-to-vote-100-years-ago-they-didnt-start-voting-differently-from-men-until-1980/.

Thornburg v. Gingles. 478 U.S. 30. (1986).

Timpone, Richard J. (1998). "Structure, Behavior, and Voter Turnout in the United States." *American Political Science Review* 92 (1): 145–58.

Tobin, David L. (1984, 2001). "User Manual for the Coping Strategies Inventory." Accessed at https://www.academia.edu/30133319/User_Manual_for_the_COPING_STRATEGIES_INVENTORY.

TV One. (n.d.). *About TV One.* http://tvone.tv/about-tvone/.

Udo, Tomoko, and Carlos M. Grilo. (2017). "Cardiovascular Disease and Perceived Weight, Racial, and Gender Discrimination in U.S. Adults." *Journal of Psychosomatic Research* 100 (September): 83–88.

Umstead, R. Thomas. (2019). "African-Americans are Leaders in Media Consumption." *Multichannel News.*

Ursin, Holger. (1980). "Personality, Activation and Somatic Health: A New Psychosomatic Theory." In S. Levine and H. Ursin (Eds.), *Coping and Health,* 259–79. New York: Plenum.

Vaillant, George E. (1977). *Adaptation to Life.* Cambridge, MA: Harvard University Press.

Van Loon, A. Jeanne M., Marja Tijhuis, Paul G. Surtees, and Johan Ormel. (2001). "Personality and Coping: Their Relationship with Lifestyle Risk Factors for Cancer." *Personality and Individual Differences* 31 (4): 541–53.

Vasilogambros, Matt. (2016). "The Ethnic Groups that Still Believe in the American Dream." *Atlantic.*

Vedhara, Kavita, Jolanda Tuinstra, Jeremy N. V. Miles, Robbert Sanderman, and Adelita V. Ranchor. (2007). "Erratum to 'Psychosocial Factors Associated with Indices of Cortisol Production in Women with Breast Cancer and controls' [Psychoneuroendocrinology 31 (2006): 299–311]." *Psychoneuroendocrinology* 32 (7): 857.

Verba, Sidney, Nancy Burns, and Kay Lehman Schlozman. (1997). "Knowing and Caring about Politics: Gender and Political Engagement." *Journal of Politics* 59 (4): 1051–72.

Verba, Sidney, and Norman H. Nie. (1972). *Participation in America.* New York: Harper & Row.

Verba, Sidney, Kay Lehman Schlozman, and Henry E. Brady. (1995). *Voice and Equality: Civic Voluntarism in American* Politics, vol. 4. Cambridge, MA: Harvard University Press.

Vygotsky, Lev S. (1978). *Mind in Society.* In M. Cole, V. John-Steiner, S. Scribner, & Soubermans (Eds.), *The Development of Higher Psychological Processes.* Cambridge, MA: MIT Press.

Walton, Hanes. (1972). *Black Political Parties: An Historical and Political Analysis.* New York: The Free Press.

Ward, L. Monique, and Rocio Rivadeneyra. (1999). "Contributions of Entertainment Television to Adolescents' Sexual Attitudes and Expectations: The Role of Viewing Amount versus Viewer Involvement." *Journal of Sex Research* 36 (3): 223–42.

Wardle, F. Jane, William Collins, Amanda L. Pernet, Malcolm I. Whitehead, Thomas H. Bourne, and Stuart Campbell. (1993). "Psychological Impact of Screening for Familial Ovarian Cancer." *Journal of the National Cancer Institute* 85 (8): 653–57.

Watson-Singleton, Natalie N., Yara Mekawi, Kaleigh V. Wilkins, and Isatou F. Jatta. (2020). "Racism's Effect on Depressive Symptoms: Examining Perseverative Cognition and Black Lives Matter Activism as Moderators." *Journal of Counseling Psychology* 68 (1): 27–37.

Watts-Smith, Candis. (2014). *Black Mosaic: The Politics of Black Pan-Ethnic Diversity.* New York: NYU Press.

Wee, Sui-Lee, Donald G. McNeil Jr., and Javier C. Hernandez. (2020). "W.H.O. Declares Global Emergency as Wuhan Coronavirus Spreads." Updated April 16, 2020. *New York Times.* https://www.nytimes.com/2020/01/30/health/coronavirus-world-health-organization.html.

Wiist, William H., and John M. Flack. (1992). "A Test of the John Henryism Hypothesis: Cholesterol and Blood Pressure." *Journal of Behavioral Medicine* 15: 15–29.

Wilkinson, Larrell L., Olivio J. Clay, Anthony C. Hood, Eric P. Plaisance, Lakesha Kinnerson, Brandon D. Beamon, and Dominique Hector. (2020). "The Association of Emotional and Physical Reactions to Perceived Discrimination with Depressive Symptoms among African American Men in the Southeast." *International Journal of Environmental Research and Public Health* 17 (1): 322.

Williams, Brett. (1983). *John Henry: A Bio-bibliography.* Westport, CT: Greenwood Press.

Williams, David R. (1992). "Black-White Differences in Blood Pressure: The Role of Social Factors." *Ethnicity and Disease* 2 (2): 126–41.

Williams, David R., Risa Lavizzo-Mourey, and Rueben C. Warren. (1994). "The Concept of Race and Health Status in America." *Public Health Reports* 109 (1): 26–41.

Williams, Linda F. (1987). "Black Political Progress in the 1980s: The Electoral Arena." In M. B. Preston, L. J. Henderson Jr., and P. Puryear (Eds.), *The New Black Politics.* New York: Longman, 97–136.

Wilson, William Julius. (1978). *The Declining Significance of Race*. Chicago, IL: University of Chicago Press.

Wolak, Jennifer, and David A. M. Peterson. (2020). "The Dynamic American Dream." *American Journal of Political Science* 64 (4): 968–81.

Wolf, Zachary B. (2021). "Watch These States as GOP Tries to Make It Harder to Vote." *CNN*. https://www.cnn.com/2021/03/16/politics/voting-rights-debates-by-state/index.html.

Wong, Paul T. P., and Lilian C. J. Wong. (2006). *Handbook of Multicultural Perspectives on Stress and Coping*. New York: Springer.

Worland, Justin. (2020). "America's Long Overdue Awakening to Systemic Racism." *Time*.

World Health Organization. (2020). "Mental Health and Psychosocial Considerations during the COVID-19 Outbreak." *WHO*. https://www.who.int/docs/default-source/coronaviruse/mental-health-considerations.pdf.

Wright, Lynda B., Frank A. Treiber, Harry Davis, and William B. Strong. (1996). "Relationship of John Henryism to Cardiovascular Functioning at Rest and During Stress in Youth." *Annals of Behavioral Medicine* 18 (3): 146–50.

Xiong, Chao. (2020). "A Timeline of Events Leading to George Floyd's Death as Outlined in Charging Documents." *Star Tribune*.

Yang, Allie. (2020). "Christian Cooper Accepts Apology from Woman at Center of Central Park Confrontation." *ABC News*. May 28.

Ye, Zhi, Xueying Yang, Chengbo Zeng, Yuyan Wang, Zijiao Shen, Xiamoing Li, and Danhua Lin. (2020). "Resilience, Social Support, and Coping as Mediators between COVID-19-Related Stressful Experiences and Acute Stress Disorder among College Students in China." *Applied Psychology: Health and Well-Being* 12 (4): 1074–94.

Yeh, Christine J., Agnes Kwong Arora, and Katherine A. Wu. (2006). "A New Theoretical Model of Collectivistic Coping." In Paul T. P. Wong and Lilian C. J. Wong (Eds.), *Handbook of Multicultural Perspectives on Stress and Coping*. New York: Springer.

Yeh, Christine J., T. Chang, A. B. Kim, Agnes Kwong Arora, and T. Xin. (2003). "Reliability, Validity, and Factor Analysis of the Collectivistic Coping Scale." Poster presented at the annual meeting of the American Psychological Association, Toronto, Canada.

Index

Page numbers in *italics* denote figures.
Page numbers followed by n denote notes.